Ready®

4 Mathematics
INSTRUCTION

Indiana

IAS Edition
Built for the Indiana
Academic Standards

$$\frac{3}{2} = \frac{1}{2} + \frac{1}{2} + \frac{1}{2}$$

120°

Vice President of Education: Adam Berkin
Editorial Director: Cynthia Tripp
Director, Customization and Correlations: Abigail Jungreis
Executive Editors: Penny Dowdy, Kathy Kellman
Edito: Kathryn Bresnahan, Ruth Estabrook, Pam Halloran, Sarah Kraus, Djana Paper, Lauren Van Wart
Project Managers: Deborah Golumbek, Grace Izzy, Sherry Pilkerton
Cover Design: Matt Pollock
Cover Illustrator: O'Lamar Gibson
Book Design: Jeremy Spiegel, Timothy Theriault
Composition: Edward Scanlon, Mark Nodland, Scott Hoffman

NOT FOR RESALE

ISBN 978-1-4957-4282-8
©2017–Curriculum Associates, LLC
North Billerica, MA 01862

Table of Contents

Standards in boldface are the focus standards that address major lesson content.

Table of Contents continued

Standards in boldface are focus standards that address major lesson content.

Standards in boldface are the focus standards that address major lesson content.

PROCESS STANDARDS HANDBOOK

We use our math thinking to figure out all kinds of problems, even hard problems from real life.

There are eight math habits that will help make your math thinking grow stronger.

Keep practicing! You'll be learning to think like a math pro. Then you'll be ready to take on any problem.

THE 8 MATH HABITS

1 Solve problems.
Keep looking for clues until you solve the problem.

2 Think and reason.
Make sense of the words and the numbers in a problem.

3 Show and explain.
Share your math ideas to help others understand you.

4 Use math in the real world.
Solve problems in real life.

5 Choose a tool.
Decide when to use tools like a diagram, a ruler, or mental math.

6 Be clear and precise.
Try to be exactly right in what you say and do.

7 Zoom in and zoom out.
Look for what's the same and what's different.

8 Use patterns.
Look for patterns in math to find shortcuts.

Read more about each math habit on the pages that follow.

MATH HABIT ①

PS 1 Make sense of problems and persevere in solving them.

Solve problems.

Keep looking for clues until you solve the problem.

For some math problems, you may not know where to start. Try different ways to find a solution and look for clues about which way works best. Then check that your answer makes sense.

To solve problems

Ask Yourself

- Can I say what the problem is asking for?
- Can I ask questions to understand it better?
- Can I think about what does or doesn't make sense?
- Can I try a different way if I need to?

Then, Discuss with a Partner

- I thought the problem didn't make sense until I asked …
- I know my answer makes sense because …

MATH HABIT ②

PS 2 Reason abstractly and quantitatively.

Think and reason.

Make sense of the words and the numbers in a problem.

Reasoning is a way of thinking that puts ideas together.
If you know one thing, then you know another thing.
Reasoning is using math rules and common sense together.

To use reasoning to solve a problem

Ask Yourself

- Can I show how multiplication and division are related?

- When I see an equation, can I think of a story that would go with it?

- When I read a problem, can I write an equation to find the answer?

- Can I try out my answer to see if it makes sense in the story?

Then, Discuss with a Partner

- I turned the problem into numbers when I wrote …

- I showed how adding and subtracting go together when I …

MATH HABIT ③

PS 3 Construct viable arguments and critique the reasoning of others.

Show and explain.

Share your math ideas to help others understand you.

When you explain your math ideas to others, it helps you understand them even better. And that helps you solve other problems later. When you listen to other people, you get new ideas too.

To help explain your ideas or listen to others

Ask Yourself

- Can I use words to show how to solve the problem?
- Can I use pictures or act out the problem with objects?
- Can I ask questions to understand another person's ideas better?

Then, Discuss with a Partner

- I showed my ideas when I wrote …
- I explained my ideas when I said …

MATH HABIT ④

PS 4 Model with mathematics.

Use math in the real world.

Solve problems in real life.

One of the best ways to use your math thinking is to solve real problems. Words tell the story for the problem. Math can turn the words into a model, such as a picture or an equation.

You can use models to solve problems about shopping, art projects, sports, cooking, or ... almost anything!

To solve a real-life problem

Ask Yourself

- Can I draw a picture, write an equation, or use a different model to show the math?
- Can I use my math model to solve the problem?
- Can I check that my answer makes sense?

Then, Discuss with a Partner

- I used a math model to show the problem when I ...
- I know my answer makes sense because ...

MATH HABIT ⑤

PS 5 Use appropriate tools strategically.

Choose a tool.

Decide when to use tools like a diagram, a ruler, or mental math.

There are many tools to use in math. You can use a pencil to do a lot of math. Sometimes you need a ruler, or maybe a diagram. Often you can just do the math in your head.

To choose the best tools

Ask Yourself

- Can I do some problems in my head?
- Can I write the problem on paper?
- Can I make a table or a diagram?
- Can I use a ruler to solve the problem?

Then, Discuss with a Partner

- The tools I chose for this problem are …
- I chose these tools because …

MATH HABIT ⑥

PS 6 Attend to precision.

Be clear and precise.

Try to be exactly right in what you say and do.

Everybody likes to be right when they do math. But sometimes people make mistakes. So it's good to check your work. And it's good to say exactly what you mean when you talk about your math ideas.

To be exactly right

Ask Yourself

- Can I use words that will help everyone understand my math ideas?
- Can I ask questions to understand the meaning of math words I don't know?
- Can I find different ways to check my work when I multiply or add?
- Can I always think about whether my answer makes sense?

Then, Discuss with a Partner

- I was careful to use the right words when I …
- I checked my answer by …

MATH HABIT ⑦

Zoom in and zoom out.

Look for what's the same and what's different.

Math follows rules. Think about these equations:

$2 + 0 = 2$
$3 + 0 = 3$

You can *zoom out* to look at what's the *same* about problems.
They show that any number plus 0 is that number.

You can also *zoom in* to see what's *different* about problems.
The number added to 0 is different in each problem.

To zoom in and zoom out

Ask Yourself

- Can I see how different whole numbers are made from hundreds, tens, and ones?
- Can I see how multiplication is different from addition but is related to addition?
- Can I see how shapes are different but are made from other shapes that are the same?

Then, Discuss with a Partner

- I zoomed out and used a math rule when I …
- I zoomed in and found a difference when I looked at …

MATH HABIT ⑧

PS 8 Look for and express regularity in repeated reasoning.

Use patterns.

Look for patterns in math to find shortcuts.

It's important in math to pay close attention. You might find a pattern or see a math idea.

Think about the pattern you see when you count by tens:

10, 20, 30, 40, 50 …

You can use the pattern to make a good guess about what comes next.

To use patterns

Ask Yourself

- Can I find a pattern in a math problem?
- Can I use clear math words to describe my pattern?
- Can I make a good guess about what is next?

Then, Discuss with a Partner

- I saw a pattern in this problem when I looked at …
- I made a good guess about the pattern when I …

Unit 1
Number Sense—Whole Numbers

Let's learn about adding and subtracting multi-digit numbers.

Real-World Connection Understanding how things are built is an important skill. Engineers need to know how all of the parts of a bridge fit together to make a safe passage for people and cars. Bakers need to know the correct amounts of each ingredient to build a recipe for a tasty loaf of bread.

Building numbers in different ways is a helpful skill, too. You might notice that 50 is 5 tens. 500 is 5 hundreds, but it is also 50 tens. 5,000 is 5 thousands, but it is also 50 hundreds. You could also say 5,000 is 500 tens.

In This Unit You will use your understanding of how numbers can be built up or broken down to compare numbers and solve problems in simpler ways.

✓ Self Check

Before starting this unit, check off the skills you know below. As you complete each lesson, see how many more skills you can check off!

I can:	Before this unit	After this unit
read and write numbers using number names, for example: 495 is *four hundred ninety-five*.	☐	☐
read and write numbers using expanded form, for example: 352 = 300 + 50 + 2.	☐	☐
compare two multi-digit whole numbers, for example: 6,131 > 6,113.	☐	☐
add multi-digit whole numbers, for example: 3,966 + 7,550 = 11,516.	☐	☐
subtract multi-digit whole numbers, for example: 25,082 − 11,919 = 13,163.	☐	☐
round multi-digit whole numbers, for example: 3,528 rounded to the nearest hundred is 3,500.	☐	☐

Think It Through

What exactly does place value mean?

Place value is the value of a digit, or amount the digit is worth, based on its position in a number. You can use a place-value chart to help understand the value of each digit. The chart below shows the number 27,138.

Hundred Thousands	Ten Thousands	Thousands	Hundreds	Tens	Ones
	2	7	1	3	8

The 2 has a value of 2 ten-thousands, or 20,000.
The 7 has a value of 7 thousands, or 7,000.
The 1 has a value of 1 hundred, or 100.
The 3 has a value of 3 tens, or 30.
The 8 has a value of 8 ones, or 8.

Think How are place values related to one another?

Our number system is based on a pattern of tens. A digit in any place has 10 times the value it would have in the place to its right.

Hundred Thousands	Ten Thousands	Thousands	Hundreds	Tens	Ones
		3	3	3	3

The **3** in the tens place has a value of **30**.
That is 10 times the value of the 3 in the ones place. $30 = 10 \times 3$

Circle the digit in the table that has a value of 30.

The **3** in the hundreds place has a value of **300**.
That is 10 times the value of the 3 in the tens place. $300 = 10 \times 30$

The **3** in the thousands place has a value of **3,000**.
That is 10 times the value of the 3 in the hundreds place. $3,000 = 10 \times 300$

Think How can a place-value chart help you think about numbers?

The digits in numbers are in groups of three places called **periods**. Commas are used to separate the periods.

To read numbers with four or more digits you need to know how to read three-digit numbers and the names of the periods. How do you read 467,882?

A place-value chart can help you read and write numbers.

Thousands Period			Ones Period		
Hundred Thousands	Ten Thousands	Thousands	Hundreds	Tens	Ones
4	6	7	8	8	2

To read 467,882, start at the left and read to the comma. Then say the name of the period.

four hundred sixty-seven thousand

Then read the three-digit number in the ones period. Do not say the name of the ones period.

eight hundred eighty-two

Here is the number in **word form**.

four hundred sixty-seven thousand, eight hundred eighty-two

Standard form is the way you usually see a number written, using digits.

467,882

Expanded form is a way to write a number to show the place value of each digit.

400,000 + 60,000 + 7,000 + 800 + 80 + 2

▶ Reflect

1 Compare the values of the two 8s in the number 467,882.

_____

_____

Think About > **Place Value**

🔍 **Let's Explore the Idea** Use the place-value chart to help you think about the value of each digit.

Hundred Thousands	Ten Thousands	Thousands	Hundreds	Tens	Ones
	2	5	0	4	9

2 Write the number in expanded form.

_____

3 Write the number in word form.

_____

4 What digit is in the thousands place? _____

5 What is the value of the digit in the thousands place? _____

6 What would be the value of the digit from problem 4 if it were in the hundreds place? _____

Now try these two problems.

7 Find the next two numbers in the following pattern.

600,000   60,000   6,000   600   _____   _____

8 Write the numbers from the pattern in problem 7 in the following place-value chart. The first one is done for you.

Hundred Thousands	Ten Thousands	Thousands	Hundreds	Tens	Ones
6	0	0	0	0	0

Let's Talk About It

Solve the problems below as a group.

9 Look at the numbers in problem 8 on the previous page. What is the same about all of the numbers?

_____

_____

What is different about all of the numbers?

_____

_____

10 Complete the following to show different ways you can make 2,079.

2,079 = _____ thousands + _____ hundreds + _____ tens + _____ ones

2,079 = _____ hundreds + _____ tens + _____ ones

2,079 = _____ tens + _____ ones

2,079 = _____ ones

11 Solve the following base-ten riddles. Show your work.

- I have 18 ones, 15 hundreds, 15 tens, and 8 thousands.
  What number am I? _____

- I have 14 tens, 6 hundreds, 7 ten-thousands, and 15 ones.
  What number am I? _____

▶ Try It Another Way

12 What number is ten thousand less than 842,719? _____

13 What number is one thousand more than 700,012? _____

Connect ▶ Ideas About Place Value

Talk through these problems as a class, then write your answers below.

14 Explain Emma wrote thirty-six thousand, forty-two as 3,642. Explain what she did wrong. Then write the number correctly.

_____

_____

_____

_____

15 Demonstrate Suppose you only have hundreds, tens, and ones blocks. What are two different ways you could make the number 1,718?

_____

_____

_____

_____

16 Apply Place value is important to know when you are talking about prices. What items have prices that are in the hundreds of dollars? thousands of dollars? tens of thousands of dollars? Think about the prices of items with place values in the hundreds, thousands, and ten-thousands. Give at least two examples of each.

Hundreds Place: _____

Thousands Place: _____

Ten-Thousands Place: _____

Apply ▶ **Ideas About Place Value**

17 Put It Together Use what you have learned to complete this task.

You are playing a game that includes the following cards.

| 1 | 5 | 2 | 7 | 0 | 4 | 8 | 6 |

Part A Choose six cards. Circle the cards you choose.

 i Make the greatest number possible using each of the six cards only once. Write your answer in standard form and in expanded form.

Standard Form: _____

Expanded Form: _____

 ii Make the least number possible using the same six cards. If the 0 card is one of your cards, do not use it as the first digit in your number. Write your answer in standard form and in expanded form.

Standard Form: _____

Expanded Form: _____

Part B Look at the standard form of your answers to Part A. Circle a digit that you used in both numbers. Did the value of the digit change between the two numbers? Explain why or why not.

_____

_____

_____

_____

_____

↻ Use What You Know

You have already learned how to compare numbers up to 999. Take a look at this problem that compares numbers in the thousands.

Students in Mrs. Allen's math class are divided into teams. Each team collects points by doing projects and playing math games.

Team A has 1,347 points. Team B has 1,295 points.

Which team has more points?

	Thousands	Hundreds	Tens	Ones
Team A				
Team B				

a. Write the numbers in the place-value chart.

b. Look at the digits in the hundreds, tens, and ones places. How could you compare 347 and 295 to decide which is more?

_____

_____

_____

c. If you add 1,000 to 347 and to 295, you get 1,347 and 1,295. Explain how you can tell that 1,347 > 1,295.

_____

_____

_____

_____

▷▷ Find Out More

In the problem about the teams, you compared 2 four-digit numbers to find out which team had more points. You can also compare numbers to make a decision, such as which size package to buy.

- Sometimes the numbers you are comparing have the same number of digits. Compare place by place, starting with the greatest place-value position, until you can tell which number is greater.

Compare 1,250 and 1,500. Both numbers have 1 thousand, so compare hundreds. One number has 5 hundreds and the other has 2 hundreds. Since 5 hundreds > 2 hundreds, 1,500 > 1,250.

- Sometimes the numbers you are comparing don't have the same number of digits.

Compare 985 and 1,402. You don't need to compare digits because you are comparing a number in the hundreds to a number in the thousands. Even the least number in the thousands (1,000) is greater than the greatest number in the hundreds (999).
So, $1,402 > $985.

▶ Reflect

1 Explain how to find which number is less, 2,400 or 2,300.

_____

_____

_____

Learn About ▷ Comparing Multi-Digit Numbers

Read the problem below. Then explore different ways to compare multi-digit numbers.

> There were 23,643 fans at a football game last week and 23,987 fans at the football game this week. Which game had fewer fans?

▶ **Model It** **You can use a place-value chart to compare multi-digit numbers.**

Ten Thousands	Thousands	Hundreds	Tens	Ones
2	3	6	4	3
2	3	9	8	7

When the numbers are in a place-value chart, it is easy to look down the columns and compare the digits. Start at the greatest place value.

The ten-thousands digits are the same. The thousands digits are the same. The hundreds digits are different. So, compare the digits in the hundreds place.

6 hundreds < 9 hundreds

▶ **Model It** **You can break down numbers by place value to compare multi-digit numbers.**

23,643 = **20,000 + 3,000 + 600** + 40 + 3

23,987 = **20,000 + 3,000 + 900** + 80 + 7

Compare the numbers place by place. The ten thousands and thousands are the same. The hundreds are different.

600 < 900

Connect It   Now you will solve the problem from the previous page using what you know about place value to compare the numbers.

2 Write the numbers 23,643 and 23,987 so they line up by place value. Explain how to line them up.

_____

_____

_____

_____

3 In what place-value position do you begin comparing the two numbers?

_____

_____

4 What is the first place in which the numbers are different? _____

5 Explain how to compare the numbers. Then write the comparison using $>$ or $<$. Tell which game had fewer fans.

_____

_____

_____

Try It   Use what you just learned to solve these problems.

6 There are two baby macaw parrots at a zoo. Zeke has a mass of 1,582 grams, and Tao has a mass of 819 grams. Which bird has a greater mass? Use $>$, $<$, or $=$ to write a comparison.

_____

7 Write the symbol that makes the statement true.

91,146 ◯ 908,043

Practice ▶ **Comparing Whole Numbers**

Study the example below. Then solve problems 8–10.

Example

Millennium Force and Formula Rossa are two famous roller coasters. Millennium Force is 6,595 feet long and Formula Rossa is 6,562 feet long. Which roller coaster is shorter? Use >, <, or = to write a comparison.

Look at how you could show your work using a place-value chart.

Thousands	Hundreds	Tens	Ones
6	5	9	5
6	5	6	2

Solution ___6,595 > 6,562 or 6,562 < 6,595; Formula Rossa___
is shorter.

The student used a place-value chart to compare the digits in the two numbers.

 Pair/Share
How else could you solve this problem?

---

8 A tile factory shipped 342,085 ceramic tiles in 2010. In 2011, they shipped 342,805 tiles. In which year did the tile factory ship more tiles? Use >, <, or = to write a comparison.

Show your work.

What is the first place in which the digits are different?

 Pair/Share
How did you and your partner decide where to start comparing?

Solution _____

_____

9 Val's Video Games sold 11,806 new games and 10,899 used games from May to July. Did Val's Video Games sell more new games or more used games? Use >, <, or = to write a comparison.

Show your work.

I think the comparison can be shown in different ways.

Pair/Share
What are some different ways to state this comparison?

Solution _____

_____

10 Kara has twenty-four thousand, five hundred sixty stickers in her album. Raul has 20,000 + 4,000 + 500 + 60 stickers in his collection.

Which statement correctly compares Kara's and Raul's stickers? Who has more stickers? Circle the letter of the correct answer.

To compare the two numbers, I can write them both in standard form.

A 2,456 < 24,560; Raul has more stickers.

B 24,560 > 24,506; Kara has more stickers.

C 24,560 < 24,650; Raul has more stickers.

D 24,560 = 24,560; They each have the same number.

Anna chose **A** as the correct answer. How did she get that answer?

_____

_____

_____

_____

Pair/Share
Does Anna's answer make sense?

Lesson 2 Compare Whole Numbers   **13**

Practice ▶ **Comparing Whole Numbers**

Solve the problems.

1 Dalton has 1,168 marbles, Juan has 1,079 marbles, Gilbert has 967 marbles, and Lydia has 199 marbles. Who has the greatest number of marbles?

A Dalton

B Juan

C Gilbert

D Lydia

2 A company made 189,909 stuffed animals in 2009. In 2010, the company made 198,909 stuffed animals. Which statement correctly compares the numbers of stuffed animals that were made?

A $189,909 > 198,909$

B $198,909 < 189,909$

C $189,909 < 198,909$

D $198,909 = 189,909$

3 Mr. Hunter wrote the following comparison on the board:

$96,341 < \square\square,\square\square\square$

Use the digits in the tiles below to come up with a number that makes the comparison true. Fill in the boxes in the comparison using each digit below only once.

2 3 5 6 9

4 Selena organized her music files into four online albums. Album A has one thousand eleven songs, Album B has $1000 + 100 + 10$ songs, Album C has 1,101 songs, and Album D has eleven hundred songs.

Write the number of songs in the four albums in the place-value chart.

	Thousands	Hundreds	Tens	Ones
Album A				
Album B				
Album C				
Album D				

Which album has the most songs? _____

5 North Elementary School collected 4,128 cans of soup during a food drive. South Elementary School collected 4,210 cans. Which school collected more cans? Use >, <, or = to write a comparison.

Show your work.

_____

6 One airplane is flying at an altitude of 31,710 feet. A second airplane is flying at 31,820 feet. Use symbols and words to write comparison statements for these numbers.

Show your work.

_____

_____

 **Self Check** Go back and see what you can check off on the Self Check on page 1.

Add and Subtract Whole Numbers

🅖 Use What You Know

In this lesson, you will use place-value understanding and basic facts to add and subtract numbers. Take a look at this problem.

Katie has 3,437 stamps in her collection and Steve has 942 stamps in his collection. How many stamps do Katie and Steve have in all?

a. What operation can you use to find the number of stamps Katie and Steve have in all? _____

b. What is the sum of the digits in the ones place? _____

c. What is the sum of the digits in the tens place? _____

d. What is the sum of the digits in the hundreds place? _____

e. What is the sum of the digits in the thousands place? _____

f. Which place value has a sum greater than 10? _____

g. Explain how you can find the number of stamps Katie and Steve have in all.

_____

_____

_____

_____

_____

▷▷ Find Out More

There are many different ways to add numbers. For example, you can use base-ten blocks, or place-value drawings. You can also break numbers apart and add the parts. When you add numbers in the thousands, some methods are more convenient than others.

To add numbers, you can stack them and line up place values. Here is one way to find the sum in the problem on the previous page. Add from right to left. Add the ones, add the tens, add the hundreds, and then add the thousands.

3,437
+   942

9 ⟶ 7 ones + 2 ones = 9 ones
70 ⟶ 3 tens + 4 tens = 7 tens
1,300 ⟶ 4 hundreds + 9 hundreds = 13 hundreds, or 1 thousand + 3 hundreds
+3,000 ⟶ 3 thousands
4,379

Katie and Steve have 4,379 stamps in all.

▶ Reflect

1 The same problem is solved below by adding left to right: thousands, hundreds, tens, ones. Describe how the methods are alike and how they are different.

3,437
+   942

3,000
1,300
70
+   9
4,379

Learn About ▶ Adding Whole Numbers

Read the problem below. Then explore different ways to add four-digit numbers.

> At a fair, 4,657 ride tickets were sold on Saturday and 3,804 were sold on Sunday. How many tickets were sold in all during those two days?

▶ **Model It** **You can use place value to add. Add ones to ones, tens to tens, hundreds to hundreds, and then thousands to thousands.**

$$
\begin{array}{r}
4{,}657 \\
+\ 3{,}804 \\
\end{array}
$$

        11 ⟶ 7 ones + 4 ones = 11 ones, or 1 ten + 1 one
        50 ⟶ 5 tens + 0 tens = 5 tens
   1,400 ⟶ 6 hundreds + 8 hundreds = 14 hundreds, or 1 thousand + 4 hundreds
+ 7,000 ⟶ 4 thousands + 3 thousands = 7 thousands

   8,461

▶ **Model It** **You can record the sums by showing regrouping above the problem.**

$$
\begin{array}{r}
^{1} \\
4{,}65\mathbf{7} \\
+\ 3{,}80\mathbf{4} \\
\end{array}
$$

    1 ⟶ **7 ones + 4 ones** = 11 ones, or **1 ten + 1 one**

$$
\begin{array}{r}
^{1} \\
4{,}657 \\
+\ 3{,}804 \\
\end{array}
$$

  61 ⟶ **1 ten + 5 tens + 0 tens = 6 tens**

$$
\begin{array}{r}
^{1}\ \ ^{1} \\
4{,}657 \\
+\ 3{,}804 \\
\end{array}
$$

 461 ⟶ **6 hundreds + 8 hundreds** = 14 hundreds, or **1 thousand + 4 hundreds**

$$
\begin{array}{r}
^{1}\ \ ^{1} \\
4{,}657 \\
+\ 3{,}804 \\
\end{array}
$$

8,461 ⟶ **1 thousand + 4 thousands + 3 thousands = 8 thousands**

Connect It Now you will see how to solve the problem by showing all the steps at once.

2 Here is what the second *Model It* looks like showing all the steps at once.

$$\begin{array}{r} \overset{1\ 1}{4,657} \\ +\ 3,804 \\ \hline 8,461 \end{array}$$

The sum of the ones values is 11. Where do you see the 11 in the equation above?

_____

3 The sum of the hundreds values is 1,400. Where do you see the 1,400 in the equation above?

_____

4 Why is there a 1 above the tens place and above the thousands place?

_____

_____

_____

5 Explain how to add two four-digit numbers if you need to regroup ones and hundreds. _____

_____

_____

_____

Try It Use what you just learned to solve this problem. Show your work two ways on a separate sheet of paper.

6 A video game company sold 5,680 copies of its new game on the first day and 3,235 copies on the second day. In those two days, how many copies of the game did the company sell? _____

Learn About > # Subtracting Whole Numbers

Read the problem below. Then explore different ways to subtract numbers.

Last week, Mr. Diaz flew 4,002 miles for work. This week, he flew 2,153 miles. How many more miles did Mr. Diaz fly last week than this week?

▶ **Model It** **You can use place value to subtract 4,002 − 2,153.**

You cannot subtract 3 from 2. So you need to regroup. Write 4,002 in a place-value chart. There are zeros in the tens and hundreds places. So you cannot regroup the tens or hundreds yet. Start by regrouping the thousands place. Keep regrouping until you can subtract.

Thousands	Hundreds	Tens	Ones
④	0	0	2

4 thousands = 3 thousands + 10 hundreds

3	⑩	0	2

10 hundreds = 9 hundreds + 10 tens

3	9	⑩	2

10 tens = 9 tens + 10 ones

3	9	9	10 + 2 = 12

Now you can subtract.

	Thousands	Hundreds	Tens	Ones
	3	9	9	12
−	2	1	5	3
	1	8	4	9

Connect It   Now you will solve the problem from the previous page by showing regrouping.

$$\begin{array}{r} 4{,}002 \\ -\ 2{,}153 \end{array} \longrightarrow \begin{array}{r} \overset{3\ \ 10}{4{,}\cancel{0}02} \\ -\ 2{,}153 \end{array} \longrightarrow \begin{array}{r} \overset{\ \ 9}{\overset{3\ \ 10\ 10}{4{,}\cancel{0}\cancel{0}2}} \\ -\ 2{,}153 \end{array} \longrightarrow \begin{array}{r} \overset{9\ \ 9}{\overset{3\ \ 10\ 10\ 12}{4{,}\cancel{0}\cancel{0}\cancel{2}}} \\ -\ 2{,}153 \\ \hline 1{,}849 \end{array}$$

7 How is regrouping thousands shown in the problem above? _____

_____

8 Why is the **10** crossed out in the hundreds column? _____

_____

9 Explain the regrouping shown in the tens column. _____

_____

10 Why are **12 ones** shown in the ones column? _____

_____

11 Explain how to subtract two four-digit numbers if you need to regroup in all places. _____

_____

_____

_____

Try It   Use what you just learned to solve these problems. Show your work on a separate sheet of paper.

12 There were 11,402 fans at the Hawks game and 9,617 fans at the Bulls game. How many more fans attended the Hawks game than the Bulls game? _____

13 129,027 − 98,918 = _____

Practice ▶ **Adding and Subtracting Whole Numbers**

Study the example below. Then solve problems 14–16.

Example

Sallie earned $4,580 last month. Her bills for that month totaled $3,178. How much money does Sallie have left after she pays her bills?

Look at how you could show your work.

$$
\begin{array}{r}
\overset{710}{4,5\cancel{8}\cancel{0}} \\
-\ 3,178 \\
\hline
1,402
\end{array}
$$

Solution _____$1,402_____

The student regrouped 1 ten as 10 ones.

Pair/Share
What is another way you could solve this problem?

---

14 The population of Turtle Valley is 407,989. The population of Art Creek is 86,966. What is the total population of the two cities?

Show your work.

What operation can you use to solve this problem?

Pair/Share
How did you decide which operation to use?

Solution _____

▷▷ Find Out More

You round numbers to estimate and to make numbers easier to work with when you don't need an exact answer.

You can use a number line to round 36,219 to the nearest thousand. The closest thousand less than 36,219 is 36,000. The closest thousand greater than 36,219 is 37,000. Which thousand is 36,219 closer to?

36,219

36,000   36,500   37,000

The number **36,219** rounded to the nearest thousand is **36,000** because it is closer to 36,000 than to 37,000.

What if 36,500 customers were surveyed? That number is exactly halfway between 36,000 and 37,000. Follow the rounding rule, "If a number is exactly halfway between, round up."

So, the number 36,500 rounded to the nearest thousand is 37,000.

▶ Reflect

1 Use the rule, "If a number is exactly halfway between, round up" to explain how to round 1,500 to the nearest thousand.

_____

_____

_____

_____

_____

_____

Learn About ▶ **Rounding Whole Numbers**

Read the problem below. Then explore how to use a number line to solve a problem that involves rounding.

> Last year, Tanaka's Toys spent $117,290 developing a new video game. This year, the company spent $175,000 on the game. Round the amounts spent to the nearest ten thousand. Then, find about how much more Tanaka's Toys spent on the game this year than last year.

▶ **Model It** **You can use a number line to round $117,290 to the nearest ten thousand.**

Find the closest ten thousands that are less than 117,290 and greater than 117,290. 117,290 is between 110,000 and 120,000.

117,290 is closer to **120,000**.

$117,290 rounded to the nearest ten thousand is $120,000.

▶ **Model It** **You can use a number line to round $175,000 to the nearest ten thousand.**

Find the closest ten thousands that are less than 175,000 and greater than 175,000. 175,000 is between 170,000 and 180,000.

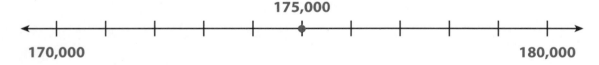

175,000 is exactly halfway between 170,000 and 180,000. Follow the rule. Round up to **180,000**.

$175,000 rounded to the nearest ten thousand is $180,000.

Connect It Now you will solve the problem from the previous page.

2 Why do you round $117,290 up to $120,000?

_____

3 Why do you round $175,000 up to $180,000?

_____

4 After you round both amounts, how do you estimate how much more Tanaka's Toys spent on the game this year than last year?

_____

5 About how much more did Tanaka's Toys spend this year? _____

6 Choose any five-digit number. Write it here. _____

Explain how to round a five-digit number to the nearest ten thousand.

_____

_____

_____

Try It Use what you just learned to solve these problems. Show your work on a separate sheet of paper.

7 Mr. Ruiz's class wants to collect 2,000 water bottles to recycle. So far, they have collected 1,376 water bottles. Round each amount to the nearest hundred. Then find about how many more bottles the class needs to collect. _____

8 Round 649,418

to the nearest ten: _____

to the nearest hundred: _____

to the nearest thousand: _____

to the nearest ten thousand: _____

to the nearest hundred thousand: _____

Practice ▸ **Rounding Whole Numbers**

Study the example below. Then solve problems 9–11.

Example

The tallest building in Martin's city is 1,729 feet tall. The tallest building in Peggy's city is 1,065 feet tall. To the nearest hundred feet, about how much taller is the building in Martin's city than the building in Peggy's city?

Look at how you could show your work using number lines.

Round each number to the nearest hundred.

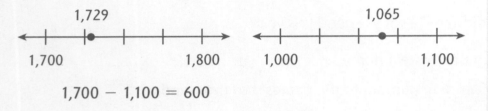

$$1,700 - 1,100 = 600$$

Solution _about 600 feet_

> The student rounded 1,729 and 1,065 to the nearest hundred, then subtracted the rounded amounts.

 Pair/Share
How can you decide which two hundreds a number is between?

---

9 Smallville has 12,548 people registered to vote. In the last election, only 4,685 people voted. To the nearest thousand, about how many registered voters did not vote?

Show your work.

> What operation do I use after I round each number?

 Pair/Share
How did you decide whether to round up or round down?

Solution _____

10 Grandview Golf makes wooden golf tees. In 2010, they made 380,285 tees. In 2011, they made 512,525 tees. To the nearest ten thousand, how many tees did they make in the two years?

Show your work.

What should I do first to solve this problem?

Solution _____

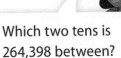

Pair/Share
Could the answer be greater than 900,000?

11 Movie Mart shipped 264,398 DVDs to its customers last year. To the nearest ten, how many DVDs did Movie Mart ship? Circle the letter of the correct answer.

A 264,300

B 264,390

C 264,400

D 265,000

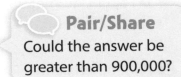

Which two tens is 264,398 between?

Elin chose **C** as the correct answer. Explain how she got her answer.

_____

_____

_____

_____

 Pair/Share
Do you agree with Elin's answer?

Lesson 4 Round Whole Numbers   **31**

Practice ▶ **Rounding Whole Numbers**

Solve the problems.

1 The distances four hot air balloons traveled are listed below.

Balloon A: 6,559 kilometers   Balloon C: 6,547 kilometers
Balloon B: 6,545 kilometers   Balloon D: 6,553 kilometers

Leah rounds the distances the balloons traveled to the nearest ten. Which distance does NOT round to 6,550 kilometers?

A   6,559 kilometers

B   6,545 kilometers

C   6,547 kilometers

D   6,553 kilometers

2 Phoebe's Bait and Tackle sold 128,107 live worms in April and 102,278 live worms in May. To the nearest thousand, how many worms did Phoebe's Bait and Tackle sell in April and May together?

A   200,000

B   230,000

C   230,400

D   230,390

3 Which numbers have been rounded correctly to the nearest thousand? Circle the letter for all that apply.

A   12,500 ⟶ 13,000

B   1,445 ⟶ 2,000

C   29,607 ⟶ 30,000

D   498 ⟶ 500

4 A is an unknown number. When you round A to the nearest thousand, you get 21,000. When you round A to the nearest hundred, you get 20,500.

Write A in the box that shows its location on the number line.

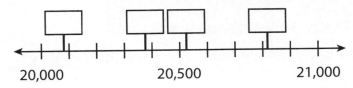

5 Round 5,563 to the nearest thousand, to the nearest hundred, and to the nearest ten. If you could pay a $5,563 bill with a rounded amount, which place value would you rather round to? If you could choose a rounded amount for a $5,563 prize in a contest, which place value would you rather round to?

Show your work.

6 Nadia's father bought a new camera, lens, and case. He rounded the cost of all the items to estimate how much money he would need. He rounded the cost of the camera to $800, the cost of the lens to $500, and the cost of the case to $200. The actual cost of all three items was $1,489. What could the actual costs of the items be?

Show your work.

Answer camera _____ lens _____ case _____

✓ **Self Check** **Go back and see what you can check off on the Self Check on page 1.**

Unit 1
MATH IN ACTION

👥 **Introduction**
Work with Whole Numbers

PS1 Make sense of problems and persevere in solving them.

Study an Example Problem and Solution

Read this problem about adding whole numbers. Then look at Max's solution to this problem.

Blog Site Visitors

Max posts the number of visitors to his gaming blog.

Max's Video Game Blog

Gaming Blog Visitors
▶ **January Visitors**
  30,000 + 2,000 + 50 + 1
▶ **February Visitors**
  28,486
▶ **March Visitors**
  thirty thousand eighteen

In his April blog, Max will post hints about a popular new computer game. He sets some goals for the number of visitors he hopes to get in April.

• Get more than the total of two of the months combined.
• Get between 999 and 9,999 more visitors than this total.

What is a number of visitors that would meet Max's goal? Tell why your number works.

Read the sample solution on the next page. Then look at the checklist below. Find and mark parts of the solution that match the checklist.

✏️ **Problem-Solving Checklist**

☐ Tell what is known.
☐ Tell what the problem is asking.
☐ Show all your work.
☐ Show that the solution works.

a. Circle something that is known.

b. Underline something that you need to find.

c. Draw a box around what you do to solve the problem.

d. Put a checkmark next to the part that shows the solution works.

Max's Solution

▷ **I need to find the total visitors for two months combined.**

I know that I can pick any two months. I'll use February and March.

▷ **Next, I write the number for March in standard form.**

thirty thousand eighteen = 30,018

▷ **Then, I add the numbers for February and March.**

$$
\begin{array}{r}
28{,}486 \\
+\ 30{,}018 \\
\hline
14 \\
90 \\
400 \\
8{,}000 \\
50{,}000 \\
\hline
58{,}504
\end{array}
$$

▷ **For April I want between 999 and 9,999 more visitors than 58,504 visitors.**

I can round 999 to 1,000 and 9,999 to 10,000.

▷ **5,000 is about halfway between 1,000 and 10,000.**

I had to choose a number that met the goal.

▷ **Last, I add to find the goal.**

Two-month total:
Number used to set goal:

$$
\begin{array}{r}
{\scriptstyle 1} \\
58{,}504 \\
+\ 5{,}000 \\
\hline
63{,}504
\end{array}
$$

I added 5,000 to the total for February and March.

▷ **My goal for April is 63,504 visitors.**

The number of visitors for both February and March is about 30,000. I want an extra 5,000 visitors.

$$30{,}000 + 30{,}000 + 5{,}000 = 65{,}000.$$

My goal of 63,504 makes sense.

I rounded to check that my answer makes sense.

Try ▶ Another Approach

There are many ways to solve problems. Think about how you might solve the Blog Site Visitors problem in a different way.

Blog Site Visitors

Max posts the number of visitors to his gaming blog.

Max's Video Game Blog

Gaming Blog Visitors
▶ **January Visitors**
30,000 + 2,000 + 50 + 1
▶ **February Visitors**
28,486
▶ **March Visitors**
thirty thousand eighteen

In his April blog, Max will post hints about a popular new computer game. He sets some goals for the number of visitors he hopes to get in April.

• Get more than the total of two of the months combined.
• Get between 999 and 9,999 more visitors than this total.

What is a number of visitors that would meet Max's goal? Tell why your number works.

▶ Plan It Answer these questions to help you start thinking about a plan.

A. What are all the possible pairs of months? Which pairs are different than the ones used in the example problem?

_____

_____

B. What steps will you take to set a goal for April?

_____

_____

Solve It Find a different solution for the Blog Site Visitors problem.
Show all your work on a separate sheet of paper.

You may want to use the problem-solving tips to get started.

Problem-Solving Tips

- ### Models

Ten Thousands	Thousands	Hundreds	Tens	Ones

- ### Word Bank

add	thousands	tens
total	hundreds	ones
less than	greater than	

- ### Sentence Starters

  - _____ is greater than _____

  - Write the number _____

Problem-Solving Checklist
Make sure that you . . .
- ☐ tell what you know.
- ☐ tell what you need to do.
- ☐ show all your work
- ☐ show that the solution works.

Reflect
Use Process Standards As you work through the problem, discuss these questions with a partner.

- **Use Structure** How can your understanding of place value help you find a number that is between two given numbers?

- **Use a Model** How can you use a place-value chart to help you think about the numbers?

Discuss Models and Strategies

Read the problem. Write a solution on a separate sheet of paper. Remember, there are lots of ways to solve a problem!

Max's Summary

Max met his goal for April! He added the information to his blog site.

Max's Video Game Blog

Gaming Blog Visitors

▶ **January Visitors**
30,000 + 2,000 + 50 + 1

▶ **February Visitors**
28,486

▶ **March Visitors**
thirty thousand eighteen

▶ **April Visitors**
50,000 + 9,000 + 600 + 30 + 2

Max wants you to write a summary about the number of visitors to his blog site from January to April. He wants the summary to tell about how many visitors he had. So, he doesn't want to use exact numbers. Then Max needs help setting a goal for the number of visitors he hopes to get in May.

What should your summary say? What number of visitors should Max set for his May goal?

Plan It and Solve It Find a solution to Max's Summary problem.

Write a detailed plan and support your answer. Be sure to include:

- a sentence about your estimate that Max could put in his summary.
- a goal for the number of visitors he hopes to get in May.
- how you decided on the goal for May.

You may want to use the problem-solving tips to get started.

Problem-Solving Tips

- **Questions**
  - Will I round to the nearest hundred? Nearest thousand?
  - Will I round the numbers first or add first?

- **Word Bank**

round	close to	less than
estimate	greater than	just under
about	a little more than	

- **Sentence Starters**
  - From January to April there were about _____
  - The goal for the number of visitors in May _____

Problem-Solving Checklist

Make sure that you . . .

☐ tell what you know.

☐ tell what you need to do.

☐ show all your work.

☐ show that the solution works.

Reflect

Use Process Standards As you work through the problem, discuss these questions with a partner.

- **Be Precise** Why is an estimate appropriate for the situation in the problem?

- **Make Sense of Problems** What is your first step in solving the problem? Why?

Persevere   On Your Own

Read the problems. Write a solution on a separate sheet of paper. Remember, there are many different ways to solve a problem!

Yearly Blog Visits

Max's blog site now shows the monthly visitors through June. He asks you to write a report about the number of visitors he had during this time. He also wants you to estimate numbers for the whole year.

Max's Video Game Blog

Gaming Blog Visitors

▶ **January Visitors**
30,000 + 2,000 + 50 + 1

▶ **February Visitors**
28,486

▶ **March Visitors**
thirty thousand eighteen

▶ **April Visitors**
50,000 + 9,000 + 600 + 30 + 2

▶ **May Visitors**
62,187

▶ **June Visitors**
sixty-three thousand nine hundred two

How many visitors should Max expect to get on his blog site in one year?

▶ **Solve It** **Write a report for Max about visitors to his blog site.**

Use rounding and estimation to help you write a report. Include:

• the approximate number of visitors each month and a 6-month total.

• a prediction of the total number of visitors there will be for the whole year.

• an explanation of how you made the total year prediction.

▶ **Reflect**

Use Process Standards   After you complete the task, choose one of these questions to discuss with a partner.

• **Look for Structure**   What number patterns helped you make a prediction?

• **Make an Argument**   Why is your prediction a reasonable estimate?

Blog Topics

Max recorded the number of visitors to his blog site for the rest of the year. This time he listed the major topics that he reported on each month.

Month	Number of Visitors	Major Topics
July	49,467	art reviews, characters
August	65,118	strategies, walkthroughs
September	60,096	story/narrative
October	68,734	strategies
November	70,643	walkthroughs
December	48,942	characters, reviews

Which of Max's major blog topics are the most and least popular?

▶ **Solve It** Help Max decide which blog topics are the most popular and which topics are the least popular.

Compare the actual numbers of monthly visitors to Max's blog site.

- List the months in order, either from the greatest to least number of visitors or from the least to greatest number of visitors.
- Find the difference between the least and greatest number of visitors.
- Tell which topics seem to be the most popular and which seem to be the least popular. Explain your reasoning.

▶ **Reflect**

Use Process Standards After you complete the task, choose one of these questions to discuss with a partner.

- **Make an Argument** How did you use the monthly numbers to explain which topic is the most popular?

- **Be Precise** Why did you use actual numbers for this problem and not rounded numbers?

Solve the problems.

1 The population of a city in North Carolina is 403,892. What is 403,892 rounded to the nearest thousand?

A 410,000

B 404,000

C 403,000

D 400,000

2 A survey reported that 713,298 people visited the local Science Museum last year. How can 713,298 be written in word form?

A seventy-one thousand, three hundred twenty-nine

B seven hundred thirteen thousand, two hundred ninety-eight

C seven hundred thirteen, two ninety-eight

D seven hundred thirty thousand, two hundred ninety-eight

3 What is the sum of 7,447 and 1,027?

A 84,641

B 84,614

C 8,474

D 8,464

4 What is the expanded form of 9,787?

A $9 + 7 + 8 + 7$

B $9,000 + 780 + 7$

C $9,000 + 700 + 87$

D $9,000 + 700 + 80 + 7$

5 Which number sentence is true? Circle the letter for all that apply.

A $386 + 752 = 1,038$

B $14,000 < 14,999$

C $8,573 = 8,000 + 570 + 3$

D $98,997 > 100,001$

6 This set of base-ten blocks represents a number. The value of this number can be represented in many different ways.

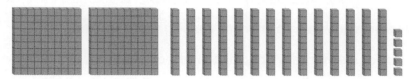

Choose *Yes* or *No* to show whether the value is equivalent to the number represented by the base-ten blocks.

a. two hundred forty-five   ☐ Yes   ☐ No

b. 200 + 140 + 5   ☐ Yes   ☐ No

c. 3 hundreds + 4 tens + 5 ones   ☐ Yes   ☐ No

7 The four highest mountains in the world are listed below.

K2 (Godwin-Austen)	**Kangchenjunga**	**Everest**	**Lhotse**
28,250 feet	28,169 feet	29,035 feet	27,940 feet

Part A Write the heights in the boxes to arrange them from greatest to least number of feet.

Part B When Lina rounded the heights, she got the same number for all four mountains. When Adam rounded, he got the same number for three of the mountains and a different number for the fourth. Can they both be correct? Explain why or why not.

_____

_____

_____

Part C The fifth highest mountain is Makalu. Its height, rounded to the nearest hundred, is 27,800 feet. What is the highest that this mountain can be? How do you know?

_____

_____

Performance Task

Answer the questions and show all your work on separate paper.

The students at Water Street Elementary School have been given a "Million Minute Reading Challenge." Students record the number of minutes that they read each day and their teachers find the total for each grade. The chart below shows the number of minutes read in the first four months of the challenge.

	First Grade	Second Grade	Third Grade	Fourth Grade	Fifth Grade
Number of Minutes	98,050	30,451	100,870	145,689	120,270

Checklist

Did you . . .

☐ show the original data and all calculations?

☐ explain how you made your estimate?

☐ write a complete letter?

The principal of Water Street Elementary School wants a report on the school's progress. She wants to know each grade's totals to the nearest thousand and approximately how close the school is to reaching one million minutes. Write a letter to the principal describing how close students are to their goal and estimating how much more time they need. In the letter you should show your work and explain your reasoning.

Reflect

Use Process Standards After you complete the task, choose one of the following questions to answer.

- **Persevere** Which information given in this problem helped you decide how to begin?

- **Reason Mathematically** How does rounding help you to solve this problem?

Unit 2
Algebraic Thinking

> Let's learn about finding patterns and relationships in numbers.

Real-World Connection Playing around with numbers can help you discover some interesting patterns and relationships. There are 24 eggs in two dozen. Three groups of 8 cupcakes are a total of 24 cupcakes. Four 6-inch pieces of ribbon are 24 inches of ribbon. Six 4-packs of yogurt make 24 yogurts, and twelve pairs of mittens are 24 mittens. Can you see a relationship among all of these facts?

In This Unit You will learn about many different patterns and relationships in numbers and shapes. You will also learn about different properties of multiplication. You will see a lot of problems that may seem difficult at first. But, what you know about numbers, shapes, multiplication, and division will help you be a star problem-solver.

✔ Self Check

Before starting this unit, check off the skills you know below. As you complete each lesson, see how many more skills you can check off!

I can:	Before this unit	After this unit
multiply and divide to solve comparison problems, for example: 28 is 4 times as many as 7.	☐	☐
understand and use properties of multiplication.	☐	☐
identify factor pairs for a number, for example: 4 and 5 are a factor pair for 20.	☐	☐
identify multiples of a number, for example: 42 is a multiple of 6.	☐	☐
identify prime or composite numbers, for example: 16 is composite.	☐	☐
describe rules in number and shape patterns, for example: the pattern "3, 10, 17, 24, . . . " has the rule "add 7" and the numbers go back and forth between odd and even.	☐	☐
model and solve multi-step word problems using equations, for example: $(6 \times 3) - 11 + 2 = 9$.	☐	☐

💭 Think It Through

What are some ways to think about multiplication?

You have looked at multiplication as joining equal groups. When you know the number of groups and the number of objects in each group, you can multiply to find the total.

If you have **3 groups** of **5 stars** each, you have 15 stars in all.

The multiplication equation that shows the total number of stars is $3 \times 5 = 15$.

Think Multiplication is also a way to compare two numbers.

If you want to find the number that is 3 times as many as 5, you also multiply.

You can draw a model to represent the situation.

Show **5 stars**.

Show **3 times as many**.

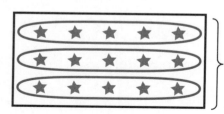

3 times as many as 5 is 15.

The model shows that 15 is 3 times as many as 5. You can write that comparison as a multiplication equation.

$$15 = 3 \times 5$$

✏️ In the comparison equation, **circle** the number that compares 15 to 5.

Think When you multiply, the order of the factors does not matter.

You can draw a model to show 5 times as many as 3.

Show **3 stars**.

5 and 3 are the factors.
15 is the product.

Show **5 times as many**.

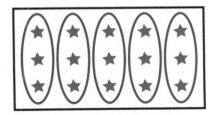

The model shows that 15 is 5 times as many as 3. You can write that comparison as a multiplication equation: $15 = 5 \times 3$.

You can think about any multiplication equation as two comparisons.
For example, the equation $5 \times 7 = 35$ shows two comparisons:

    35 is 5 times as many as 7.

    35 is 7 times as many as 5.

Now you'll have a chance to think more about multiplication as a comparison.
You may find that using models can help you explain your thinking.

▶ Reflect

1 On the lines below, use words to describe the two ways you can think about
$8 \times 5 = 40$ as a comparison.

_____

_____

Think About **Multiplication**

🔍 **Let's Explore the Idea** You can use bar models to help you understand multiplication as a comparison.

2 Look at the following model.

2			
2	2	2	2

8

Describe the comparison the model shows.

Use words: 8 is _____ times as many as _____ .

Use an equation: _____

3 Tucker and Abel are brothers. Tucker is 6 years old. Abel is 3 times as old as Tucker. Label the bar model below to show the relationships between the numbers in the problem.

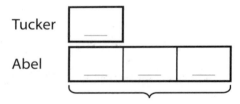

Now try these two problems.

4 Draw and label a bar model to show a number that is 4 times as many as 8.

5 Draw and label a bar model to show a number that is 6 times as many as 9.

Let's Talk About It

Solve the problems below as a group.

6 Write a word problem that the bar model in problem 2 could represent.

_____

_____

_____

7 Gabby read 4 times as many books as Mark. Mark read 5 books. Draw a bar model that represents the number of books Gabby read.

8 Yao blew up 8 balloons. Flora blew up 2 times as many balloons as Yao. Write an equation that represents the number of balloons Flora blew up.

_____

▶ **Try It Another Way** Work with your group to write a word problem that could be modeled by each of the following equations.

9 $4 \times 6 = 24$

_____

_____

_____

10 $5 \times 8 = 40$

_____

_____

_____

Connect **Ideas About Multiplication**

Talk through these problems as a class, then write your answers below.

11 Explain Mia planted 8 seeds. Her sister planted 6 times as many seeds. How could you find the number of seeds Mia's sister planted?

_____

_____

_____

_____

12 Compare How is 4 times as many as 7 related to 7 times as many as 4? Explain your reasoning.

_____

_____

_____

_____

13 Analyze Ben found 4 pennies on the ground. His sister said she found 2 times as many pennies. Ben figured out that his sister found 6 pennies.

What did Ben do wrong?

_____

_____

_____

_____

14 **Put It Together** Use what you have learned to complete this task.

> Paige and Ben each babysat last weekend. Paige babysat for 3 times as many hours as Ben. Ben babysat for 4 hours.

Part A Draw a bar model to represent the situation.

Part B Look at your model. Now write a different word problem that could also be represented by the model. Then, write an equation that the model represents.

_____

_____

_____

_____

_____

Equation _____

Use Multiplication Properties

Use What You Know

In this lesson you will learn how to use ordering, grouping, and renaming of factors to solve multiplication problems. Take a look at this problem.

For a balloon toss, one class had 6 teams of 3 students. For a relay race, another class had 3 teams of 6 students. How does the number of students on each team compare?

Balloon Toss

Relay Race

a. What multiplication equation could you write to find how many students tossed balloons? _____

b. What multiplication equation could you write to find how many students ran the relay race? _____

c. What do you know about the total number of students playing each game?

_____

d. What is the same about the equations in parts a and b? What is different?

_____

_____

e. Is the product of any pair of factors the same no matter what order the factors are written in? Give two examples that support your answer.

_____

▷▷ Find Out More

On the previous page you saw that when you multiply two factors, the product is the same no matter what order the factors are written in.

When you multiply three numbers, you can use parentheses ( ) to group together the two factors you want to multiply first. Look at the problem below.

> For the relay race, there were 3 teams with 6 students from one class. There were also 3 teams with 6 students from another class. How many students ran the relay race altogether?

- **One way** to think about this is to first find how many students are in each class. Then multiply by the number of classes.

Class A   **Class B**

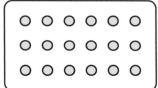

6×3 is 18. There are 18 students in each class.
$(6 \times 3) \times 2 = 36$
18 students in each of 2 classes is 36 students.

- **Another way** to solve this is to find the total number of teams. Then multiply by the number of students on each team.

Class A   **Class B**

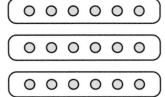

3×2 is 6. There are 6 teams in all.
$6 \times (3 \times 2) = 36$
6 teams with 6 students on each is 36 students.

▶ Reflect

1 Explain how to multiply three numbers together. _____

_____

_____

Learn About	**Using Order to Multiply**

Read the problem below. Then explore ways to show you can multiply factors in an equation in any order.

> The Rackey family raked leaves each day for 7 days. They filled 4 bags each day.
> The Tang family raked leaves each day for 4 days. They filled 7 bags each day.
> The total number of bags each family filled is the same. How do you know this?

▶ **Picture It** **You can use arrays to help show the two numbers are the same.**

Each row in the arrays shows the number of bags the Rackey family or the Tang family filled each day.

Rackey Family   **Tang Family**

▶ **Model It** **You can use multiplication expressions to show two ways to solve the problem.**

7 days, 4 bags each day $\longrightarrow$ 7 × 4

4 days, 7 bags each day $\longrightarrow$ 4 × 7

Connect It   Now you will solve the problem on the previous page using equations.

2 How are the arrays shown in *Picture It* alike? How are they different?

_____

_____

3 How are the expressions shown in *Model It* alike? How are they different?

_____

_____

4 What multiplication equation can you write to find the number of bags filled by the Rackey family? _____

5 What multiplication equation can you write to find the number of bags filled by the Tang family? _____

6 Describe how you know each family filled the same number of bags.

_____

7 The next week the Rackey family filled 5 bags a day for 7 days. The Tang family filled 7 bags a day for 5 days. How do you know they filled the same number of bags without multiplying? _____

_____

Try It   Use what you learned about ordering factors to solve these problems.

8 Meg has 5 boxes with 6 books in each box. Jack has 6 boxes with 5 books in each box. Explain how you know Meg and Jack have the same number of books.

_____

9 Devon has a storage shelf for his building cubes. It has 8 rows with 4 drawers in each row. Jayla has a storage shelf with the same number of drawers. It has 4 rows. How many drawers are in each row in Jayla's storage box? _____

Learn About ▶ **Using Grouping to Multiply**

Read the problem below. Then explore different ways to group factors to help you multiply three numbers.

> Sara places sandwiches on trays for the cafeteria. On each tray she places 3 sandwiches in a row, and she makes 4 rows on each tray. She fills 5 trays. How many sandwiches in all does Sara put on the trays?

▶ **Picture It** **You can draw a diagram to decide which two factors to multiply first.**

One way:

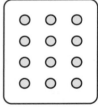    

4 × **3** sandwiches on each tray. So, **12** sandwiches × 5 trays.

Another way:

 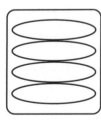 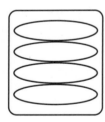 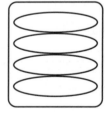 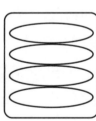

4 × **5** rows in all. So, **20** rows × 3 sandwiches.

▶ **Model It** **You can write the multiplication problem with parentheses.**

Parentheses show which two factors you will multiply first.

One way: (3 × 4) × 5 ⟶   ?

Another way: 3 × (4 × 5) ⟶   ?

Connect It Now you will solve the problem on the previous page using equations.

10 What is the difference between the two expressions in the *Model It* section?

_____

_____

11 Complete the multiplication in the parentheses in each expression. Then write the resulting expressions. _____

12 Which way would you choose to find the product? Explain your choice.

_____

_____

What is the total number of sandwiches that Sara put on the trays? _____

13 Remember that you can change the order of factors and not change the product. Change the order of the factors in $3 \times 4 \times 5$. Then use parentheses to show a third way to group the factors. _____

Try It Use what you just learned about grouping factors to solve these problems.

14 At a food bank, Eva opened 2 boxes of donated food. Inside each box there were 8 packages of granola bars. Each package held 6 granola bars. How many granola bars were donated? Show two different ways to solve the problem.

_____

_____

15 People picking apples at Red Maple Farm ride to the orchard in wagons. Each wagon has 5 rows of seats. Each row has 5 seats. The farm has 6 wagons. How many seats are there in all? Show two different ways to solve the problem.

_____

_____

Learn About ▶ **Renaming Numbers to Multiply**

Read the problem below. Then explore how to rename one of the factors to make multiplying easier.

> Ramon plans to set up chairs for a soccer club dinner. There will be 3 tables, and 9 players will sit at each table. How many chairs does Ramon need? Rename one of the numbers to find the answer.

▶ **Picture It** **You can use an array to help you understand the problem.**

Break apart an array to show numbers that are easier to multiply.

```
X X X X X X X X X          X X X X X          X X X X
X X X X X X X X X    →     X X X X X          X X X X
X X X X X X X X X          X X X X X          X X X X
```

3 groups of 9　　　　**3 groups of 5**　and　**3 groups of 4**

Add to an array to show numbers that are easier to multiply.

```
X X X X X X X X X          X X X X X X X X X X
X X X X X X X X X    →     X X X X X X X X X X
X X X X X X X X X          X X X X X X X X X X
```

3 groups of 9　　　　　　**3 groups of 10**

▶ **Model It** **You can write the multiplication problem and use parentheses.**

The numbers in the parentheses show how you renamed one of the factors.

Rename using addition: 3×9

$$3(5 + 4) \quad \text{or} \quad (3 \times 5) + (3 \times 4)$$

Rename using subtraction: 3×9

$$3(10 - 1) \quad \text{or} \quad (3 \times 10) - (3 \times 1)$$

Connect It Now you will solve the problem from the previous page.

16 What two numbers did Ramon use when he renamed 9 using addition? _____

17 What two multiplication expressions did Ramon use then? _____

18 Show how to use those two multiplication expressions to solve the problem.

_____

19 What two numbers did Ramon use when he renamed 9 using subtraction?

_____

20 Write the two expressions Ramon used then and use them to solve the problem.

_____

21 Explain how to rename the factors in 3×9 in a different way to solve the problem.

_____

_____

Try It Use what you just learned about renaming numbers to solve these problems.

22 Maxine needs to multiply 4 and 8. She knows the answer to 4×6. How can that help her find the answer to 4×8? Draw a model and show the math equations you used.

_____

23 Ali knows the answer to 7×10. How can that help him find the answer to 7×9? Show the math equations you used.

_____

Practice > **Using Order, Grouping, and Renaming to Multiply**

Study the example below. Then solve Problems 24–26.

Example

Erica is making 2 posters. Each poster has 4 snowmen on it. Each snowman has 6 buttons. Erica uses a bead for each button. Show how to group the factors to find the total number of beads she needs.

Look at how you could show your work using a picture.

4 snowmen × 2 posters

So, 8 snowmen × 6 beads each.

Solution: $(4 \times 2) \times 6 \longrightarrow 8 \times 6 = 48$. Erica needs 48 beads.

The student drew a picture showing you to multiply the first two factors to find the total number of snowmen.

 Pair/Share
What are two other ways you could group the factors?

---

24 Tom is displaying his collection of keychains. He makes 9 rows and puts 6 keychains in each row. Then he decides to change it so that there are only 6 rows. If he displays the same number of keychains, how many keychains does he put in each row?

Show your work.

The total number of keychains is the same in both displays. What else is the same?

 Pair/Share
Did you need to find the product of 9 × 6 to find the answer? Tell why or why not.

Solution: _____

25 At a book fair, graphic novels are placed in bins. 8 novels are placed in each bin. Gavin places bins on 3 tables, and puts 5 bins on each table. How many graphic novels are in the bins on the tables?

Show your work. Include parentheses in your work.

Do you want to change the order of the factors before you group them?

Pair/Share
How did you decide which two factors to group together?

Solution: _____

---

26 To find the product 8 × 4, Ella drew the model shown.

Which of the following shows the next steps in finding the product 8 × 4? Circle the letter of the correct answer.

```
X  X  X  X  X
X  X  X  X  X
X  X  X  X  X
X  X  X  X  X
X  X  X  X  X
X  X  X  X  X
X  X  X  X  X
X  X  X  X  X
```

Which factor did Ella rename? Did she use addition or subtraction?

A $(8 \times 4) + (8 \times 1)$

B $(8 \times 5) + (8 \times 1)$

C $(8 \times 5) - (8 \times 1)$

D $(8 \times 4) - (8 \times 1)$

Vinny chose **B** as the correct answer. How did he get that answer?

_____

_____

_____

_____

_____

Pair/Share
What is another way Ella could have renamed one of the factors to make multiplying easier?

Practice ▸ Using Order, Grouping, and Renaming to Multiply

1 Pictures made by students in an art class are arranged in 4 rows on the bulletin board. There are 6 pictures in each row. Which of the following expressions or arrays could be used to find the total number of pictures? Circle the letter of all that apply.

A $6 \times 6 \times 6 \times 6$

B 6×4

C 4×6

D
```
O O O O
O O O O
O O O O
O O O O
O O O O
O O O O
```

E
```
O O O O O O
O O O O O O
O O O O O O
O O O O O O
```

2 A coach bought sports drinks for his teams. The drinks are sold in packs of 8. He put the drinks in 2 bags. He put 2 packs in each bag. How many sports drinks did he buy?

A 12

B 16

C 24

D 32

3 Tell whether the expression could be used to find the answer to $9(10 - 1)$. Choose *Yes* or *No*.

a. $90 - 1$ ☐ Yes ☐ No

b. $90 - 9$ ☐ Yes ☐ No

c. $(9 \times 10) - (9 \times 1)$ ☐ Yes ☐ No

d. $(9 \times 10) - 9$ ☐ Yes ☐ No

4 One way to multiply $3 \times 6 \times 5$ is to first multiply 3 and 6, then multiply that product by 5. Describe in words another way to multiply these three numbers. Then show how to find the product.

_____

_____

_____

_____

5 Find the answer: $7(3 + 5)$

Show your work.

Answer _____

✓ **Self Check** **Go back and see what you can check off on the Self Check on page 45.**

🔄 Use What You Know

Earlier, you thought about equations that compare numbers using multiplication. In this lesson, you will solve problems by comparing numbers. Take a look at this problem.

Hannah scored 3 goals last season. She scored 4 times as many goals this season. How many goals did Hannah score this season?

Last season

This season

a. How many goals did Hannah score last season? _____

b. Count to find the number of goals she scored this season. _____

c. How can you skip count to find the number of goals Hannah scored this season?

_____

d. Besides addition, what operation can you use to solve the problem?

_____

e. What is 4 times as many as 3? _____

You will often need to figure out some unknown amount, like when you found the number of goals Hannah scored. You used skip counting to find 4 times 3. You can also use a bar model.

Last season | 3

This season | 3 | 3 | 3 | 3
?

The bar model can help you write an equation to solve the problem.

4 × **goals last season** = **goals this season**

Goals last season is known (**3**). Goals this season is unknown. You can use a **symbol**, such as an empty box or a question mark, to stand for what is **unknown** in the equation.

4 × **3** = ☐

▶ **Reflect**

1 How would the bar model above change if Hannah scored only 2 goals last year instead of 3? Describe with words what would change. Then draw the bar model to show that.

_____

_____

_____

Learn About ▷ Multiplication in Word Problems

Read the problem below. Then explore different ways to understand it.

> Janelle's Market sells bags of 8 oranges. Simone needs 5 times that amount. Write and solve an equation to find the number of oranges Simone needs.

▶ **Model It** **You can use a model to help understand the problem.**

Number in one bag

8

Number Simone needs

8	8	8	8	8

?

Skip count to find the total Simone needs: 8, 16, 24, 32, 40.

▶ **Model It** **You can use the bar model to make an equation to help understand the problem.**

5 × oranges in one bag = total oranges needed

The number of oranges in one bag is known (**8**). The total number of oranges needed is unknown.

$5 \times 8 = \square$

Connect It Now you will solve the problem from the previous page using an equation.

2 You don't know how many oranges Simone needs. What symbol on the bar model shows how many she needs? _____

3 How does the bar model show how many oranges are in one bag?

_____

4 How does the bar model show how many oranges Simone needs?

_____

5 How can you find "*5 times as many*" as 8? _____

6 Write an equation using numbers to show how many oranges Simone needs.

_____

Simone needs _____ oranges.

7 Explain how you can write a multiplication equation from a bar model.

_____

_____

_____

Try It Use what you just learned to solve these problems. Show your work on a separate sheet of paper.

8 Neil and Vincent are collecting cans. Neil has collected 10 cans and Vincent has collected 3 times as many cans as Neil. Write and solve an equation to find the number of cans Vincent has collected.

_____

9 Mimi ate 6 times as many raisins as Mary. Mary ate 11 raisins. Write and solve an equation to find the number of raisins Mimi ate.

_____

Learn About ▶ Division in Word Problems

Read the problem below. Then explore different ways to understand it.

> Juan found 3 times as many seashells at the beach as Jeremy found. Juan found 24 shells. Write and solve an equation to find the number of shells Jeremy found.

▶ **Model It** **You can use a model to help understand the problem.**

Jeremy found one group of seashells. Juan found 3 times as many shells as Jeremy.

Jeremy's shells | ? |

Juan's shells | ? | ? | ? |
                   ⎵⎵⎵⎵⎵
                     24

Divide 24 by 3 to find the number of seashells in each group.

▶ **Model It** **You can use the model to make an equation to help understand the problem.**

3 × Jeremy's shells = Juan's shells

The number of shells Juan found is known (24). The number Jeremy found is not known.

3 × ☐ = **24**

Connect It Now you will solve the problem from the previous page using an equation.

10 You don't know the number of shells Jeremy found. In the bar model, what part shows the number of shells Jeremy found?

_____

11 How does the bar model show how many shells Juan found?

_____

12 How does the bar model show that 24 is 3 times another number?

_____

13 How can you find what number times 3 is 24?

_____

14 Write a division equation using numbers to show how many shells Jeremy found.

_____

Jeremy found _____ shells.

15 Explain how you can write a division equation from a model.

_____

_____

_____

Try It Use what you just learned to solve these problems. Show your work on a separate sheet of paper.

16 Monique and Wint are both reading the same book. Monique read 63 pages last weekend. She read 7 times as many pages as Wint. Write and solve an equation to find the number of pages Wint read. _____

17 The winning baseball team scored 4 times as many runs as their opponent. The winning team scored 8 runs. Write and solve an equation to find the number of runs their opponent scored. _____

Practice ▶ **Multiplying and Dividing in Word Problems**

Study the example below. Then solve problems 18–20.

Example

Karina is 6 feet tall. Her cousin is 3 feet tall. How many times as tall as her cousin is Karina?

Look at how you could show your work using a bar model.

Cousin's height | 3 |

Karina's height | 3 | 3 |
                     ⎵_____⎵
                        6

☐ × 3 = 6; ☐ = 2

Solution _Karina is 2 times as tall as her cousin._

 There are twice as many boxes in the model for Karina's height as there are for her cousin's height.

💬 **Pair/Share**
How else could you solve this problem?

---

18 A small shrimp taco has 5 shrimp. There are 3 times as many shrimp in a large taco. How many shrimp are in a large taco? Write and solve an equation to find the answer.

Show your work.

 What does it mean when the problem says 3 times as many?

💬 **Pair/Share**
Did you and your partner write the same, or different, equations?

Solution _____

19 Christina read 7 pages in a magazine. She read 5 times as many pages in a book. How many pages did Christina read altogether?

Show your work.

> I think this problem has more than one step.

Solution _____

Pair/Share
How can you check your answer?

---

20 Aida swam 7 laps in a pool. Kaya swam 28 laps. How many times the number of laps Aida swam did Kaya swim? Circle the letter of the correct answer.

A 4

B 21

C 35

D 196

> I can use multiplication or division to solve this problem.

Jae Ho chose **D** as the correct answer. How did he get that answer?

_____

_____

_____

_____

_____

Pair/Share
How did you and your partner know what operation to use?

Practice ▶ Multiplying and Dividing in Word Problems

Solve the problems.

1 Kyle sold 28 boxes of fruit for a fundraiser. Omar sold 2 times as many boxes of fruit as Kyle sold. What is the total number of boxes that Kyle and Omar sold?

   A 84

   B 56

   C 42

   D 14

2 Raoul biked 11 miles last week. Jackson biked 22 miles last week. Jackson biked how many times as many miles as Raoul? Which equation can help you answer the question?

   A $22 - 11 = \square$

   B $22 \div 11 = \square$

   C $11 \times 22 = \square$

   D $11 + 22 = \square$

3 Which problems can be solved using the equation $3 \times 9 = A$? Circle the letter of all that apply.

   A Pam is 9 years old. She is 3 times as old as Kate. How old is Kate?

   B Marco is making 9 apple tortes. He needs 3 apples for each torte. How many apples does he need?

   C Three groups of actors are performing plays at a festival. There are 9 actors in each group. How many actors are performing?

   D An art class meets 3 times a week for 9 weeks. How many times does the art class meet?

   E Judy found 3 acorns. Aaron found 3 times as many acorns as Judy. How many acorns did Aaron find?

4 Maria has 32 postcards. Henry has *h* postcards. Maria has 4 times as many postcards as Henry. Choose *Yes* or *No* to indicate whether each statement is true.

a. The number of postcards Henry has can be represented by the expression $32 \div 4$.

☐ Yes ☐ No

b. Henry has 6 postcards.

☐ Yes ☐ No

c. The number of postcards Henry has can be found by solving the equation $32 = 4 \times h$.

☐ Yes ☐ No

5 Last week Viet learned 25 new spelling words. That was 5 times as many words as Max. How many words did Max learn last week? Draw a bar model to find the number of words Max learned.

Show your work.

Answer Max learned _____ new spelling words last week.

6 Mr. Naik traveled 18 days on vacation last summer. Miss Cooper traveled 3 days on vacation last summer. How many times as many days did Mr. Naik travel on vacation as Miss Cooper? Write an equation to find the answer.

Show your work.

Answer Mr. Naik traveled _____ times as many days on vacation as Miss Cooper.

✓ **Self Check** Go back and see what you can check off on the Self Check on page 45.

Lesson 7 👥 Introduction
Multiples and Factors

Ⓖ Use What You Know

In previous lessons, you multiplied and divided numbers. Now you can use multiplication and division to find factors and multiples, and then learn a way to classify a number by how many factors it has. Take a look at this problem.

A garden has several rows of pumpkin plants. Each row has 10 plants. How many pumpkin plants could be in the garden?

a. How many pumpkin plants are in each row? _____

b. How many pumpkin plants would be in 2 rows? _____

   In 4 rows? _____

   In 5 rows? _____

c. How do you know there are not a total of 45 pumpkin plants in the garden?

_____

_____

d. How can you describe how many pumpkin plants there could be?

_____

_____

▷▷ Find Out More

If there were 5 rows of 10 pumpkin plants, there would be 50 plants. The numbers 5 and 10 are a **factor pair** of 50 because they are two factors whose product is 50. To find other factor pairs of 50, think of other ways 50 pumpkin plants could be planted in equal rows.

You could have 2 rows of 25.

$2 \times 25 = 50$

You could also have 1 row of 50.

$1 \times 50 = 50$

50 has three factor pairs: 1 and 50, 2 and 25, 5 and 10. So, 50 has 6 factors: 1, 2, 5, 10, 25, and 50.

When you multiply numbers, the product is a **multiple** of each factor. So, 50 is a multiple of each of its factors. You can use skip counting to check if a number is a multiple of another number. If you start at 0 and count by 5s, you will reach 50. So, 50 is a multiple of 5.

Numbers like 50 that have more than one factor pair are called **composite numbers**. **Prime numbers** have only one factor pair: the number and 1. The number 1 is neither prime nor composite.

 There is only one way to plant 11 bean plants in equal rows. 11 is a prime number.

 There is more than one way to plant 24 onion plants in equal rows. 24 is a composite number.

▶ Reflect

1 Describe the difference between prime numbers and composite numbers.

_____

_____

Learn About ▸ Multiples

Read the problem below. Then explore different ways to use multiples to solve it.

> Leona has 5 cups of oats. She needs 2 cups of oats for one full batch of oatmeal muffins. Can she use all of her oats by making multiple full batches of muffins?

▶ **Picture It** **You can use a model to help understand the problem.**

The model shows the oats Leona has, divided into 2-cup measuring cups.

▶ **Model It** **You can also use a number line to help understand the problem.**

The number line shows multiples of 2 circled. To find the multiples of 2, you can start at 0 and skip count by 2s. You can see that the **multiples of 2** are even numbers.

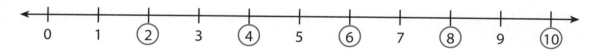

Connect It ▶ Now you will further explore the problem from the previous page.

2 Why does the model use measuring cups that hold 2 cups of oats?

_____

_____

3 How can you tell from the measuring cup model that Leona can't use all 5 cups of oats in 2-cup batches? _____

_____

_____

4 What do the circled numbers on the number line represent? _____

5 How can you tell from the number line that 5 is not a multiple of 2?

_____

_____

6 How many cups of oats would Leona use in 3 batches of muffins? _____

7 Explain how you can find out whether a number, such as 5, is a multiple of 2.

_____

_____

_____

Try It ▶ Use what you just learned to solve these problems. Show your work on a separate sheet of paper.

8 There are 4 bottles of water in a pack. Patrick needs 20 bottles of water for his soccer team. Can he buy exactly 20 bottles in packs of 4? _____

9 What are the first five multiples of the number 9? _____

Learn About **Factors and Factor Pairs**

Read the problem below. Then explore different ways to use factor pairs to solve it.

Alfred is arranging 40 model cars into rows and wants to put the same number of cars in each row. Find all the ways he can arrange the cars.

▶ **Model It** **You can use arrays to help understand the problem.**

One way Alfred can arrange his cars is in 8 rows of 5.

8 and 5 are a factor pair for 40. This means Alfred could also arrange the cars in 5 rows of 8.

▶ **Model It** **You can also use area models to help understand the problem.**

Two more ways Alfred can arrange the cars are 10 rows of 4 or 2 rows of 20.

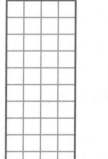 

10 and 4 are a factor pair for 40. This means Alfred could also arrange the cars in 4 rows of 10.

2 and 20 are another factor pair for 40. So Alfred could also arrange the cars in 20 rows of 2.

Connect It   Now you will explore the problem from the previous page further.

10 What are two more ways to arrange the cars into even rows?

_____

11 List all of the factor pairs of 40: _____

12 Each number in a factor pair is a factor. How many factors does 40 have?

_____

13 Why might it be helpful to always start with the number 1 and work up when finding factors? _____

_____

_____

14 Explain how to use arrays or area models to find factor pairs.

_____

_____

_____

_____

Try It   Use what you just learned to solve these problems. Show your work on a separate sheet of paper.

15 Brad is playing with blocks. He has 18 blocks and wants to make an array with the same number of blocks in each row. What are all the different ways he could arrange the blocks? _____

_____

16 What are the factors of the number 27? _____

Learn About ▶ Prime and Composite Numbers

Read the problem below. Then explore different ways to understand it.

> Janae has 36 pennies. Nate has 23 pennies. Who has a composite number of pennies?

▶ **Picture It** **You can use models to help understand the problem.**

Janae

Nate

36 pennies can be divided into 3 equal stacks of 12.

23 pennies can't be divided into equal stacks.

▶ **Model It** **You can also use area models to help understand the problem.**

With composite numbers, you can make area models that have more than one equal-sized row.

Janae

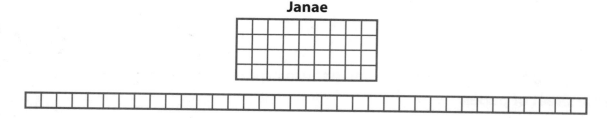

With prime numbers, you can only make one area model that has one equal-sized row.

Nate

Connect It Now you will explore the problem from the previous page further.

17 What factor pair is shown by Janae's stacks of pennies? _____

18 Is 36 a prime or composite number? _____

How do you know? _____

_____

_____

19 Is 23 a prime or composite number? _____

How do you know? _____

_____

_____

20 Explain how you can use models to decide if a number is prime or composite.

_____

_____

_____

_____

_____

Try It Use what you just learned to solve these problems. Show your work on a separate sheet of paper.

21 Mrs. Reynaldo is picking up 17 playground balls after recess and she wants to put the same number of balls into each ball bin. What are the different ways she could group the balls?

_____

22 Is 17 a prime number or a composite number? _____

Practice ▷ **Using Multiples and Factors**

Study the example below. Then solve problems 23–25.

Example

School pictures are sold with 9 pictures on a sheet. Hallie needs 45 pictures for her family and classmates. Can she buy exactly 45 pictures in sheets of 9? If so, how many sheets does she need?

Look at how you could show your work using a picture.

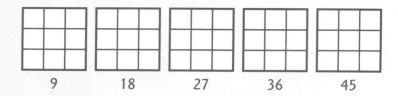

9   18   27   36   45

Solution: Hallie can buy exactly 45 pictures. She needs 5 sheets.

Any number that has 0 or 5 in the ones place is a multiple of 5!

💬 **Pair/Share**
How else could you solve this problem, without using models?

---

23 There are 12 levels in Liang's new video game. If he plays the same number of levels each day, what are all the possibilities for the number of days he could spend playing the game without repeating a level?

Show your work.

I notice that 2 is a factor of every even number!

💬 **Pair/Share**
Why do you need to find the factors of 12 to solve this problem?

Solution _____

24 A basketball team scored 37 points in one quarter. Is the number 37 prime or composite?

Show your work.

Starting with 1 is a good way to find factors!

Solution _____

---

25 Grant walks 2 miles every day. Which could NOT be the number of miles that Grant has walked after some number of days? Circle the letter of the correct answer.

A 2

B 3

C 10

D 18

What do you know about multiples of 2?

Noelle chose **B** as the correct answer. How did she get that answer?

Lesson 7 Multiples and Factors   **83**

Practice ▸ **Using Multiples and Factors**

Solve the problems.

1 Simon is organizing his 36 toy cars into equal-sized piles. Which list shows all of the possible numbers of cars that could be in each pile?

A 2, 3, 4, 6

B 1, 2, 3, 4, 6

C 2, 3, 4, 6, 9, 12, 18

D 1, 2, 3, 4, 6, 9, 12, 18, 36

2 Reggie ate 31 raisins. Which correctly describes 31 as a prime number or a composite number and tells the number of factor pairs 31 has?

A 31 is a prime number because it has 0 factor pairs.

B 31 is a prime number because it has 1 factor pair.

C 31 is a composite number because it has 1 factor pair.

D 31 is a composite number because it has 2 factor pairs.

3 Sara is playing a memory card game with 24 cards. She wants to lay the cards out in rows. Shade in 24 boxes below to show one way that she could lay out the cards.

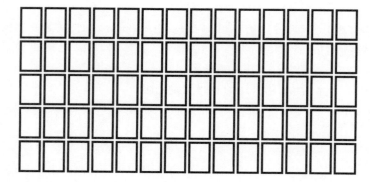

4 Tell whether each sentence is *True* or *False*.

a. The number 96 is a multiple of 8. That means all of the factors of 8 are also factors of 96. ☐ True ☐ False

b. The number 1 is prime. ☐ True ☐ False

c. The number 1 is composite. ☐ True ☐ False

d. The number 2 is prime. ☐ True ☐ False

e. The number 9 has four factors. ☐ True ☐ False

5 There are 15 cousins playing a game. They need to divide evenly into teams. Draw a model to show one way they can split into teams. Then decide if 15 is a prime number or a composite number.

Show your work.

Answer   15 is a _____ number.

6 A pack of toy cars contains 12 cars. If Sylvia buys some packs, what are two possible numbers of cars that she could buy?

Show your work.

Answer   Sylvia could buy _____ cars or _____ cars.

✓ **Self Check**   **Go back and see what you can check off on the Self Check on page 45.**

Number and Shape Patterns

 **Use What You Know**

You have used rules to describe patterns in numbers. In this lesson, you will explore patterns further. Take a look at this problem.

> What are the next two numbers in the pattern below?
>
> 5, 10, 15, 20, 25, _____ , _____

a. What are two ways to get from 5 to 10?

_____

b. How do you get from 10 to 15?

_____

c. What rule works for all of the numbers in the pattern?

_____

d. How can you find the number that comes after 25?

_____

e. What are the next two numbers in the pattern?

_____

"Add 5" is not the only relationship between the numbers in the pattern on the previous page. Take another look at the numbers, along with the model of the numbers below.

5, 10, 15, 20, 25

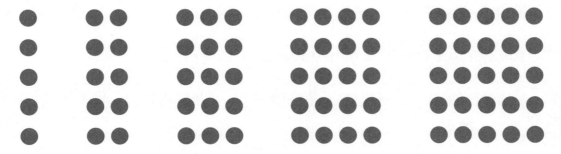

- Look at the digits in the ones place in the numbers. The digits alternate between 5 and 0.

- Look at the number of dots in the models. The number of dots alternates between odd and even.

The pattern below also follows the rule "add 5."

17, 22, 27, 32, 37, 42

- The numbers in this pattern also alternate between odd and even.

- The ones digits alternate between 7 and 2 instead of between 5 and 0.

So, two sets of numbers can share some patterns or rules, such as "add 5," but not share others, such as having the last digit alternate between 5 and 0.

Reflect

1 Describe a pattern that you have noticed in the real world.

_____

_____

_____

_____

Learn About Number Patterns

Read the problem below. Then explore different ways to understand it.

> Orlando does push-ups every day. This week, he wants to do 4 more push-ups each day than the day before. Find out how many push-ups Orlando will do each weekday if he does 20 push-ups on Monday.

▶ **Picture It** You can use a table to help understand the problem.

Day	Monday	Tuesday	Wednesday	Thursday	Friday
Number of Push-ups	20				

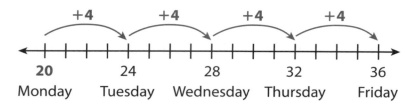

+4   +4   +4   +4

▶ **Model It** You can also use a number line to help understand the problem.

```
        +4        +4        +4        +4
    ┌──────┐  ┌──────┐  ┌──────┐  ┌──────┐
←───┼──┼──┼──┼──┼──┼──┼──┼──┼──┼──┼──┼──┼──┼───→
   20        24        28        32        36
 Monday   Tuesday  Wednesday Thursday   Friday
```

Start at 20, which is the number of push-ups Orlando does on Monday. Then count on 4 more for each day.

Connect It Now you will explore the problem from the previous page further.

2 How many push-ups did Orlando do each day?

Monday: _____ Tuesday: _____ Wednesday: _____ Thursday: _____ Friday: _____

3 What is the rule for the pattern? _____

4 What does the pattern show you about what happens when you start with an even number and add an even number? _____

_____

_____

5 Describe another pattern you see in this set of numbers. _____

_____

_____

_____

6 Explain how you found the additional pattern(s). _____

_____

_____

_____

Try It Use what you just learned to solve these problems. Show your work on a separate sheet of paper.

7 The first time Lori played a certain game she scored 100 points. She doubled her previous score each of the next 3 times she played the game. What were Lori's scores the first 4 times she played the game?

_____

8 What is one additional pattern in Lori's scores? _____

_____

Learn About ▶ **Shape Patterns**

Read the problem below. Then explore different ways to understand it.

> Camille made a shape pattern with pattern blocks that goes back and forth between a triangle and a square. Draw the pattern that Camille made.

▶ **Picture It** **You can use models to help understand the problem.**

Start by describing the pattern with words. Repeat the pattern at least 3 times.

triangle   square   triangle   square   triangle   square

Now draw the shapes in the order you named them.

▶ **Model It** **You can also use pattern blocks to help understand the problem.**

Use pattern blocks in the shapes Camille used to create her pattern.

Connect It   Now you will explore the shape pattern from the previous page further.

9 How many sides does a triangle have? _____

10 How many sides does a square have? _____

11 How could you describe the pattern using the number of sides the shapes have?

_____

_____

12 What would the 10th shape in the pattern be? _____

13 Explain how you can figure out what the 85th shape in the pattern would be without drawing all 85 shapes. _____

_____

_____

_____

_____

Try It   Use what you just learned to solve this problem. Show your work on a separate sheet of paper.

14 Describe any rules you see in the shape pattern below.

_____

_____

_____

_____

Learn About ❯ **Patterns with Equations**

Read the problem below. Then explore different ways to understand it.

Kyle uses pattern blocks to make a different pattern than Camille. He has 1 triangle followed by 4 squares, repeated vertically. The multiplication equation $S = 4 \times T$ describes the relationship between the number of squares, S, Kyle needs for T triangles. How many squares does Kyle need if he uses 5 triangles? 6 triangles? 7 triangles?

▶ **Picture It** **You can use pattern blocks to help understand the problem.**

Use pattern blocks to show 3 rows of Kyle's pattern.

▶ **Model It** **You can also use a table to help understand the problem.**

The equation $S = 4 \times T$ describes the relationship between the **number of squares** and the **number of triangles**.

Number of Triangles, T	Number of Squares, S
1	4
2	8
3	12
4	16
5	
6	
7	

Connect It Now you will explore the equation from the previous page.

Consider the equation $S = 4 \times T$.

15 What does S stand for? _____

What does T stand for? _____

16 What does "$4 \times T$" mean? _____

17 Look at *Model It*. Describe the number of squares as a multiple of the number of triangles.

_____

18 Explain how to use the equation to figure out how many squares Kyle needs if he

uses 5 triangles. _____

_____

_____

19 How many squares does Kyle need if he uses 6 triangles and 7 triangles?
Complete the table on the previous page. _____

_____

20 Explain why the equation describes the rule for Kyle's pattern.

_____

_____

Try It Use what you just learned about equations with two variables to solve these problems. Show your work on a separate sheet of paper.

21 Rita wants 2 cupcakes for each guest plus 4 extra cupcakes. The equation $C = (2 \times G) + 4$ describes the relationship between the total number of cupcakes, C, and the number of guests, G. How many cupcakes will Rita need for 5, 6, and 7 guests? _____

22 Use the equation $y = 3x - 1$ to complete the table.

x	y
1	2
2	
3	
4	

Practice **Using Number and Shape Patterns**

Study the example below. Then solve problems 23–25.

Example

Hungry Heath's sells four different sizes of sandwiches: small, medium, large, and jumbo. The small sandwich costs $3. Each size after that costs $2 more than the size before it. How much does each sandwich cost?

Look at how you could show your work using a picture.

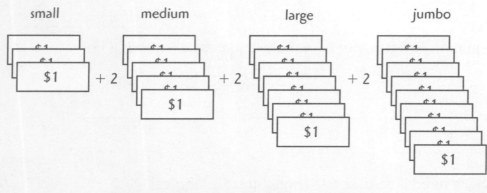

The student used the rule "add 2" because each sandwich is $2 more than the one before.

Pair/Share
Are there any other patterns in this set of numbers?

Solution small: $3, medium: $5, large: $7, jumbo: $9

---

23 Draw the next two shapes in the shape pattern shown below.

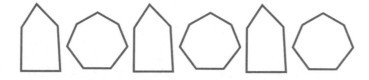

There is more than one pattern in these shapes!

Pair/Share
Are your shapes the same as your partner's?

Solution _____

24 Eva drew a shape pattern that goes back and forth between rectangles and ovals.

There are several ways to describe a pattern!

What are two other rules that describe this set of shapes?

Solution _____

_____

_____

_____

_____

_____

Pair/Share
Did your partner find the same rules in the pattern as you did?

---

25 Lana wrote the pattern below.

7, 14, 21, 28, 35

If the pattern continues, what would be the next number in the pattern? Circle the letter of the correct answer.

A 40

B 42

C 49

D 70

Diego chose **D** as the correct answer. How did he get that answer?

You can check your answer by working backward!

_____

_____

_____

_____

Pair/Share
What would be the next three numbers in the pattern?

Practice ⟩ **Using Number and Shape Patterns**

Solve the problems.

1 What would be the 99th number in the pattern shown below?

10, 20, 30, 40, 50

A 99

B 900

C 909

D 990

2 Nia drew the shape pattern shown below.

Which does NOT describe Nia's shape pattern?

A Each shape has one more side than the shape before it.

B The shapes in the odd-numbered spots have an odd number of sides.

C The sides in a shape are all the same length.

D The hexagon only appears in spots that are multiples of 4.

3 Use the equation $y = 5x - 2$ to complete the table.

x	y
2	
3	
4	
5	

4 Tell whether each sentence is *True* or *False*.

   a. A number pattern that follows the rule "add 3" has both odd and even numbers. □ True □ False

   b. A number pattern that starts with 5 cannot include the number 3. □ True □ False

   c. A number pattern that follows the rule "start at 20 and subtract 4" has only even numbers. □ True □ False

   d. A number pattern that follows the rule "multiply by 2" must have even numbers only. □ True □ False

5 Draw a shape pattern that follows the rule that the shapes go back and forth between four sides and five sides.

Show your work.

Solution _____

6 Write a number pattern that follows the rule "subtract 6" and also has all odd numbers.

Show your work.

Solution _____

✓ **Self Check**   **Go back and see what you can check off on the Self Check on page 45.**

Use What You Know

You know how to solve two-step problems. Now, you will extend those skills to multi-step problems. Take a look at this problem.

Tia mowed Ms. Vega's lawn 4 days last month. Each day she worked 2 hours in the morning and 1 hour in the afternoon. Write an equation to find how many hours Tia worked mowing Ms. Vega's lawn.

	Morning	Afternoon
Day 1	2 hours	1 hour
Day 2	2 hours	1 hour
Day 3	2 hours	1 hour
Day 4	2 hours	1 hour

a. Write an expression to show how many hours Tia worked each day.

_____

b. What will you need to do to the expression above to find out how many hours Tia worked all 4 days? _____

c. Write an expression for the number of hours she worked one day and put parentheses around it. Then show this amount multiplied by 4.

_____

d. Choose a letter to represent the total hours that Tia worked.

_____

e. Write an equation to show how you would find the total number of hours Tia worked. _____

Parentheses help you remember what part of an equation to solve first. Think about the problem on the previous page. You first need to find out how many hours Tia worked each day, which is **(2 + 1)**. Then you multiply the sum by **4** to find the total number of hours for all 4 days. The final equation looks like this:

(2 + 1) × 4 = H

A bar model can help you see each part of the equation.

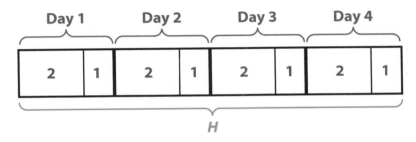

If Tia was paid $10 for each hour she worked, how could you find out how much she earned in all? You would need to multiply the total number of hours by the amount she was paid each hour. Let *E* be the total amount she earned.

E = H × 10

Equations can be helpful in real-world situations. For example, an equation can help you find the cost of something you want to do, like go to a movie with 2 friends and an adult.

▶ Reflect

1 Describe a real-world situation that you could represent with an equation.

_____

_____

_____

_____

_____

Learn About ▶ **Writing Equations**

Read the problem below. Then explore different ways to model it.

> Garrett is paid $4 for every hour he babysits. Mrs. Becker paid him for 5 hours of babysitting. On the way home, Garrett spent $9 on a book and $6 on a puzzle. How much money did Garrett have left from the money he received from Mrs. Becker?

▶ **Model It** **You can use a bar model to help understand the problem.**

$4	$4	$4	$4	$4
$9		$6		?

The top part of the model shows the amount Garrett was paid for every hour and the number of hours he babysat.

The bottom part of the model shows the total amount he spent. You do not know how much money he has left.

▶ **Model It** **You can use the bar model to write equations for the problem.**

Let **B** equal the amount Mrs. Becker paid Garrett.

$B = 5 \times 4$

He spent $9 on the book and $6 on the puzzle, so the amount he spent is **9 + 6**.

Let **L** be the amount he has left after buying the book and puzzle.

$L = B - (9 + 6)$

Connect It Now you will explore the problem from the previous page further.

2 Look at the second *Model It*. What is represented by $\times 4$ in the equation $B = 5 \times 4$?

_____

3 Why are the two amounts that Garrett spent in parentheses in the equation $L = B - (9 + 6)$? _____

_____

4 Alissa combined the two equations into one equation: $L = 20 - (9 + 6)$. What does the 20 in her equation represent?

_____

5 Ben used the equation $L = (4 \times 5) - 9 - 6$. Is his equation correct? Explain.

_____

_____

6 Explain how it's possible for two equations to look different but still show the same problem. _____

_____

_____

_____

Try It Use what you just learned to solve this problem. Show your work on a separate sheet of paper.

7 There were 4 vans and 2 cars going to a museum. Each van carried 9 people. Each car carried 3 people.

Write an equation to represent the number of people who traveled in a van, *V*. Then write an equation to represent the total number of people who went to the museum, *T*.

_____

Study the example below. Then solve problems 8–10.

Example

Tulio's plant was 40 inches tall in May. In June it grew 3 inches. In July, it grew 2 times as much as it grew in June.

Write an equation to show how tall Tulio's plant is now. Use *P* to represent the unknown quantity.

Look at how you could show your work using a picture.

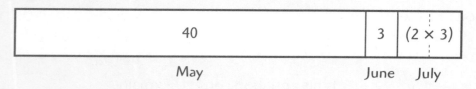

40	3	(2 × 3)
May	June	July

Solution 40 + 3 + (2 × 3) = P

There is more than one way to write the equation!

💬 **Pair/Share**

How could you solve this problem without using a model?

---

8 Olivia drove 170 miles each way (there and back) to visit her cousin. On the trip, Olivia drove an extra 20 miles to see the Grand Canyon. She also drove an extra 45 miles to see Lake Powell.

Write an equation to represent the total number of miles, *M*, Olivia drove on her trip.

Show your work.

How do you show that she drove 170 miles each way?

💬 **Pair/Share**

Did you and your partner write the equation the same way?

Solution _____

_____

9 Lucy bought 2 sandwiches for $4 each and 1 small salad for $3. She handed the clerk $20.

Write an equation to show the total cost of Lucy's food, *F*. Then write an equation to show the amount of change, *C*, Lucy will get.

Show your work.

You can use parentheses to show which part you would do first!

Solution _____

_____

Pair/Share
How did you show that Lucy bought 2 sandwiches?

---

10 The Martinez family recycled 37 cans one week and 24 cans the next week. The Zhang family recycled twice as many cans as the Martinez family.

Which equations could be used to find the total number of cans both families recycled? Let *M* stand for the Martinez family and *B* stand for both families. Circle the letter of the correct answer.

A $M = 2 \times (37 + 24)$
$B = 2 \times M$

B $M = 37 + 24$
$B = 2 \times M$

C $M = 37 + 24$
$B = M + (37 \times 2)$

D $M = 37 + 24$
$B = M + (2 \times M)$

You can label each part in the equation to help you keep track of the numbers!

Cassie chose **B** as the correct answer. How did she get that answer?

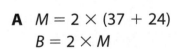 _____

_____

Pair/Share
Paulo chose **C** as the correct answer. Discuss Paulo's mistake.

Practice **Modeling Multi-Step Problems**

Solve the problems.

1 Celia and Jake bought 4 pizzas that cost $7 each and breadsticks that cost $3. They split the cost between them. Which equations could be used to find how much each paid? Let *T* stand for the total cost and *E* stand for the amount each paid.

A $T = (4 \times 7) + 3; E = T \times 2$

B $T = (4 \times 7) + 3; E = T \div 2$

C $T = (7 + 3) \times 4; E = T \div 2$

D $T = (4 + 7) \times 3; E = T \div 2$

2 Ty bought 2 watermelons for $6 each and a cantaloupe for $4. He paid with a $20 bill. Which equations could be used to find how much change Ty received? Let *T* stand for the total cost and *C* stand for the change.

A $T = (2 \times 6) + 4; C = 20 - T$

B $T = (6 + 4) \times 2; C = 20 - T$

C $T = (2 \times 6) + 4; C = T - 20$

D $T = (2 + 6) \times 4; C = T - 20$

3 Jane bought 3 magnets and 9 bookmarks at the craft fair. The magnets cost $5 each and the bookmarks cost $2 each. Which equations could you use to find out how much money, *M*, she spent? Circle the letter for all that apply.

A $M = (9 \times 2) + (3 \times 5)$

B $M = (3 \times 9) + (5 \times 2)$

C $M = (5 \times 3) + (2 \times 9)$

D $M = (3 + 5) \times (9 + 2)$

E $M = (3 + 9) \times (5 + 2)$

4 A farm stand sells strawberries in 1-pound, 2-pound, and 5-pound baskets. Use the information in the table below to write an equation for *S*, the number of pounds of strawberries sold.

Pounds per Basket	Number of Baskets Sold
1	9
2	5
5	7

Solution _____

5 Gymnastics lessons cost $10 per session, plus a one-time fee of $25. Shawn went to 7 sessions. Write an equation that can be used to find how much Shawn paid, *P*.

Show your work.

Solution _____

6 Landon bought 5 packs of baseball cards. Each pack had 8 cards. His sister gave him 12 more cards. Then he sold 4 cards. Write an equation that can be used to find how many baseball cards, *C*, Landon has left.

Show your work.

Solution _____

✔ **Self Check**   **Go back and see what you can check off on the Self Check on page 45.**

Use What You Know

In Lesson 9, you learned how to write equations for multi-step problems. In this lesson, you will solve those equations. Take a look at this problem.

On a test, Lola scored 6 points on each of the first 3 questions and 4 points on each of the other 2 questions. Write an equation to find Lola's total score.

Question	Score
1	6 points
2	6 points
3	6 points
4	4 points
5	4 points

a. Write an expression that represents Lola's score on the first 3 questions.

_____

b. Write an expression that represents Lola's score on the other 2 questions.

_____

c. What operation can be used to combine her scores on the first 3 questions with her scores on the other 2 questions? _____

d. Choose a letter to represent Lola's total score and write an equation that could be used to solve the problem. _____

e. What was Lola's total score on the first 3 questions? _____

f. What was Lola's total score on the last 2 questions? _____

g. What was Lola's total score on all 5 questions? _____

▶▶ Find Out More

There is often more than one way to find the answer to a problem.

- **One Way** The bar model below shows one way to think about the problem about Lola's scores.

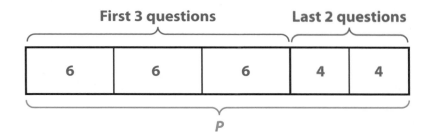

First 3 questions   Last 2 questions

| 6 | 6 | 6 | 4 | 4 |

P

- **Another Way** You can also represent the problem with an equation. Sometimes you can write more than one equation to represent a problem. Both of the equations below show a correct way to solve a problem.

$$(3 \times 6) + (2 \times 4) = P \qquad (6 \times 3) + 4 + 4 = P$$
$$18 \quad + \quad 8 \quad = P \qquad 18 \quad + 4 + 4 = P$$
$$26 = P \qquad\qquad\qquad 26 = P$$

Lola's total score was 26 points.

How can you tell if the answer is reasonable? Lola scored 6 points on some questions and 4 points on others. You could think of it as scoring 5 points for each question. $5 \times 5 = 25$, so the answer of 26 makes sense.

▶ Reflect

1 How would the bar model change if Lola scored 5 points on each of the last 2 questions? How would the first equation change?

_____

_____

_____

_____

Learn About ▶ Solving Multi-Step Problems

Read the problem below. Then explore different ways to understand it.

> Ms. Dennison is packing up the books in her classroom for the summer. Each box holds 9 books. She has 24 math books and 27 science books to pack. How many boxes will she need?

▶ **Model It** You can use a number line to help understand the problem and write an equation.

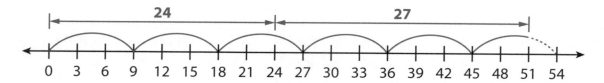

The total number of books is shown above the number line (24 + 27). The number line shows jumps of 9 because each box holds 9 books.

Let *X* equal the number of boxes needed. Remember to use parentheses to show what to do first.

$X = (24 + 27) \div 9$

▶ **Solve It** You can solve the equation that represents the problem.

$X = (24 + 27) \div 9$
$X = 51 \div 9$

When a number doesn't divide evenly, you have some left over. The amount left over is called a **remainder**, shown with an R.

$51 \div 9 \longrightarrow 5\ \text{R}6$

Connect It Now you will explore the problem from the previous page further.

2 What does the 5 in the solution 5 R6 mean? _____

What does the R6 mean? _____

3 How many books are left over that do not make a full box? _____

Is another box needed to hold the 6 left over books? _____

4 How many boxes will Ms. Dennison need? _____

5 Check the solution to the equation:

_____ boxes × _____ books per box + _____ books = 51 total books

6 How could you estimate to make sure your answer is reasonable? _____

_____

_____

7 Explain why the solution to an equation is not always the answer to a problem when there is a remainder. _____

_____

_____

Try It Use what you just learned to solve these problems. Show your work on a separate sheet of paper.

8 Cadence ordered a $4 sandwich, a $2 drink, and a $3 smoothie for lunch. She has $10. Write and solve an equation to find out if she has enough money for lunch.

_____

9 In the problem above, will Cadence get any change back from her $10? Explain how you know. _____

_____

Practice ▶ **Solving Multi-Step Problems**

Study the example below. Then solve problems 10–12.

Example

Myron and Suzanne are making banana bread. Each batch uses 3 bananas. Myron has 5 bananas and Suzanne has 8 bananas. Write and solve an equation to find out how many batches of banana bread they can make. Will they have bananas left over?

Look at how you could show your work using a model.

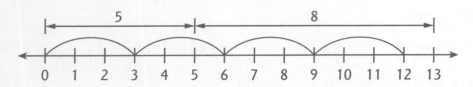

Let B = number of batches

$(5 + 8) \div 3 = B$

$13 \div 3 \longrightarrow 4\ R1$

Solution <u>They can make 4 batches with 1 banana left over.</u>

The student could estimate the answer to check whether it is reasonable!

Pair/Share
Discuss the reasonableness of the answer.

---

10 A pet store has 17 rabbits. They have 5 fewer cats than rabbits. Write and solve an equation to find how many rabbits and cats the store has altogether.

Show your work.

How many cats does the store have?

Pair/Share
Do you get the same answer if you write the equation a different way?

Solution _____

_____

11 Taylor earns $5 each time she walks her neighbor's dog. She has already earned $25. Write and solve an equation to find out how many more times Taylor needs to walk the dog to earn enough to buy a bike that costs $83.

Show your work.

What does the remainder tell you?

Solution _____

_____

_____

Pair/Share
What would happen if Taylor didn't think about the remainder?

12 Lindsay sold 47 boxes of oranges for a fundraiser. Tim sold 12 fewer boxes than Lindsay. How many more boxes of oranges does Tim need to sell to have sold 60 boxes? Circle the letter of the correct answer.

A 1

B 25

C 35

D 48

Shonda chose **A** as the correct answer. How did she get that answer?

A picture can help make sense of all the numbers!

_____

_____

_____

_____

Pair/Share
Compare the strategies you both used to solve the problem.

Practice ▷ **Solving Multi-Step Problems**

Solve the problems.

1 Franklin uses 3 eggs to make a large omelet and 2 eggs to make a small omelet. How many eggs would he need to make 5 large omelets and 4 small omelets?

A 14 eggs

B 22 eggs

C 23 eggs

D 26 eggs

2 The student council needs drinks for the annual Fun Run. They can buy water, juice, or sports drinks. The table shows how many people will be participating.

Grade	Total Number of People
4th Graders	28
5th Graders	23
6th Graders	24

Water
24 bottles per pack

Juice
8 boxes per pack

Sports drink
6 bottles per pack

Which combinations will provide enough drinks so that each participant can have at least one drink? Circle the letter for all that apply.

A 3 packs of water

B 2 packs of water, 2 packs of juice, 2 packs of sports drink

C 2 packs of water, 5 packs of sports drink

D 1 pack of water, 8 packs of juice

E 1 pack of water, 6 packs of sports drink

3 Petra walked 9 miles the first week of this month, twice that far the second week, and 6 miles the third week. How many miles did Petra walk altogether? _____

4 Ms. Ruiz planted 14 flowers in 3 pots. She planted 4 flowers in the 1 blue pot and split the rest equally between the 2 red pots.

Write and solve an equation to find the number of flowers Ms. Ruiz planted in each of the 2 red pots.

Show your work.

_____

_____

5 Gabriel owns 27 fiction books and 23 non-fiction books. If 8 books fit on each shelf, how many shelves does he need for all of his books?

Solve the problem and explain how the remainder affected your answer.

Show your work.

_____

_____

_____

_____

✓ **Self Check** **Go back and see what you can check off on the Self Check on page 45.**

Study an Example Problem and Solution

Read this problem about comparing numbers. Then look at G.O.'s solution to this problem.

Pine Cones and Needles

G.O. is with his friend Azul at a wildlife park. A worker at the nature center is arranging pine cones and pine needles in pairs for a display. Here are the rules.

Rules for Pairing Objects
· One length is a multiple of another length.
· The longer length is no more than 5 times the shorter length.
· Cones or needles can be paired with other cones or needles.

Kind of Tree	Sugar Pine	Jack Pine	Ponderosa Pine	Longleaf Pine
Cone Length	50 cm	5 cm	8 cm	24 cm
Needle Length	10 cm	4 cm	15 cm	40 cm

Use an object only once. Find three possible pairs of objects that fit the rules. Tell why these pairs work.

Read the sample solution on the next page. Then look at the checklist below. Find and mark parts of the solution that match the checklist.

 Problem-Solving Checklist

☐ Tell what is known.
☐ Tell what the problem is asking.
☐ Show all your work.
☐ Show that the solution works.

a. Circle something that is known.
b. Underline something that you need to find.
c. Draw a box around what you do to solve the problem.
d. Put a checkmark next to the part that shows the solution works.

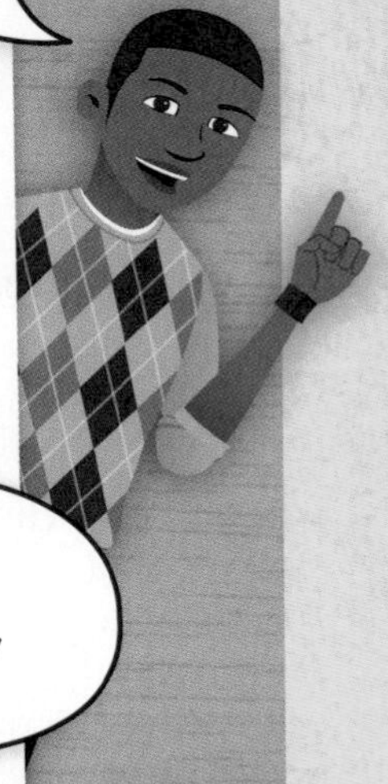

G.O.'s Solution

Hi, I'm G.O. Here's how I solved this problem.

▷ **I already know** that the length of one object in the pair has to be a multiple of the length of the other object. So one length is multiplied by a factor to get the other length as the product.

▷ **I can think about any two numbers in the table.**

I need to find pairs in which one number is a multiple of the other. I'll make a chart with some multiplication facts I can write using the lengths.

I made a table to organize my thinking.

Shorter Length	x Number	Longer Length
10 cm	x 5	50 cm
5 cm	x 2	10 cm
5 cm	x 3	15 cm
8 cm	x 3	24 cm
4 cm	x 6	24 cm

The longer length is no more than 5 times the shorter length. These pairs all work.

24 is 6 times 4, and 6 times is more than 5 times. This doesn't work.

▷ **Now I can pick three pairs that work and name the objects and lengths.**

Pair 1:
sugar pine needle (10 cm)
sugar pine cone (50 cm)

Pair 2:
jack pine cone (5 cm)
ponderosa pine needle (15 cm)

Here's my final answer.

Pair 3:
ponderosa pine cone (8 cm)
longleaf pine cone (24 cm)

Try **Another Approach**

There are many ways to solve problems. Think about how you might solve the Pine Cones and Needles problem in a different way.

Pine Cones and Needles

G.O. is with his friend Azul at a wildlife park. A worker at the nature center is arranging pine cones and pine needles in pairs for a display. Here are the rules.

Rules for Pairing Objects
- One length is a multiple of another length.
- The longer length is no more than 5 times the shorter length.
- Cones or needles can be paired with other cones or needles.

Kind of Tree	Sugar Pine	Jack Pine	Ponderosa Pine	Longleaf Pine
Cone Length	50 cm	5 cm	8 cm	24 cm
Needle Length	10 cm	4 cm	15 cm	40 cm

Use an object only once. Find three possible pairs of objects that fit the rules. Tell why these pairs work.

▶ **Plan It** Answer these questions to help you start thinking about a plan.

A. Look at the sample answer. What are some other factors of the numbers in the Longer Length column?

_____

_____

B. Can you pair the cone of each kind of tree with its needle? Why or why not?

_____

_____

Solve It Find a different solution for the Pine Cones and Needles problem. Show all your work on a separate sheet of paper.

You may want to use the problem-solving tips to get started.

Problem-Solving Tips

- **Models** You may want to use . . .
  - a table.

- **Word Bank**

factor	multiply	length
multiple	product	times

- **Sentence Starters**

  - _____ is _____ times

  - _____ is a multiple

  - I can pair _____

Reflect

Use Process Standards As you work through the problem, discuss these questions with a partner.

- **Use Reasoning** How is your partner's reasoning different than your own?

- **Make Sense of Quantities** Look at the lengths in the pairs you made. How do you know how many times as many one number is than the other?

Read the problem. Write a solution on a separate sheet of paper. Remember, there are lots of ways to solve a problem!

Numbers in Nature

The nature center is planning a display called "Numbers in Nature." It will show animals and plants that represent different types of numbers.

> **Number Categories**
> · Prime Numbers
> · Composite Numbers
> · Even Numbers
> · Odd Numbers

One part of the display shows the number of petals that flowers have. G.O. is sorting these flowers into the number categories listed above.

| A | B | C | D |

| E | F | G | H |

How can G.O. arrange these flowers?

Plan It and Solve It   Find a solution to G.O.'s Numbers in Nature problem.

Help G.O. sort the flowers. Be sure to . . .

- find the number of petals each flower has.

- identify all the categories that each number fits in.

- study all the numbers and categories. Tell what you notice about how even and odd numbers relate to prime and composite numbers.

You may want to use the problem-solving tips to get started.

Problem-Solving Tips

- **Questions**
    - Do some numbers fit in more than one category?
    - Are there any numbers that fit in only one category?

- **Word Bank**

prime	odd	divide
composite	factor	add
even	factor pair	

- **Sentence Starters**
    - The flower has _____
    - This number belongs to _____

Problem-Solving Checklist

Make sure that you . . .

- ☐ tell what you know.
- ☐ tell what you need to do.
- ☐ show all your work.
- ☐ show that the solution works.

Reflect

Use Process Standards   As you work through the problem, discuss these questions with a partner.

- **Use a Model** How can you create a model that will help you see the relationship between the different types of numbers?

- **Make an Argument** How can you justify the relationships that you describe?

Read the problems. Write a solution on a separate sheet of paper.
Remember, there are many different ways to solve a problem!

G.O.'s Planting Project

By the 1950s, almost all American chestnut trees in the country had been
destroyed by a fungus. Now a conservation group plants groves of chestnut
trees in suitable places. They hope the trees will make a strong comeback.

G.O. volunteers for a planting project at the park. Below is G.O.'s plan.

My Planting Plan
· Plant 48 chestnut trees.
· Plant the trees in rows.
· Include an equal number of trees in each row.
· Plant a tree every 10 feet in the row.
· Leave 20 feet of space between rows.

How many rows of trees will G.O.'s plan make? How many trees
are in each row?

▶ **Solve It** Describe a way to plant the 48 trees that works with the plan.
- Draw and label a diagram.
- Tell how many rows there are and how many trees are in each row.
- Tell the length and width of the rectangular area you need for your plan.
- Explain why your plan works.

▶ **Reflect**

Use Process Standards After you complete the task, choose one
of these questions to discuss with a partner.

- **Make Sense of Problems** What was your first step in solving the
  problem? Why?

- **Use Tools** What tools did you use to help you find the length and width
  of the rectangular area?

Unit 3
Computation

Real-World Connection Understanding how to calculate with numbers is an important skill. You use math in many different ways in everyday life. For a school field day, how many bottles of water would be needed for all the students? If the bottles of water come in packages, how many packages would be needed? And, what if the field day includes students playing games in teams? To find out how many teams there will be, you'll need to divide the number of students in the school by the number of students you want on each team.

In This Unit You will multiply and divide with whole numbers. You will use your understanding of place value to help you multiply and divide. You will also use models and what you know about how multiplication and division are related to help you solve word problems.

> Let's learn about multiplying and dividing multi-digit numbers.

✓ Self Check

Before starting this unit, check off the skills you know below. As you complete each lesson, see how many more skills you can check off!

I can:	Before this unit	After this unit
multiply a four-digit number by a one-digit number, for example: 2,810 × 3 = 8,430.	☐	☐
multiply a two-digit number by a two-digit number, for example: 62 × 33 = 2,046.	☐	☐
divide a four-digit number by a one-digit number, for example: 6,328 ÷ 4 = 1,582.	☐	☐
use area models and equations to explain calculations, for example: 7 × 240 = (7 × 200) + (7 × 40).	☐	☐

⟲ Use What You Know

You have learned how to multiply one-digit numbers by multiples of ten. Take a look at this problem.

There are 100 stickers on each roll, and a box of stickers has 3 rolls. How many stickers are there in 4 boxes?

a. How many boxes are there? _____

b. How many rolls of stickers are in each box? _____

c. Write a multiplication expression to show how many rolls of stickers there are in all the boxes. _____

d. How many stickers are on each roll? _____

e. Write a multiplication expression to show how many stickers there are in all.

_____

f. How can you show 100 using tens as factors? _____

Write an expression that is equal to the one above using tens as factors.

_____

g. Explain how to use what you know about multiplying by 10 to solve the problem.

_____

_____

_____

To multiply with three-digit and four-digit numbers, you need to understand how to multiply by multiples of 10, 100, and 1,000. Take a look at the chart below.

Expression	Think of it as...	Think of it as...	Product
4 × 3	4 × 3 ones	12 ones	12
4 × 30	4 × 3 tens	12 tens	120
4 × 300	4 × 3 hundreds	12 hundreds	1,200
4 × 3,000	4 × 3 thousands	12 thousands	12,000

Notice that in each expression one factor is 4 and the other is 3 times 10, 100, or 1,000. You can use the basic fact 4 × 3 = 12 to find each product.

The factor 30 is ten times 3, so the product 4 × 30 is ten times 12: 4 × 30 = 120.

The factor 300 is one hundred times 3, so the product 4 × 300 is one hundred times 12: 4 × 300 = 1,200.

The factor 3,000 is one thousand times 3, so the product 4 × 3,000 is one thousand times 12: 4 × 3,000 = 12,000.

▶ **Reflect**

1 Choose a basic multiplication fact that you know. Show how to multiply the product of the fact by 10, 100, and 1,000. Explain how you know your answer is correct.

_____

_____

_____

_____

Learn About ▶ **Multiplying by a One-Digit Number**

Read the problem below. Then explore different ways to multiply a four-digit number by a one-digit number.

> Ezekiel has 3 building sets. Each set includes 1,125 pieces. How many pieces are in all 3 sets?

▶ **Picture It** **You can use an area model to help understand the problem.**

	1,000	+	100	+ 20	+ 5
3	$3 \times 1{,}000$		3×100	3×20	3×5

$$3 \times 1{,}125 = (3 \times 1{,}000) + (3 \times 100) + (3 \times 20) + (3 \times 5)$$
$$= 3{,}000 + 300 + 60 + 15$$
$$= 3{,}375$$

▶ **Model It** **You can also multiply the numbers using partial products.**

```
      1,125
   ×      3
   ─────────
        15 ──→ 3 × 5 ones
        60 ──→ 3 × 2 tens
       300 ──→ 3 × 1 hundred
  +  3,000 ──→ 3 × 1 thousand
   ─────────
     3,375
```

The **partial products** are **15**, **60**, **300**, and **3,000**. The product is the sum of the partial products: $15 + 60 + 300 + 3{,}000 = 3{,}375$.

Connect It Now you will explore the problem from the previous page further.

2 What is the expanded form of 1,125? _____ + _____ + _____ + _____

3 Where do you see the expanded form in the area model?

_____

4 How is the expanded form used in the equation in *Picture It*?

_____

5 The partial products in *Model It* shows first multiplying the 3 by the value of the digit in the ones column. Would the product change if you first multiplied the 3 by the value of the digit in the thousands column? Explain. _____

_____

_____

_____

6 Describe how the factor 3 is used with the factor 1,125 to find the product.

_____

_____

_____

7 Explain how you multiply a four-digit number by a one-digit number. _____

_____

_____

_____

Try It Use what you just learned to solve these problems. Show your work on a separate sheet of paper.

8 $2{,}041 \times 6 =$ _____

9 $5{,}342 \times 4 =$ _____

Learn About ⟩ **Multiplying by Two-Digit Numbers**

Read the problem below. Then explore different ways to multiply a two-digit number by a two-digit number.

> Folding chairs are set up in a school auditorium for a play. There are 16 rows of chairs, each with 28 chairs. How many folding chairs are there?

▶ **Picture It** **You can use an area model to multiply two-digit numbers.**

To solve this problem, multiply 16×28.

	10	+	6
20	20×10 2 tens $\times$ 1 ten = 2 hundreds 200		20×6 2 tens $\times$ 6 = 12 tens 120
+ 8	8×10 8×1 ten = 8 tens 80		$8 \times 6 = 48$

$200 + 80 + 120 + 48 = 448$

▶ **Model It** **You can also multiply two-digit numbers using partial products.**

$$
\begin{array}{r}
16 \\
\times\ 28 \\
\hline
48 \\
80 \\
120 \\
+\ 200 \\
\hline
448
\end{array}
$$

48 ⟶ 8 ones $\times$ 6 ones
80 ⟶ 8 ones $\times$ 1 ten
120 ⟶ 2 tens $\times$ 6 ones
200 ⟶ 2 tens $\times$ 1 ten

Connect It Now you will explore the problem from the previous page further.

10 Why is the area model divided into four sections? _____

_____

_____

11 How do the four steps in the multiplication using partial products in *Model It* relate to the four sections in the area model in *Picture It*? _____

_____

_____

12 Would the product change if $20 + 8$ on the left side of the area model were changed to $10 + 10 + 8$? Explain. _____

_____

_____

_____

_____

13 List two different ways that you could break up the numbers in 34×12 to find the product. Explain why both ways would have the same product.

_____

_____

_____

Try It Use what you just learned to solve these problems. Show your work on a separate sheet of paper.

14 $27 \times 21 =$ _____

15 $37 \times 23 =$ _____

Practice ▶ **Multiplying Whole Numbers**

Study the example below. Then solve problems 16–18.

Example

An aquarium has 6 female sea turtles. Each turtle lays up to 1,785 eggs a year. If each turtle lays 1,785 eggs this year, how many eggs will there be in all?

Look at how you could show your work using an area model.

	1,000	+	700	+	80	+	5
6	6 × 1,000		6 × 700		6 × 80		6 × 5

$6 \times 1{,}785 = (6 \times 1{,}000) + (6 \times 700) + (6 \times 80) + (6 \times 5)$
$= 6{,}000 + 4{,}200 + 480 + 30$
$= 10{,}710$

Solution ___10,710 eggs___

The student multiplied 6 by the value of the digit in each place in 1,785.

Pair/Share
How else could you solve this problem?

---

16 A deli is preparing trays of sandwiches. There are 15 trays, each with 24 sandwiches. How many sandwiches are there?

Show your work.

Should you multiply 15 × 24 or 24 × 15?

Pair/Share
How did you decide which method to use to help you solve the problem?

Solution _____

17 The owner of 12 bookstores is buying 32 copies of a new book for each of the stores. How many books is the owner buying in all?

Show your work.

Could you use an area model to help solve the problem?

Solution _____

Pair/Share
How is this problem different than the one modeled on the previous page?

---

18 A hardware store has 147 containers of paint. If each container holds 5 gallons of paint, how many gallons of paint are at the store? Circle the letter of the correct answer.

A 235

B 505

C 735

D 905

Dale chose **A** as the correct answer. How did he get that answer?

Multiply 5 by the value of the digit in each place in 147.

_____

_____

_____

Pair/Share
Does Dale's answer make sense?

Practice ▶ **Multiplying Whole Numbers**

Solve the problems.

1 A person blinks about 16 times per minute. About how many times does a person blink in 3 hours? [Hint: 1 hour = 60 minutes]

A 48

B 96

C 960

D 2,880

2 Mr. Larson is planning a pizza party for 273 people. He plans on 3 slices of pizza for each person. How many slices of pizza is this in all?

A 276

B 546

C 619

D 819

3 Can the expression be used to solve 29×14? Choose *Yes* or *No* for each expression.

a. $(9 \times 4) + (20 \times 4) + (9 \times 1) + (20 \times 1)$ ☐ Yes ☐ No

b. $(14 \times 9) + (14 \times 20)$ ☐ Yes ☐ No

c. $(9 \times 4) + (20 \times 4) + (9 \times 10) + (20 \times 10)$ ☐ Yes ☐ No

d. $(29 \times 4) + (29 \times 10)$ ☐ Yes ☐ No

4 Which model(s) below could represent the solution to the problem 45 × 15? Circle the letter for all that apply.

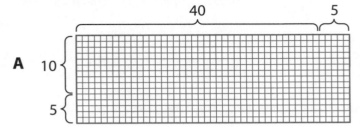

A 10, 5 (40, 5)

B 0 15 30 45

C (4 × 1) + (4 × 5) + (5 × 1) + (5 × 5)

D (4 × 1) + (5 × 5)

E

0 45 90 135 180 225 270 315 360 405 450 495 540 585 630 675

5 Mo had 14 tutoring sessions. Each session was 35 minutes long. How many minutes did Mo spend in the 14 sessions combined?

Show your work.

Answer Mo spent _____ minutes in the 14 sessions.

6 Fourth grade students held a recycling drive. During one week they collected 1,238 water bottles each day. How many water bottles did the fourth graders collect that week? [Hint: There are 7 days in one week.]

Show your work.

Answer The fourth grade students collected _____ water bottles.

✓ **Self Check** Go back and see what you can check off on the Self Check on page 125.

🔄 Use What You Know

You have learned how to multiply one-digit numbers by multiples of 10, 100, and 1,000. Take a look at this problem.

> The Chase family is driving 3,000 miles across the country. They plan on driving for 5 days, traveling the same distance each day. How many miles will the Chase family drive each day?
>
>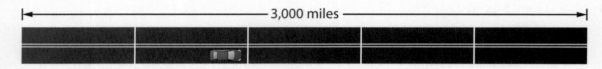
>
> |← ——————————————— 3,000 miles ——————————————— →|

a. What division equation can be used to solve this problem? _____

b. What is the related multiplication equation? _____

c. What basic multiplication fact can you use to help find the answer? _____

d. If you divide 30 hundreds into 5 equal groups, how many hundreds are in each group? _____

e. How can the basic fact help find 3,000 ÷ 5? _____

_____

_____

f. Explain how to find the number of miles the Chase family will drive each day.

_____

_____

_____

▷▷ Find Out More

The area model below shows the numbers for the Chase family trip.

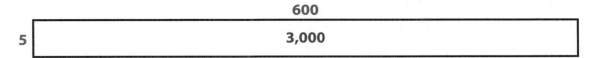

	600
5	3,000

An area model shows both multiplication (**5 × 600 = 3,000**) and division (**3,000 ÷ 5 = 600**). Here are two possible ways you could break apart the factor **600** and the total **3,000**.

	300	+	300
5	1,500		1,500

	100	+	100	+	100	+	100	+	100	+	100
5	500		500		500		500		500		500

When you look at this as a model for division, the sum of the numbers in red is the **quotient**, or the result of the division problem. The sum of the numbers inside the area model is the **dividend**, or the total you are dividing. The number at the side of the model is the **divisor**, or the number you are dividing by.

Sometimes numbers don't divide evenly. The amount left over is the **remainder**. If you divided 17 baseballs equally among 4 brothers, each brother would get 4 baseballs and there would be 1 baseball left over. This is written as:

$$4 \overline{)17} \quad \begin{array}{c} 4 \text{ R1} \end{array}$$

▶ Reflect

1 Explain how an area model shows both multiplication and division.

_____

_____

_____

_____

Learn About ▸ Dividing Three-Digit Numbers

Read the problem below. Then explore different ways to divide three-digit numbers by one-digit numbers.

> There are 150 students going on a field trip. Students are put in equal groups of 6. How many groups are there? Are there any students left over?

▶ **Model It** **You can use an area model to help understand the problem.**

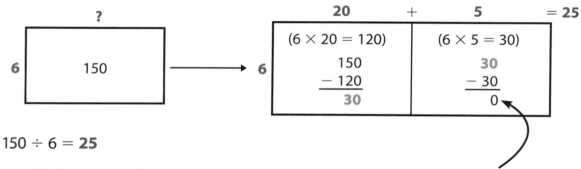

$150 \div 6 = 25$

Use multiplication to check:

There is no remainder.

$$25 \times 6 = (20 \times 6) + (5 \times 6)$$
$$= 120 + 30$$
$$= 150$$

There are 25 groups and 0 students left over.

▶ **Model It** **You can also subtract partial products to divide the numbers.**

$$
\begin{array}{r}
150 \\
-\ 120 \quad \longleftarrow 6 \times 20 \\
\hline
30 \\
-\ 30 \quad \longleftarrow 6 \times 5 \\
\hline
0 \quad \longleftarrow \text{no remainder}
\end{array}
$$

Stop subtracting when you reach zero or a number less than the divisor (**6**). The quotient is the sum of all the numbers you multiplied by 6.

$$20 + 5 = 25$$

There are 25 groups and 0 students left over.

Connect It Now you will solve the problem from the previous page using a different area model.

2 Melinda decided to split her area model into five sections that each show $6 \times 5 = 30$. Draw Melinda's area model below. Then show how to subtract the partial products to find the answer.

3 Can you use Melinda's model to solve the problem? Why or why not?

_____

_____

_____

_____

4 Explain how an area model can help you break apart a division problem to make it easier to solve. _____

_____

_____

_____

_____

Try It Use what you just learned to solve these problems. Show your work on a separate sheet of paper.

5 $132 \div 3 =$ _____

6 $364 \div 7 =$ _____

Learn About ▶ Dividing Four-Digit Numbers

Read the problem below. Then explore different ways to divide four-digit numbers by one-digit numbers.

> A factory has 2,125 DVD players to ship to electronics stores. They ship 4 DVD players in each box. How many full boxes can they ship?

▶ **Model It** **You can use an area model to help understand the problem.**

$$500 \; + \; 25 \; + \; 6 \; = 531$$

$(4 \times 500 = 2,000)$	$(4 \times 25 = 100)$	$(4 \times 6 = 24)$
2,125	125	25
− 2,000	− 100	− 24
125	25	1 remainder

?

4 | 2,125 ⟶ 4

▶ **Model It** **You can also find partial quotients to divide the numbers.**

Divide each place value of 2,125 by 4.

```
        6
       25
      500
   4)2,125  ⟵ How many groups of 4 in 2,000? 500
    − 2,000    Subtract 500 groups of 4.
        125 ⟵ How many groups of 4 in 100? 25
      − 100    Subtract 25 groups of 4.
         25 ⟵ How many groups of 4 in 25? 6
       − 24    Subtract 6 groups of 4.
          1
```

The **partial quotients** are **500**, **25**, and **6**. The quotient, **531**, is the sum of the partial quotients. The remainder is **1**.

Connect It Now you will explore the problem from the previous page further.

7 How many full boxes can they ship? _____

8 What does the remainder mean in this problem? _____

_____

9 If the factory could ship partially filled boxes, how would the answer change?

_____

_____

10 How is the partial quotients model on the previous page like the subtracting partial products model in the field trip problem? _____

_____

_____

_____

11 Which division model do you like better: area models, subtracting partial products, or finding partial quotients? Explain how that model helps you divide.

_____

_____

_____

_____

Try It Use what you just learned to solve these problems. Show your work on a separate sheet of paper.

12 1,010 ÷ 9 ⟶ _____

13 5,783 ÷ 6 ⟶ _____

Practice ▶ **Dividing Whole Numbers**

Study the example below. Then solve problems 14–16.

Example

In art class, 8 students share 104 scraps of felt. Each student gets the same number of pieces. How many scraps of felt does each student get?

Look at how you could show your work using an area model.

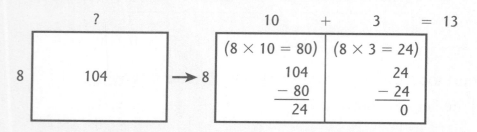

Solution _13 scraps of felt_

> The student first multiplied 8 × 10. After subtracting 80 from 104, there were still 24 left.

Pair/Share
How else could you solve this problem?

---

14 A tailor has 641 yards of material to make costumes. Each costume needs 3 yards of material. How many costumes can be made? Will there be any material left over?

Show your work.

How could you use an area model to help solve the problem?

Solution _____

Pair/Share
What does the remainder mean in this problem?

15 The Prize Place has 252 toys to be divided equally among 6 piñatas. How many toys will go into each piñata?

Show your work.

Will there be any toys left over?

Pair/Share
How else could you solve this problem?

Solution _____

---

16 There are 1,275 people trying out for a show. The director needs to put people in 5 waiting rooms. If each room has the same number of people, how many will be in each room? Circle the letter of the correct answer.

A 111

B 251

C 255

D 1,270

Awan chose **D** as the correct answer. How did he get that answer?

Can you use multiplication to help solve the problem?

_____

_____

_____

_____

Pair/Share
How can you tell that Awan's answer doesn't make sense?

Practice ▶ **Dividing Whole Numbers**

Solve the problems.

1 James, Micah, and Rebecca work at a restaurant. Last night there was $115 in the tip jar. They decided to divide the tips equally among them and leave any extra money in the jar. How much money did they leave in the jar?

A $1

B $2

C $38

D $39

2 Together Aiden and his sister saved 360 quarters. Aiden saved twice as many quarters as his sister. If Aiden plans to put his quarters into 3 equal piles, how many quarters will he put in each pile?

A 36

B 60

C 80

D 120

3 A group of 53 tourists visit a museum. Museum volunteers lead tours for groups of no more than 8 tourists. Draw a model to show the least number of groups that can be formed for these 53 tourists. Use circles to show the groups and choose a symbol to show each person.

What is the fewest number of tour groups that need to be formed? _____

4 Tell whether each equation is *True* or *False*.

    a. $8{,}675 \div 8 = 1{,}084$ ☐ True   ☐ False

    b. $493 \div 7 = 73$ ☐ True   ☐ False

    c. $3{,}604 \div 4 = 91$ ☐ True   ☐ False

    d. $675 \div 5 = 135$ ☐ True   ☐ False

5 Mrs. Long is making 7 snack bags. She has 175 almonds to share evenly among the bags. How many almonds will be in each bag? How many almonds will be left over?

Show your work.

    Answer   There will be _____ almonds in each bag.

                   There will be _____ almonds left over.

6 Trina has a box of 1,132 beads to make necklaces. She wants to use as many of the beads as possible to make 9 necklaces. If she uses the same number of beads for each necklace, how many beads will be on each one? How many beads will be left over?

Show your work.

    Answer   There will be _____ beads on each necklace.

                   There will be _____ beads left over.

✔ **Self Check**   **Go back and see what you can check off on the Self Check on page 125.**

Study an Example Problem and Solution

Read this problem about multiplying multi-digit numbers. Then look at Beau's solution to this problem.

Worm Farm

Beau likes to recycle. He wants to start a worm farm where he can recycle kitchen scraps from people in his neighborhood. He gathers this information.

My Data

· 2,000 worms can eat about 1 pound of food in 1 day.

· I can collect 50 to 65 pounds of scraps each week.

Red Worm Prices

1,050 worms $25
2,950 worms $72

Show how to find the number of worms Beau needs for this amount of scraps.

• Tell how many and what size packages Beau can buy to get this many worms.

• Give the total cost of buying the worms.

Read the sample solution on the next page. Then look at the checklist below. Find and mark parts of the solution that match the checklist.

✏️ Problem-Solving Checklist

☐ Tell what is known.

☐ Tell what the problem is asking.

☐ Show all your work.

☐ Show that the solution works.

a. Circle something that is known.

b. Underline something that you need to find.

c. Draw a box around what you do to solve the problem.

d. Put a checkmark next to the part that shows the solution works.

Beau's Solution

> Hi, I'm Beau. Here's how I solved this problem.

▷ **I already know** that the amount of kitchen scraps is between 50 and 65 pounds. I'll use 55 pounds to make an estimate.

▷ **I need to find** about how many worms are needed to recycle 55 pounds of scraps each week.

▷ **I also know** that 2,000 worms eat 1 pound of scraps in 1 day. So 2,000 worms eat 7 pounds of scraps in 7 days, or 1 week.

> Since the amount of kitchen scraps is not exact, I can estimate.

▷ **I can estimate** that 55 is about 8 times 7.
So, I need about 8 times 2,000 worms for 55 pounds of scraps.
$$2,000 \times 8 = 16,000$$
I need about 16,000 worms.

▷ **Now I can look for ways to get about 16,000 worms.**
2,950 is about 3,000 and $3,000 \times 5 = 15,000$.

▷ **I'll start with 5 packages of 2,950 worms.**
$$2,950 \times 5 = 2,000 \times 5 + 900 \times 5 + 50 \times 5$$
$$= 10,000 + 4,500 + 250$$
$$= 14,750$$

> Here I used the exact number of worms in the package.

▷ **Then, I'll subtract to find how many more worms I need.**
$$16,000 - 14,750 = 1,250$$
I need 2 packages of 1,050 worms to get 1,250 more worms.
The total number of worms is 14,750 + 2,100, or 16,850.
This is close to 16,000.

> There may be more than 55 pounds of scraps some weeks. It's okay to have more worms.

▷ **Multiply to find the total cost.**
$$\$25 \times 2 = \$\ 50$$
$$\underline{\$72 \times 5 = \$360}$$
$$\$410$$

Try > Another Approach

There are many ways to solve problems. Think about how you might solve the Worm Farm problem in a different way.

Worm Farm

Beau likes to recycle. He wants to start a worm farm where he can recycle kitchen scraps from people in his neighborhood. He gathers this information.

My Data

· 2,000 worms can eat about 1 pound of food in 1 day.

· I can collect 50 to 65 pounds of scraps each week.

Red Worm Prices

1,050 worms $25
2,950 worms $72

Show how to find the number of worms Beau needs for this amount of scraps.

• Tell how many and what size packages Beau can buy to get this many worms.

• Give the total cost of buying the worms.

▶ **Plan It** **Answer these questions to help you start thinking about a plan.**

A. Will you use a lesser or greater amount of kitchen scraps to estimate the number of worms? Explain why.

_____

_____

B. How could you solve the problem by finding the amount of kitchen scraps there will be in 1 day?

_____

_____

Solve It Find a different solution for the Worm Farm problem.
Show all your work on a separate sheet of paper.

You may want to use the problem-solving tips to get started.

Problem-Solving Tips

- **Models** You might want to use . . .
  - partial products.
  - area models.

- **Word Bank**

estimate	total	about
multiply	subtract	close to

- **Sentence Starters**

  - To make an estimate, I can use _____

  - There are _____ worms in _____

Reflect

Use Process Standards As you work through the problem, discuss these questions with a partner.

- **Be Precise** Why is it appropriate to use an estimate with this problem?

- **Make an Argument** Why did you choose the numbers you did for your estimates?

Discuss ▶ **Models and Strategies**

Read the problem. Write a solution on a separate sheet of paper. Remember, there are lots of ways to solve a problem!

Recycle It

Because of his composting work, Beau decided to start other recycling projects. He wants to promote recycling in his neighborhood. This is the slogan he will use to start a recycling campaign.

> Everyone can recycle at least 30 pounds of waste in 3 months!

Beau weighs different items that can be recycled. Here are some items he found that weigh about 1 pound:

3 medium-size cardboard boxes

105 sheets of printer paper

24 empty plastic water bottles

32 empty aluminum cans

Help Beau write a report to show ways people can recycle 30 pounds of waste in 3 months.

Plan It and Solve It Find a solution to Beau's Recycle It problem.

Use Beau's information.

- Use a combination of at least two of the items on the list.
- Explain how a person could recycle at least 30 pounds of waste in 3 months with these items.

You may want to use the problem-solving tips to get started.

Problem-Solving Tips

- **Questions**
  - What are some different ways you can combine two or three weights to have a sum of 30 pounds?
  - How can you find the number of a type of item it takes to make each of these weights?

- **Sentence Starters**
  - If you recycle _____ plastic bottles, you _____
  - If you add the weights of all the items, _____

Problem-Solving Checklist
Make sure that you . . .
- ☐ tell what you know.
- ☐ tell what you need to do.
- ☐ show all your work.
- ☐ show that the solution works.

Reflect
Use Process Standards As you work through the problem, discuss these questions with a partner.

- **Use Tools** What methods can you use to find the numbers you need in your solution?
- **Be Precise** How can you make sure that your solution shows the meaning of all the numbers in it?

Read the problems. Write a solution on a separate sheet of paper. Remember, there are many different ways to solve a problem!

Rainwater Recycling

Beau's report about recycling was very popular. He decides to write a similar report about recycling rainwater. He will post both reports on the bulletin board at the Community Center. Here is some information Beau found about this topic.

Information About Recycling Rainwater

· A 1,000 square foot roof can collect 620 gallons of water when 1 inch of rain falls.

· The typical rainfall in our area is 3 inches per month.

· It takes about . . .

50 gallons to water a 200 square foot garden.

62 gallons to water a 100 square foot area of lawn.

55 gallons of water to wash a car.

What should Beau include in his report to convince people in the area to collect rainwater?

▶ **Solve It** **Help Beau write a report about recycling rainwater.**

• Find the amount of water that a homeowner could collect in one month.

• Write a 1 paragraph report to convince people to save water.

• Tell at least two things that could be done with the rainwater.

▶ **Reflect**

Use Process Standards After you complete the task, choose one of these questions to discuss with a partner.

• **Use a Model** How could you use equations to find the numbers you need for the report?

• **Be Precise** How did you make sure that readers will see the different measurements in your report?

Let's learn about fractions and decimals.

Real-World Connection What would the world be like without fractions? Well . . . without fractions, chefs wouldn't be able to measure $\frac{2}{3}$-cup of milk, and construction workers wouldn't be able to cut a piece of wood $4\frac{1}{8}$-feet long. Without fractions, even your language would change. You wouldn't be able to talk about one-quarter or one-half of an hour.

In This Unit You will see that fractions are a lot like whole numbers. What you know about whole numbers will help you add, subtract, multiply, and compare fractions. You will explore how fractions are like whole numbers, including all the ways you can show, build, and take apart fractions to solve problems. And, you'll learn about mixed numbers and improper fractions.

✓ Self Check

Before starting this unit, check off the skills you know below. As you complete each lesson, see how many more skills you can check off!

I can:	Before this unit	After this unit
find equivalent fractions, for example: $\frac{2}{3} = \frac{4}{6}$.	☐	☐
understand whole numbers, mixed numbers, and improper fractions, for example: 2, $2\frac{1}{4}$, and $\frac{9}{4}$.	☐	☐
compare fractions with unlike denominators, for example: $\frac{2}{5} > \frac{3}{10}$.	☐	☐
add and subtract fractions with like denominators, for example: $\frac{2}{6} + \frac{3}{6} = \frac{5}{6}$.	☐	☐
multiply a fraction by a whole number, for example: $3 \times \frac{1}{2} = \frac{3}{2}$.	☐	☐
write a decimal as a fraction, for example: $0.4 = \frac{4}{10}$.	☐	☐
compare decimals, for example: $0.65 < 0.7$.	☐	☐

💭 **Think It Through**

What's really going on when fractions are equivalent?

Equivalent fractions name the same part of a whole.

Think about how you could explain to a third grader why $\frac{5}{10}$ and $\frac{1}{2}$ are equivalent.

You could shade area models to show $\frac{5}{10}$ and $\frac{1}{2}$.

Both models at the right are the same size. Both show the same amount shaded, so $\frac{5}{10}$ and $\frac{1}{2}$ are equivalent fractions.

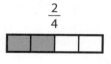

Think Equivalent fractions show the same amount in different ways.

Fractions can be written many different ways by changing the number of equal parts in the whole.

Start with a rectangle divided into 2 equal parts. Shade one part to show $\frac{1}{2}$.

$$\frac{1}{2}$$

Divide the same rectangle into 4 equal parts. There are 2 times as many parts and 2 times as many parts shaded. Now 2 out of 4 equal parts are shaded.

$$\frac{2}{4}$$

But, your rectangle still shows $\frac{1}{2}$ shaded.

Divide the original rectangle into 8 equal parts. There are 4 times as many parts and 4 times as many parts shaded. Now 4 out of 8 equal parts are shaded. Your rectangle still shows $\frac{1}{2}$ shaded.

$$\frac{4}{8}$$

So, $\frac{1}{2}$, $\frac{2}{4}$, and $\frac{4}{8}$ are all equivalent fractions, since they name the same part of a whole.

✏️ **Underline** the part that explains how to write a fraction a different way.

Think Every fraction has many equivalent fractions.

You can start with any fraction and change the way the whole is divided to get an equivalent fraction.

This model is divided into 3 equal parts.
The shaded section shows the fraction $\frac{1}{3}$.

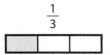
$\frac{1}{3}$

Think of 2 times as many as $\times$ 2.

$\frac{2}{6}$ has 2 times as many parts shaded and
2 times as many equal parts.

$\frac{2}{6}$

$\frac{4}{12}$ has 4 times as many equal parts and
4 times as many parts shaded as $\frac{1}{3}$.

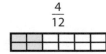
$\frac{4}{12}$

All three models have the same shaded area. So, $\frac{1}{3}$, $\frac{2}{6}$, and $\frac{4}{12}$ are equivalent fractions.

You can also multiply the numerator and denominator of $\frac{1}{3}$ by the same number to get an equivalent fraction.

2 times as many equal parts and 2 times as many parts shaded:

$$\frac{1 \times 2}{3 \times 2} = \frac{2}{6}$$

4 times as many equal parts and 4 times as many parts shaded:

$$\frac{1 \times 4}{3 \times 4} = \frac{4}{12}$$

▶ Reflect

1 Explain how you can find equivalent fractions.

_____

_____

_____

_____

Think About ▸ **Equivalent Fractions**

🔍 **Let's Explore the Idea** Dividing models is one way to think about equivalent fractions.

2 The model shows $\frac{1}{4}$. How many equal parts make up the whole? _____

Use a ruler to draw 2 more lines to make 8 equal parts.

3 Compare the 4 equal parts to the 8 equal parts.
How many times as many parts are there now? _____

Now how many parts are shaded? _____

Why are there two times as many parts shaded as there were in the $\frac{1}{4}$ model?

_____

Use the model above to answer problems 4 and 5.

4 If 3 of the original 4 parts were shaded, how many of the 8 parts would be shaded? _____

5 If all 8 parts were shaded, how many of the original 4 parts would be shaded?

_____

Now try these two problems.

6 Draw a model to show $\frac{2}{3}$ and then divide it into a different number of parts to show an equivalent fraction.

7 This model shows $\frac{30}{100}$. If the model had only 10 equal parts, how many would be shaded? _____

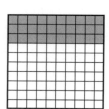

Let's Talk About It

Solve the problems below as a group.

8 Write the equivalent fractions from problems 2 and 3. _____

Multiply both the numerator and denominator of $\frac{1}{4}$ by the same number to get $\frac{2}{8}$.
What number did you use? Why does this make sense?

_____

_____

What happens if you divide both the numerator and the denominator in $\frac{2}{8}$ by 2?

_____

9 To find an equivalent fraction to $\frac{6}{8}$, Beth divided by 2 to get 4 in the denominator.
What should Beth do to find the numerator? What are the equivalent fractions?

_____

10 Fill in the missing numbers to find an equivalent fraction to $\frac{5}{6}$.

$$\frac{5 \times 2}{6 \times \square} = \frac{10}{\square}$$

▶ Try It Another Way Work with your group to model equivalent fractions.

11 Shade the model to show $\frac{2}{5}$. Then show 10 equal parts and write the
equivalent fractions.

$$\frac{\square}{\square} = \frac{\square}{\square}$$

12 Shade the model to show $\frac{1}{4}$. Then show 12 equal parts and write the
equivalent fractions.

$$\frac{\square}{\square} = \frac{\square}{\square}$$

Connect ▶ **Ideas about Equivalent Fractions**

Talk through these problems as a class, then write your answers below.

13 Compare Use different methods to find two fractions that are equivalent to $\frac{3}{3}$.

14 Illustrate Explain why you can multiply both the numerator and denominator by the same number to make an equivalent fraction. Draw a model to show an example.

_____

_____

_____

15 Choose Think about the cooking problem below.

Fia needs $\frac{3}{4}$ of a cup of brown sugar. She only has a $\frac{1}{3}$-cup measuring cup and a $\frac{1}{8}$-cup measuring cup. Which should she use and why?

_____

_____

_____

Apply ▸ **Ideas about Equivalent Fractions**

16 Put It Together Use what you have learned to complete this task.

Part A Draw a model to show the fraction $\frac{6}{10}$ and two equivalent fractions.

Part B How can you use multiplication and division to check your equivalent fractions in Part A? Why does this work?

_____

_____

_____

_____

_____

_____

_____

_____

Lesson 13B 👥 Introduction
Whole Numbers, Mixed Numbers, and Improper Fractions

🅖 Use What You Know

You know that equivalent fractions name the same part of one whole. Fractions can also name amounts that are equal to or greater than one whole. Take a look at this problem.

> Dee has green and blue ribbons that are the same length. She is going to cut them into pieces to decorate a dance costume. She cuts the green ribbon into sixths. She uses two of those pieces for her costume.
>
>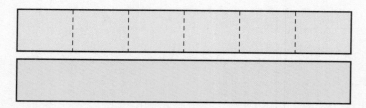
>
> Dee cuts the blue ribbon into thirds. She wants to use the same amount of green and blue ribbon. How many pieces of blue ribbon will she use?

a. Look at the picture above. What fraction of the green ribbon is each piece? _____

b. Circle two pieces to show the amount of green ribbon Dee uses. What fraction of the green ribbon is this amount? _____

c. On the picture above, draw lines on the blue ribbon to divide it into thirds. What fraction of the blue ribbon is each piece? _____

d. How many pieces of blue ribbon does Dee need to use in order to use the same amount as the green ribbon? What fraction of the blue ribbon is this? _____

_____

e. Explain how you know that $\frac{2}{6}$ of the green ribbon is equivalent to $\frac{1}{3}$ of the blue ribbon. _____

_____

In the ribbon problem you found equivalent fractions for part of a length. You can also use fractions to name whole amounts, or whole numbers.

1 length of green ribbon is $\frac{6}{6}$.

1 length of blue ribbon is $\frac{3}{3}$.

$$1 = \frac{6}{6}$$

$$1 = \frac{3}{3}$$

A number line can help you find fractions that name whole numbers, such as $\frac{6}{3}$.

Notice that the number line shows fractions greater than 1 that are not whole numbers, such as $\frac{4}{3}$, $\frac{5}{3}$, $\frac{7}{3}$ and $\frac{8}{3}$. The numerators of these fractions are greater than or equal to their denominators. They are **improper fractions**.

An improper fraction such as $\frac{4}{3}$ can be written as a **mixed number**, a number that has a whole number part and a fraction part. As a mixed number, $\frac{4}{3}$ is written $1\frac{1}{3}$.

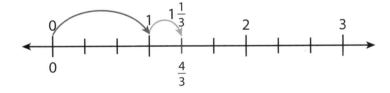

▶ Reflect

1 Suppose that the number line above was extended to show the whole number 4. What fraction would be shown below the number 4? Explain how you know.

_____

_____

Learn About ▸ Writing a Whole Number as a Fraction

Read the problem below. Then explore different ways to write a whole number as a fraction.

> Tucker visited a shop on the Hoosier Pie Trail and bought 2 pies. He cut each pie into eighths. How can you write the number 2 as a fraction to find the number of eighths Tucker has?

▶ **Picture It** **You can use models to help you write a whole number as a fraction.**

The fraction circles below show 2 wholes, each cut into eighths.

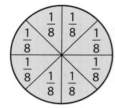 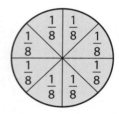

Each part is $\frac{1}{8}$ of the whole. There are 16 eighths in all.

▶ **Model It** **You can use a number line to help you write a whole number as a fraction.**

The number line below shows whole numbers on the top and eighths on the bottom.

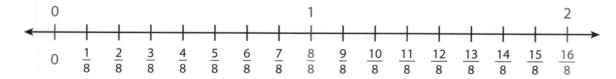

Notice that each whole number has an equivalent fraction with a denominator of 8.

Connect It   Now you will solve the problem on the previous page using number sentences.

2 Look at the fraction circles in *Picture It*. How many equal parts are shown in 1 whole?

_____

3 How many equal parts are shown in 2 wholes? Explain how you know.

_____

_____

4 Complete the sentences to show the fraction that is equivalent to 2.

Use words: Two wholes equal _____.

Use a fraction: 2 = _____

How many eighths did Tucker cut the pies into? _____

5 Explain how to find a fraction equivalent of a whole number.

_____

_____

_____

Try It   Use what you just learned about writing a whole number as a fraction to solve these problems.

6 Use the model below. Write a fraction equivalent to 4.

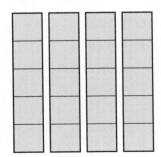

4 = _____

7 Draw a model to show $4 = \frac{16}{4}$.

Lesson 13B Whole Numbers, Mixed Numbers, and Improper Fractions

Learn About ▶ **Writing a Whole Number as a Fraction**

Read the problem below. Then explore different ways to write whole numbers as fractions with denominators of 1.

> Damari had 5 sticker sheets showing race cars. He did not cut or divide the sheets into separate stickers. How can you write the number of sticker sheets as a fraction?

▶ **Picture It** **You can use a model to help you write a whole number as a fraction with a denominator of 1.**

Each rectangle stands for 1 sticker sheet.

The sheets are not cut or divided into separate stickers, so each whole has one part.

▶ **Model It** **You can use a number line to help you write a whole number as a fraction with a denominator of 1.**

This number line shows whole numbers on the top and fractions on the bottom.

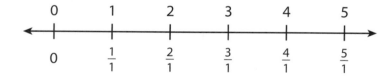

Notice that the spaces between whole numbers are not divided into parts. Each whole number has one part, so the denominator of each equivalent fraction is 1.

Connect It Now you will solve the problem from the previous page.

8 Look at the rectangles in *Picture It*. Explain how you know each whole has only 1 part.

_____

_____

9 How many parts do the 5 sticker sheets make altogether? _____

10 What does the numerator of a fraction show? _____

_____

11 What does the denominator of a fraction show? _____

_____

12 Write the number of sticker sheets as a fraction. Use the fraction below as a guide.

$$\frac{\text{Number of equal parts you have}}{\text{Number of equal parts in one whole}} = \underline{\quad}$$

13 Explain how to write a whole number as a fraction with a denominator of 1.

_____

_____

Try It Use what you just learned writing a whole number as a fraction with a denominator of 1 to solve these problems.

14 Use the number line below. Write a fraction that is equivalent to 7.

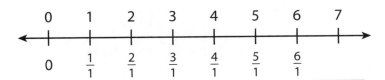

15 Draw a model to show that $10 = \frac{10}{1}$.

Learn About ▶ **Writing a Mixed Number as an Improper Fraction**

Read the problem below. Then explore different ways to write a mixed number as an improper fraction.

> Ms. Razdan is cutting boards to make bases for sculptures. Each base is one-fourth of a board. She has $2\frac{3}{4}$ boards. How can you write $2\frac{3}{4}$ as an improper fraction to find how many fourths she can cut the boards into?

▶ **Picture It** **You can use models to help you write a mixed number as an improper fraction.**

The fraction strips below show 2 wholes and $\frac{3}{4}$ of another whole.

$\frac{1}{4}$	$\frac{1}{4}$	$\frac{1}{4}$	$\frac{1}{4}$

$\frac{1}{4}$	$\frac{1}{4}$	$\frac{1}{4}$	$\frac{1}{4}$

$\frac{1}{4}$	$\frac{1}{4}$	$\frac{1}{4}$	$\frac{1}{4}$

Each part is $\frac{1}{4}$ of a whole.

▶ **Model It** **You can use a number line to help you write a mixed number as an improper fraction.**

This number line shows whole numbers on the top and fourths on the bottom.

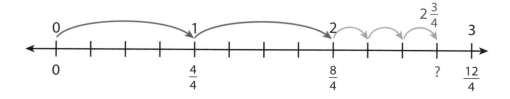

The long jumps show the wholes. The short jumps show the fractions of a whole.

Connect It Now you will solve the problem from the previous page.

16 Look at the model in *Picture It*. Explain how it shows the mixed number $2\frac{3}{4}$.

_____

_____

17 How many fourths are in 1 whole? 2 wholes? _____

18 How many fourths are shaded in the fraction strip that is not completely shaded?

_____

19 What is the total number of fourths that Ms. Razdan can cut from $2\frac{3}{4}$ boards?

_____ fourths

20 Complete the sentences to show the improper fraction that is equivalent to $2\frac{3}{4}$.

Use words: Two and three fourths equal _____ .

Use a fraction: $2\frac{3}{4} = $ _____

21 Explain how to write a mixed number as an improper fraction.

_____

_____

_____

_____

_____

Try It Use what you just learned about writing mixed numbers as improper fractions to solve these problems.

22 Use the model. Write the mixed number it shows.

_____

 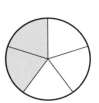

23 Use the model. Write the improper fraction it shows.

_____

Practice **Writing Mixed Numbers and Improper Fractions**

Study the example below. Then solve Problems 24–26.

Example

Jan is cutting construction paper into equal-sized parts to make name tags. Each name tag is $\frac{1}{6}$ of a sheet of paper. What fraction can Jan write to show the number of sixths he can cut from 3 pieces of paper?

Look at how you could show your work using a model.

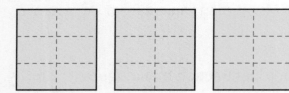

Solution: $\frac{18}{6}$

The student showed each of the 3 wholes divided into sixths.

Pair/Share
How could you solve this problem using a number line?

---

24 Blair says $\frac{6}{2}$ is equivalent to 3. Lex says $\frac{12}{4}$ is equivalent to 3.

Who is correct?

Show your work.

How many wholes can you make from 6 halves? How many wholes can you make from 12 fourths?

Pair/Share
What is another fraction equivalent to 3?

Solution: _____

25 The picture at the right shows the amount of pizza the Kang family had left over from a family celebration. Write the leftover amount of pizza as a mixed number.

Show your work.

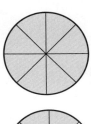

A mixed number has a whole-number part and a fraction part.

Pair/Share
Explain how the mixed number would change if 1 more slice of pizza was eaten.

Solution: _____

---

26 Each carton holds 4 cups of fruit juice. There are $5\frac{1}{4}$ cartons. Which improper fraction shows the same amount as $5\frac{1}{4}$? Circle the letter of the correct answer.

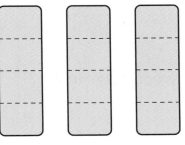
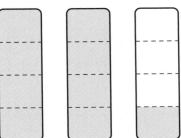

Do you count the amount of fruit juice by fourths or by fifths?

A $\frac{21}{5}$

B $\frac{21}{4}$

C $\frac{10}{4}$

D $\frac{4}{21}$

Evan chose **A** as the correct answer. How did he get that answer?

_____

_____

_____

_____

Pair/Share
Did you and your partner use the same strategy to find the answer?

Practice ▶ **Writing Mixed Numbers and Improper Fractions**

Solve the problems.

1 Which model below shows the mixed number $2\frac{5}{10}$?

A

C

B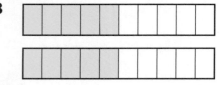

D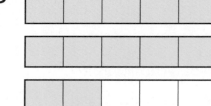

2 Which improper fraction is equivalent to $2\frac{5}{10}$?

A $\frac{10}{5}$ **C** $\frac{15}{10}$

B $\frac{12}{5}$ **D** $\frac{25}{10}$

3 Does the fraction that labels the point on the number line represent 4? Choose *Yes* or *No* for each number line.

a.

0    $\frac{3}{3}$ $\frac{6}{3}$ $\frac{9}{3}$ $\frac{12}{3}$ $\frac{15}{3}$ ☐ Yes   ☐ No

b.

0    $\frac{3}{3}$ $\frac{6}{3}$ $\frac{9}{3}$ $\frac{12}{3}$ $\frac{15}{3}$ ☐ Yes   ☐ No

c.

0    $\frac{2}{2}$ $\frac{4}{2}$ $\frac{6}{2}$ $\frac{8}{2}$ $\frac{10}{2}$ ☐ Yes   ☐ No

d.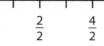

0    $\frac{2}{2}$ $\frac{4}{2}$ $\frac{6}{2}$ $\frac{8}{2}$ $\frac{10}{2}$ ☐ Yes   ☐ No

4 Is the fraction equivalent to 4? Choose *True* or *False* for each equation.

a. $4 = \frac{16}{4}$ ☐ True ☐ False

b. $4 = \frac{20}{5}$ ☐ True ☐ False

c. $4 = \frac{30}{6}$ ☐ True ☐ False

d. $4 = \frac{28}{7}$ ☐ True ☐ False

5 Write a fraction equivalent to 3 with a numerator of 3. Draw a diagram to show why your fraction is correct.

Show your work.

Answer _____

6 Polina is unpacking boxes of paint tubes. Paint tubes come in boxes of 6. Polina has unpacked $3\frac{5}{6}$ boxes.

Draw a picture to represent $3\frac{5}{6}$. Use your picture to write $3\frac{5}{6}$ as an improper fraction and explain how you used the picture.

Show your work.

Answer _____

_____

✓ Self Check Go back and see what you can check off on the Self Check on page 157.

Compare Fractions

⟳ Use What You Know

In the past, you learned to compare fractions using models. Take a look at this problem.

Adriana and June have granola bars that are the same size. Adriana ate $\frac{2}{4}$ of her granola bar. June ate $\frac{2}{5}$ of her granola bar. Which girl ate more of her granola bar?

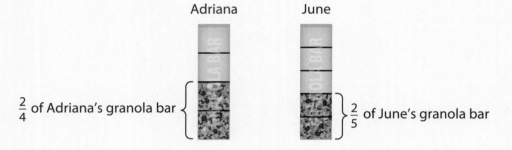

$\frac{2}{4}$ of Adriana's granola bar $\frac{2}{5}$ of June's granola bar

a. How many equal pieces of granola bar did Adriana eat? _____

b. How many equal pieces of granola bar did June eat? _____

c. Since both girls ate the same number of pieces, what can you look at to find out who ate more granola bar? _____

d. What does the size of the denominator tell you about the size of the pieces of granola bar? _____

_____

_____

e. Who ate more? Explain why. _____

_____

_____

▷▷ Find Out More

Deciding who ate more of her granola bar means comparing the fractions $\frac{2}{4}$ and $\frac{2}{5}$. To compare fractions, you must use the same-size whole.

- The granola bars were the same size, so you can compare the fractions to know who ate more. These area models compare $\frac{2}{4}$ and $\frac{2}{5}$.

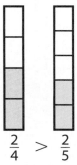
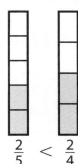

$$\frac{2}{4} > \frac{2}{5}$$

$\frac{2}{4}$ is greater than $\frac{2}{5}$.

$$\frac{2}{5} < \frac{2}{4}$$

$\frac{2}{5}$ is less than $\frac{2}{4}$.

- If the granola bars were not the same size, you could not compare the fractions to know who ate more.

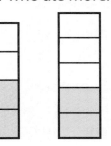 ← $\frac{1}{5}$ of the larger granola bar looks to be larger than $\frac{1}{4}$ of the smaller granola bar.

- You can use equivalent fractions to compare fractions. Rewrite one, or both, of the fractions so they have the same denominator, or a **common denominator**.

$$\frac{2 \times 4}{5 \times 4} = \frac{8}{20} \text{ and } \frac{2 \times 5}{4 \times 5} = \frac{10}{20}$$

$$\frac{8}{20} < \frac{10}{20}, \text{ so } \frac{2}{5} < \frac{2}{4}.$$

▶ Reflect

1 Explain how you can tell which fraction is greater, $\frac{2}{5}$ or $\frac{3}{10}$.

_____

_____

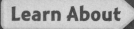

Learn About ▸ Common Numerators and Denominators

Read the problem below. Then explore different ways to understand it.

> A grasshopper weighs about $\frac{2}{100}$ of an ounce. A beetle weighs $\frac{8}{10}$ of an ounce. Which weighs more?

▶ **Picture It** **You can use models to help compare fractions.**

The model shows the fractions of an ounce that the grasshopper and beetle weigh.

Grasshopper   Beetle

    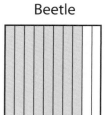

▶ **Model It** **You can use a common denominator to help you solve the problem.**

When you compare two fractions, it helps if they have a common denominator. Fractions with the same denominator are divided into the same number of equal parts. When two fractions have the same denominator, you can compare the numerators.

Compare $\frac{2}{100}$ and $\frac{8}{10}$.

The fractions do not have a common denominator. Find a fraction equivalent to $\frac{8}{10}$ that has a denominator of 100.

$$\frac{8}{10} \times \frac{10}{10} = \frac{80}{100}$$

Now, compare the numerators of $\frac{2}{100}$ and $\frac{80}{100}$.

   $80 > 2$

So, $\frac{80}{100} > \frac{2}{100}$ and $\frac{8}{10} > \frac{2}{100}$.

The beetle weighs more than the grasshopper.

Connect It Now you will solve the problem from the previous page by finding a common numerator.

2 What is an equivalent fraction for $\frac{2}{100}$ that has a numerator of 8? _____

3 One model is divided into 400 equal parts and the other is divided into 10 equal parts. Which has smaller parts?

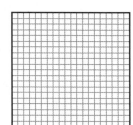 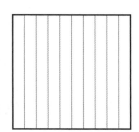

_____

_____

4 Shade 8 parts of each model.

5 Which model has a greater area shaded? _____

6 Which fraction is greater, $\frac{8}{400}$ or $\frac{8}{10}$? _____

7 Look at the denominators of $\frac{8}{400}$ and $\frac{8}{10}$. When two fractions have the same numerator and different denominators, how do you know which one is greater? Explain. _____

_____

_____

Try It Use what you just learned to solve these problems. Show your work on a separate sheet of paper.

8 Mel's tomato plant is $\frac{8}{12}$ of a foot tall. Her pepper plant is $\frac{3}{4}$ of a foot tall. Compare the heights of the plants using $<$, $>$, or $=$.

_____

9 Compare the fractions $\frac{4}{6}$ and $\frac{2}{5}$ using $<$, $>$, or $=$.

_____

Learn About ▶ Using a Benchmark to Compare Fractions

Read the problem below. Then explore different ways to use benchmarks to compare fractions.

> Jasmine's swimming lesson lasts for $\frac{2}{3}$ of an hour. It takes her $\frac{1}{6}$ of an hour to do her homework. Will Jasmine spend more time on her homework or at her swimming lesson?

▶ **Model It** **You can use a number line to help you compare fractions.**

The number line shows where the fractions $\frac{2}{3}$ and $\frac{1}{6}$ are compared to 0 and 1.

The number line shows that $\frac{1}{6}$ is closer to 0 than $\frac{2}{3}$ is, and that $\frac{2}{3}$ is closer to 1 than $\frac{1}{6}$ is. This means that $\frac{1}{6} < \frac{2}{3}$ and $\frac{2}{3} > \frac{1}{6}$.

▶ **Solve It** **You can use a benchmark fraction to solve the problem.**

Another way to compare fractions is by using a **benchmark fraction**.

Use $\frac{1}{2}$ as a benchmark to compare $\frac{1}{6}$ and $\frac{2}{3}$.

The number line shows that $\frac{1}{6}$ is less than $\frac{1}{2}$ and $\frac{2}{3}$ is greater than $\frac{1}{2}$.
So, $\frac{1}{6} < \frac{2}{3}$ and $\frac{2}{3} > \frac{1}{6}$.

Jasmine will spend more time at her swimming lesson than on homework.

Connect It Now you will solve a similar problem using 1 as a benchmark.
Think about the two fractions $\frac{11}{10}$ and $\frac{7}{8}$.

10 Which fraction, $\frac{11}{10}$ or $\frac{7}{8}$, is greater than 1? _____

11 Which fraction, $\frac{11}{10}$ or $\frac{7}{8}$, is less than 1? _____

12 Which fraction, $\frac{11}{10}$ or $\frac{7}{8}$, is greater? Explain why.

_____

_____

13 Write $<$, $>$, or $=$ to show the comparison. $\frac{11}{10}$ ◯ $\frac{7}{8}$

14 Explain how you can use benchmarks to compare fractions.

_____

_____

_____

_____

_____

Try It Use what you just learned to solve these problems. Show your work on a separate sheet of paper.

15 Use $<$, $>$, or $=$ to complete the comparison. Explain how you found your answer. $\frac{5}{10}$ ◯ $\frac{3}{4}$

_____

_____

16 Nathan walked $\frac{10}{10}$ of a mile. Sarah walked $\frac{19}{20}$ of a mile. Who walked a greater distance? Explain.

_____

Practice ▶ **Comparing Fractions**

Study the example below. Then solve problems 17–19.

Example

Becker catches a fish that is $\frac{3}{12}$ of a yard long. To keep the fish, it has to be longer than $\frac{1}{3}$ of a yard. Can Becker keep his fish?

Look at how you could show your work using a number line.

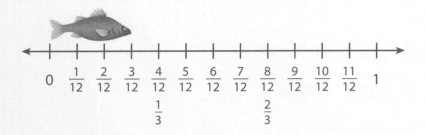

Solution ___Since $\frac{3}{12}$ is less than $\frac{1}{3}$, Becker can't keep his fish.___

It is important that both measurements use the same unit!

Pair/Share
How else could you solve this problem?

---

17 Myron and Jane are working on the same set of homework problems. Myron has finished $\frac{7}{9}$ of the problems and Jane has finished $\frac{2}{3}$ of the problems. Who has finished more of their homework problems?

Show your work.

Which strategy for comparing do you think works best with these fractions?

Pair/Share
How did you and your partner choose what strategy to use to solve the problem?

Solution _____

18 Compare the fractions $\frac{3}{10}$ and $\frac{7}{12}$ using the benchmark fraction $\frac{1}{2}$.
Show your work.

You already know about how big $\frac{1}{2}$ is!

Solution _____

 Pair/Share
Draw a model to check your answer.

---

19 Janelle walked $\frac{3}{6}$ of a mile. Pedro walked $\frac{6}{10}$ of a mile. Which statement shows how to find the greater fraction? Circle the letter of the correct answer.

There are several ways to compare fractions!

A $\frac{3}{6} = \frac{6}{12}$ and $\frac{6}{12} < \frac{6}{10}$

B $\frac{3}{6} = \frac{6}{12}$ and $\frac{6}{12} > \frac{6}{10}$

C $\frac{6}{10} = \frac{3}{5}$ and $\frac{3}{5} < \frac{3}{6}$

D $\frac{3}{6} < \frac{1}{2}$ and $\frac{6}{10} > \frac{1}{2}$

Tina chose **B** as the correct answer. How did she get that answer?

_____

_____

_____

_____

 Pair/Share
How can you find the answer using a benchmark fraction?

Practice Comparing Fractions

Solve the problems.

1 Grant needs $\frac{2}{3}$ cup of raisins and $\frac{3}{4}$ cup of almonds to make trail mix. Which statement can be used to find out if there are more raisins or almonds in the mix?

A $\frac{2}{3} = \frac{8}{12}$ and $\frac{3}{4} = \frac{9}{12}$

B $\frac{2}{3} = \frac{4}{6}$ and $\frac{3}{4} = \frac{4}{5}$

C $\frac{2}{3} = \frac{6}{9}$ and $\frac{3}{4} = \frac{6}{12}$

D $\frac{2}{3} = \frac{6}{9}$ and $\frac{3}{4} = \frac{6}{7}$

2 Tell whether each comparison is *True* or *False*.

a. $\frac{2}{5} < \frac{6}{15}$ ☐ True ☐ False

b. $\frac{7}{10} > \frac{7}{8}$ ☐ True ☐ False

c. $\frac{1}{2} > \frac{3}{8}$ ☐ True ☐ False

d. $\frac{2}{4} = \frac{4}{6}$ ☐ True ☐ False

e. $\frac{30}{500} = \frac{3}{50}$ ☐ True ☐ False

3 Fill in the circle with one of the symbols below to correctly compare $\frac{5}{10}$ and $\frac{5}{8}$.

$<$ $=$ $>$

$\frac{5}{10}$ ◯ $\frac{5}{8}$

4 Sam's music teacher told him to practice his trombone for $\frac{5}{10}$ of an hour. He spent $\frac{2}{6}$ of an hour practicing. Did he practice long enough?

Show your work.

Answer Sam _____ practice long enough.

5 Olivia and Eleanor each made the same amount of lemonade to sell at a lemonade stand. Olivia poured all of her lemonade into 10 equal-size glasses. Eleanor poured all of her lemonade into 5 equal-size glasses. Olivia sold 7 glasses of lemonade and Eleanor sold 2 glasses. Which girl sold a greater fraction of her lemonade? Compare the fractions using a symbol.

Show your work.

Answer _____ sold a greater fraction of her lemonade.

6 Rachel and Sierra are selling boxes of fruit as a fundraiser. Rachel has sold $\frac{9}{10}$ of her boxes of fruit and Sierra has sold $\frac{5}{8}$ of her boxes. Which girl has sold a greater fraction of her boxes of fruit? Draw a model to show your answer.

Show your work.

Answer _____ has sold a greater fraction of her boxes of fruit.

✓ **Self Check** **Go back and see what you can check off on the Self Check on page 157.**

💭 Think It Through

What's really going on when we add numbers?

Adding means joining or putting things together.

Think about how you could explain adding 2 + 3 to a first grader. You could start at 2, count on 3 more, and see where you end up: 2 . . . 3 . . . 4 . . . 5.

Or, you could put a segment with a length of 2 and a segment with a length of 3 next to each other on a number line to show **2 + 3**.

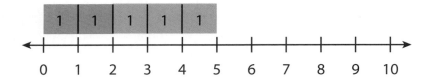

When you add 2 + 3, you are putting ones together.

Think Adding fractions means putting together parts of the same whole.

You can put a segment with a length of $\frac{2}{4}$ and a segment with a length of $\frac{3}{4}$ next to each other to show $\frac{2}{4} + \frac{3}{4}$.

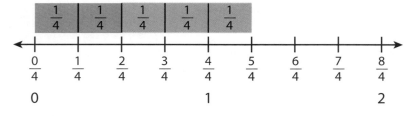

When you add $\frac{2}{4} + \frac{3}{4}$, you are putting one-fourths together.

> ✏️ **Underline** the sentence that explains what adding fractions means.

Think Subtracting means separating or taking away.

On a number line, you can start with a segment of length 5 and take away a segment of length 2 to show **5 − 2.**

Look at the whole numbers. Now look at the numerators of the fractions. I think I see a connection.

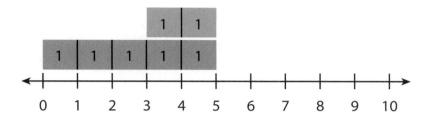

When you subtract 5 − 2, you are taking away ones.

You can show subtracting fractions on a number line. Start with a segment of length $\frac{5}{4}$ and take away a segment of length $\frac{2}{4}$ to show $\frac{5}{4} - \frac{2}{4}$.

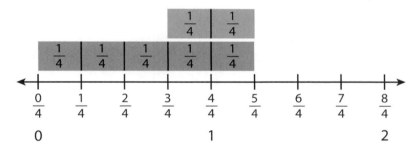

When you subtract $\frac{5}{4} - \frac{2}{4}$, you are taking away one-fourths.

Now you'll have a chance to think more about how adding or subtracting fractions is like adding or subtracting whole numbers. You may find that using number lines or area models can help you explain your thinking.

▶ Reflect

1 Use your own words to describe what you just learned about adding and subtracting fractions.

_____

_____

_____

Think About ▶ **Adding and Subtracting Fractions**

Let's Explore the Idea Counting on and using a number line are two ways to think about adding fractions.

2 Count by fourths to fill in the blanks: $\frac{1}{4}$, $\frac{2}{4}$, _____, $\frac{4}{4}$, $\frac{5}{4}$, _____, _____, _____, _____

Now label the number line.

0    $\frac{1}{4}$ $\frac{2}{4}$ _____ $\frac{4}{4}$ $\frac{5}{4}$ _____ _____ _____ _____ $\frac{10}{4}$

3 Count by fifths to fill in the blanks: $\frac{1}{5}$, $\frac{2}{5}$, _____, _____, _____

Now label the number line.

0    $\frac{1}{5}$ $\frac{2}{5}$ _____ _____ _____ $\frac{6}{5}$

Use the number lines above to answer problems 4 and 5.

4 What is $\frac{1}{4}$ more than $\frac{6}{4}$? _____

5 What is $\frac{1}{5}$ more than $\frac{3}{5}$? _____

Now try these two problems.

6 Label the number line below and use it to show $\frac{2}{4} + \frac{1}{4}$.

7 Label the number line below and use it to show $\frac{3}{4} + \frac{1}{4}$.

Let's Talk About It

Solve the problems below as a group.

8 Look at your answers to problems 2 and 3. How is counting with fractions the same as counting with whole numbers?

_____

_____

_____

How is it different?

_____

_____

9 Label the number line below and use it to show $\frac{7}{8} - \frac{2}{8}$.

10 Label the number line below and use it to show $\frac{5}{6} - \frac{1}{6}$.

▶ Try It Another Way Work with your group to use the area models to show adding or subtracting fractions.

11 Show $\frac{1}{8} + \frac{2}{8}$.

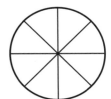

12 Show $\frac{6}{10} - \frac{2}{10}$.

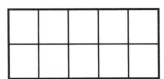

Connect ▶ **Ideas about Adding and Subtracting Fractions**

Talk through these problems as a class, then write your answers below.

13 Compare Draw two different models to show $\frac{2}{3} - \frac{1}{3}$.

14 Explain Rob had a large pizza and a small pizza. He cut each pizza into fourths. He took one fourth from each pizza and used the following problem to show their sum: $\frac{1}{4} + \frac{1}{4} = \frac{2}{4}$. What did Rob do wrong?

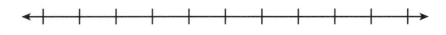

15 Demonstrate Think about how you would add three whole numbers. You start by adding two of the numbers. Then you add the third number to that sum. You add three fractions the same way.

Use the number line and area model below to show $\frac{1}{10} + \frac{3}{10} + \frac{4}{10}$.

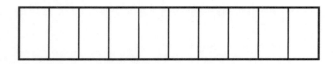

Apply ▶ **Ideas about Adding and Subtracting Fractions**

16 Put It Together Use what you have learned to complete this task.

> Jen has $\frac{4}{10}$ of a kilogram of dog food. Luis has $\frac{3}{10}$ of a kilogram of dog food. A large dog eats $\frac{2}{10}$ of a kilogram in one meal.

Part A Write two different questions about this problem that involve adding or subtracting fractions.

Question 1: _____

_____

Question 2: _____

_____

Part B Choose one of your questions to model. Circle the question you chose. Show the addition or subtraction using a number line and an area model.

Lesson 16 👥 Introduction
Add and Subtract Fractions

🔄 Use What You Know

In Lesson 15, you learned that adding fractions is a lot like adding whole numbers. Take a look at this problem.

> Lynn, Paco, and Todd split a pack of 12 baseball cards. Lynn gets 4 cards, Paco gets 3 cards, and Todd gets the rest of the cards. What fraction of the pack does Todd get?

a. How many cards do Lynn and Paco get altogether? _____

b. How many cards does Todd get? _____

c. There are 12 cards in the pack. What fraction represents the

whole pack of cards? _____

d. If Lynn gets 4 cards out of 12, that means she gets $\frac{4}{12}$ of the pack. If Paco gets

3 cards out of 12, what fraction of the pack does he get? _____

e. What fraction of the pack do Lynn and Paco get altogether? _____

f. Explain how you could find the fraction of the pack that Todd gets.

_____

_____

_____

We often use **fractions** in real life. Fractions can describe something that has several equal parts, as in the baseball card problem. In that problem the "whole" is the pack of cards. Since there are 12 cards in the pack, each card represents $\frac{1}{12}$ of the whole.

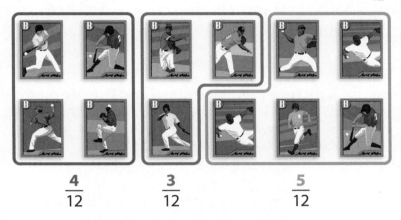

$$\frac{4}{12} \qquad \frac{3}{12} \qquad \frac{5}{12}$$

Fractions in real life can also describe the equal parts of a single object, such as a pizza cut into 8 equal slices. The pizza is the "whole," and all the slices of pizza are equal parts of the same whole. Since there are 8 equal-sized slices, each slice is $\frac{1}{8}$ of the pizza. Even if a person takes away one or more slices, the "whole" is still the same 8 slices.

Reflect

1 Give another example of a "whole" object with equal parts that can be described by fractions.

_____

_____

_____

_____

Lesson 16 Add and Subtract Fractions

Learn About ▶ **Adding Fractions**

Read the problem. Then explore different ways to understand adding fractions.

> Josie and Margo are painting a fence green. Josie starts at one end and paints $\frac{3}{10}$ of the fence. Margo starts at the other end and paints $\frac{4}{10}$ of it. What fraction of the fence do they paint?

▶ **Picture It** **You can use a picture to help understand the problem.**

Think what the fence might look like. It has 10 equal-sized parts.

Each part is $\frac{1}{10}$ of the whole. ⌐

The girls paint 3 tenths and 4 tenths of the fence.

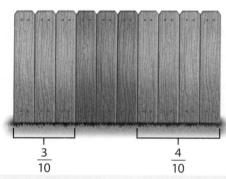

$\frac{3}{10}$ $\frac{4}{10}$

▶ **Model It** **You can also use a number line to help understand the problem.**

The number line below is divided into tenths, with a point at $\frac{3}{10}$.

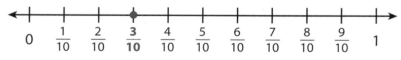

Start at $\frac{3}{10}$ and count 4 tenths to the right to **add** $\frac{4}{10}$.

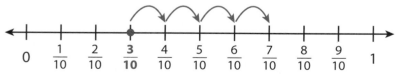

Connect It Now you will solve the problem from the previous page using equations.

2 How do you know that each section of fence is $\frac{1}{10}$ of the total fence?

_____

_____

_____

3 What do the numerators, 3 and 4, tell you? _____

_____

_____

4 How many sections of the fence did Josie and Margo paint altogether? _____

5 Complete the equations to show what fraction of the fence Josie and Margo painted altogether.

Use words: **3 tenths**   +   **4 tenths**   =   ⬚ tenths

Use fractions: $\frac{3}{10}$ + $\frac{4}{10}$ = $\frac{\boxed{}}{10}$

6 Explain how you add fractions that have the same denominator.

_____

_____

Try It Use what you just learned to solve these problems. Show your work on a separate sheet of paper.

7 Lita and Otis are helping their mom clean the house. Lita cleaned $\frac{1}{3}$ of the rooms. Otis cleaned $\frac{1}{3}$ of the rooms. What fraction of the rooms did Lita and Otis clean altogether? _____

8 Mark's string is $\frac{1}{5}$ of a meter long. Bob's string is $\frac{3}{5}$ of a meter long. How long are the two strings combined? _____ of a meter

Learn About ▸ **Subtracting Fractions**

Read the problem. Then explore different ways to understand subtracting fractions.

> Alberto's 1-liter water bottle had $\frac{5}{6}$ of a liter of water in it. He drank $\frac{4}{6}$ of a liter.
> What fraction of a liter of water is left in the bottle?

▶ **Picture It** **You can use a picture to help understand the problem.**

The following model shows the water bottle divided into 6 equal parts. Five shaded parts show how much water was in the bottle.

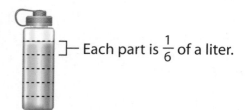

Each part is $\frac{1}{6}$ of a liter.

Alberto drank 4 sixths of a liter, so take away 4 shaded parts. The 1 shaded part that is left shows the fraction of a liter that is left.

5 sixths − 4 sixths = 1 sixth

▶ **Model It** **You can also use a number line to help understand the problem.**

The number line below is divided into sixths, with a point at $\frac{5}{6}$.

Start at $\frac{5}{6}$ and count back 4 sixths to **subtract** $\frac{4}{6}$.

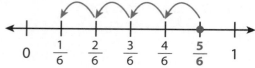

Connect It Now you will solve the problem from the previous page using equations.

9 In *Picture It*, why does $\frac{1}{6}$ represent 1 of the equal parts of the bottle?

_____

_____

_____

10 What do the numerators, 5 and 4, tell you? _____

_____

_____

11 How many sixths of a liter are left in the bottle after Alberto drank 4 sixths? _____

12 Complete the equations to show what fraction of a liter is left in the bottle.

Use words: **5 sixths** $-$ **4 sixths** $=$ $\boxed{}$ sixth

Use fractions: $\dfrac{5}{6}$ $-$ $\dfrac{4}{6}$ $=$ $\dfrac{\boxed{}}{6}$

13 Explain how you subtract fractions with the same denominator.

_____

_____

_____

Try It Use what you just learned to solve these problems. Show your work on a separate sheet of paper.

14 Mrs. Kirk had $\frac{3}{4}$ of a carton of eggs. She used $\frac{2}{4}$ of the carton to make breakfast. What fraction of the carton of eggs does Mrs. Kirk have left? _____

15 Carmen had $\frac{8}{10}$ of the lawn left to mow. She mowed $\frac{5}{10}$ of the lawn. Now what fraction of the lawn is left to mow? _____

Practice > **Adding and Subtracting Fractions**

Study the example below. Then solve problems 16–18.

Example

Jessica hiked $\frac{2}{5}$ of a mile on a trail before she stopped to get a drink of water. After her drink, Jessica hiked another $\frac{2}{5}$ of a mile. How far did Jessica hike in all?

Look at how you could show your work using a number line.

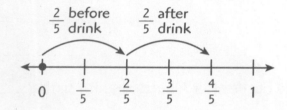

Solution _Jessica hiked $\frac{4}{5}$ of a mile._

> The student used labels and "jump" arrows to show each part of the hike on a number line. It is just like adding whole numbers!

> **Pair/Share**
> How else could you solve this problem?

---

16 Ruth made 1 fruit smoothie. She drank $\frac{1}{3}$ of it. What fraction of the fruit smoothie is left?

Show your work.

> What fraction represents the whole fruit smoothie?

> **Pair/Share**
> How did you and your partner decide what fraction to start with?

Solution _____

17 Mr. Chang has a bunch of balloons. $\frac{3}{10}$ of the balloons are red. $\frac{2}{10}$ of the balloons are blue. What fraction of the balloons are neither red nor blue?

Show your work.

I think that there are at least two different steps to solve this problem.

Pair/Share
How is this problem different from the others you've seen in this lesson?

Solution _____

---

18 Emily ate $\frac{1}{6}$ of a bag of carrots. Nick ate $\frac{2}{6}$ of the bag of carrots. What fraction of the bag of carrots did Emily and Nick eat altogether? Circle the letter of the correct answer.

A $\frac{1}{6}$

B $\frac{1}{3}$

C $\frac{3}{6}$

D $\frac{3}{12}$

To find the fraction of the bag Emily and Nick ate altogether, should you add or subtract?

Rob chose **D** as the correct answer. How did he get that answer?

_____

_____

_____

Pair/Share
Does Rob's answer make sense?

Lesson 16 Add and Subtract Fractions   **199**

Practice ▶ **Adding and Subtracting Fractions**

Solve the problems.

1 Liang bought some cloth. He used $\frac{5}{8}$ of a yard for a school project. He has $\frac{2}{8}$ of a yard left. How much cloth did Liang buy?

A $\frac{3}{8}$ of a yard

B $\frac{7}{16}$ of a yard

C $\frac{7}{8}$ of a yard

D $\frac{8}{8}$ of a yard

2 Carmela cut a cake into 12 equal-sized pieces. She ate $\frac{2}{12}$ of the cake, and her brother ate $\frac{3}{12}$ of the cake. What fraction of the cake is left?

A $\frac{1}{12}$

B $\frac{5}{12}$

C $\frac{7}{12}$

D $\frac{12}{12}$

3 Lee's muffin mix calls for $\frac{2}{3}$ cup of milk and $\frac{1}{3}$ cup of oil. How much more milk than oil does she need for the muffin mix?

_____

4 Lucy and Melody are painting a room. They divided the room into 8 equal sections. Lucy painted 2 sections and Melody painted 4 sections. Which model can be used to find the total fraction of the room they painted? Circle the letters of all that apply.

A

B

C

D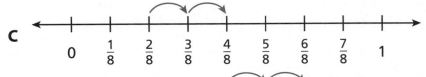

5 In all, Cole and Max picked $\frac{9}{10}$ of a bucket of blueberries. Cole picked $\frac{3}{10}$ of a bucket of blueberries. What fraction of a bucket of blueberries did Max pick?

Show your work.

Answer Max picked _____ of a bucket of blueberries.

6 A melon is cut into 8 equal slices. Together, Regan and Juanita will eat $\frac{5}{8}$ of the melon. What is one way the girls could eat that fraction of the melon?

Show your work. Write an equation to represent your answer.

Answer Regan could eat _____ of the melon, and

Juanita could eat _____ of the melon.

Equation _____

✓ **Self Check** Go back and see what you can check off on the Self Check on page 157.

Add and Subtract Mixed Numbers

🔄 Use What You Know

In Lesson 16, you learned about adding and subtracting fractions. In this lesson, you will learn about adding and subtracting whole numbers and fractions.

Raquel measured milk with a $\frac{1}{2}$-cup measuring cup. She filled the cup 5 times and poured each $\frac{1}{2}$-cup of milk in a bowl. How much milk did Raquel pour into the bowl?

| $\frac{1}{2}$ cup | $\frac{1}{2}$ cup | $\frac{1}{2}$ cup | $\frac{1}{2}$ cup | $\frac{1}{2}$ cup |

a. What fraction do you need to add? _____

b. How many times will you add the fraction? _____

c. Write an equation to represent this problem.

_____

d. What is the total amount of milk in the bowl? _____

▷▷ Find Out More

Suppose Raquel adds another 2 cups of milk to the bowl. How much milk is there now?

These cups show the $\frac{5}{2}$ cups already in the bowl. There are 2 half-cups in each whole cup.

These cups show the amount Raquel adds. There are 4 halves in 2, so 2 is equal to $\frac{4}{2}$.

There are 9 half-cups of milk.

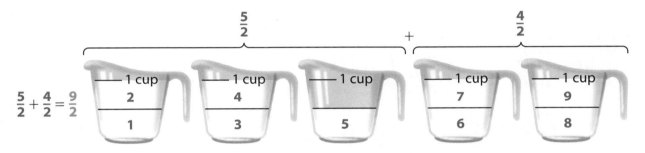

$\frac{5}{2} + \frac{4}{2} = \frac{9}{2}$

Altogether, 4 whole cups and $\frac{1}{2}$ of another cup are filled: $\frac{9}{2} = 4 + \frac{1}{2}$. You can write $\frac{9}{2}$ as a mixed number. **Mixed numbers** have a whole number part and a fraction part. Just write $4 + \frac{1}{2}$ without the +. $\frac{9}{2} = 4\frac{1}{2}$

Here is another way to add $\frac{5}{2} + 2$. You can see from the model above that $\frac{5}{2} = 2 + \frac{1}{2}$.

So, $\frac{5}{2} + 2 = 2 + \frac{1}{2} + 2$, or $2 + 2 + \frac{1}{2}$.

$2 + 2 + \frac{1}{2} = 4 + \frac{1}{2}$ or $4\frac{1}{2}$

▶ Reflect

1 Explain how you could figure out how many halves are in $3\frac{1}{2}$.

_____

_____

Learn About ▷ **Adding Mixed Numbers**

Read the problem below. Then explore different ways to add mixed numbers.

> Markers come in boxes of 8. For an art project, one group of students used $1\frac{5}{8}$ boxes of markers and another group used $1\frac{6}{8}$ boxes. How many boxes of markers did the two groups use altogether?

▶ **Picture It** **You can use models to help add mixed numbers.**

The picture shows the boxes of markers. Each marker is $\frac{1}{8}$ of the whole box.

| 1 box | $\frac{5}{8}$ box | | 1 box | $\frac{6}{8}$ box | |

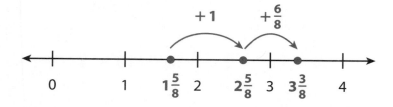

3 boxes $\frac{3}{8}$ box

▶ **Model It** **You can also use a number line to help add mixed numbers.**

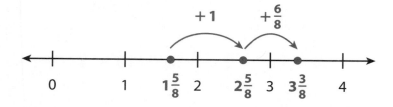

Remember that 1 whole box is 8 markers, or $\frac{8}{8}$ of a box.

Connect It Now you will solve the problem from the previous page using fractions.

2 What is the sum of just the whole number parts of $1\frac{5}{8}$ and $1\frac{6}{8}$? _____

3 What is the sum of just the fraction parts of $1\frac{5}{8}$ and $1\frac{6}{8}$? _____

4 Think about how many wholes are in $\frac{11}{8}$ and how many extra eighths there are. Complete the equations below.

$$\frac{11}{8} = \frac{8}{8} + \frac{\boxed{}}{8} \qquad \frac{8}{8} = \underline{\quad\quad} \qquad \text{So, } \frac{11}{8} = 1 + \frac{\boxed{}}{8}.$$

5 Now add the sum of the whole numbers to the sum of the fractions.

$$2 + 1 + \frac{3}{8} = \underline{\quad\quad}$$

6 Explain how you add mixed numbers. _____

_____

_____

_____

_____

_____

Try It Use what you just learned about adding mixed numbers to solve these problems. Show your work on a separate sheet of paper.

7 Mrs. Suarez sold pies for a fundraiser. She sold $3\frac{5}{6}$ pies the first day and $1\frac{3}{6}$ pies the second day. How many pies did she sell in all? _____

8 Beth went on vacation for $4\frac{1}{2}$ days in June and $8\frac{1}{2}$ days in July. How many days was Beth on vacation altogether? _____

Learn About ▶ Subtracting Mixed Numbers

Read the problem below. Then explore different ways to subtract mixed numbers.

> Ursula picked carrots and radishes from her garden. She picked $4\frac{1}{4}$ pounds of carrots and $1\frac{3}{4}$ pounds of radishes. How many more pounds of carrots did she pick than radishes?

▶ **Picture It** You can use a model to help subtract mixed numbers.

This model shows $4\frac{1}{4}$ pounds of carrots.

This model shows $4\frac{1}{4}$ pounds of carrots minus $1\frac{3}{4}$ pounds of radishes. The fourths still shaded red show the difference in weight between the carrots and radishes.

$$4\frac{1}{4} - 1\frac{3}{4} = 2\frac{2}{4}$$

▶ **Model It** You can also use a number line to help subtract mixed numbers.

To subtract using a number line, start at the number you are subtracting from and move left the amount you are subtracting.

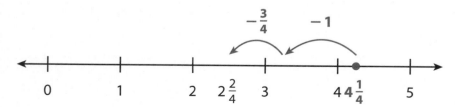

Connect It Now you will solve the problem from the previous page using equations.

$$4\frac{1}{4} - 1\frac{3}{4}$$

9 Complete the equations to write $4\frac{1}{4}$ as a fraction greater than 1.

$$4\frac{1}{4} = \frac{16}{\square} + \frac{1}{4} \qquad \text{So, } 4\frac{1}{4} = \frac{\square}{4}.$$

10 Complete the equations to write $1\frac{3}{4}$ as a fraction greater than 1.

$$1\frac{3}{4} = \frac{\square}{4} + \frac{3}{4} \qquad \text{So, } 1\frac{3}{4} = \frac{\square}{4}.$$

11 Subtract the fractions. Write an equation that shows the difference.

_____

12 How many more pounds of carrots did Ursula pick than radishes? _____

13 Explain how you can use fractions greater than 1 to subtract mixed numbers.

_____

_____

_____

_____

Try It Use what you just learned about subtracting mixed numbers to solve these problems. Show your work on a separate sheet of paper.

14 Monica rode her bike $3\frac{1}{4}$ miles on Monday. She rode $2\frac{2}{4}$ miles on Tuesday.

How much farther did Monica ride on Monday than on Tuesday? _____

15 Look at problem 14. Monica wants to ride $8\frac{2}{4}$ miles total. How many more miles

does she need to ride? _____

©Curriculum Associates, LLC   Copying is not permitted.

Lesson 17 Add and Subtract Mixed Numbers   **207**

Practice **Adding and Subtracting Mixed Numbers**

Study the example below. Then solve problems 16–18.

Example

One soccer team drank $5\frac{2}{3}$ liters of water during a game. Their opponents drank $4\frac{2}{3}$ liters of water. How much water did both teams drink?

Look at how you could show your work using models.

Solution _The teams drank $10\frac{1}{3}$ liters of water combined._

The student added the whole numbers and then combined the fractions!

💬 **Pair/Share**
How could you use a number line to help you solve this problem?

---

16 Kelly bought $4\frac{7}{8}$ pounds of apples and $2\frac{3}{8}$ pounds of oranges. How many pounds of fruit did she buy altogether?

Show your work.

What operation do you need to use?

💬 **Pair/Share**
Is there one way that works the best to solve this problem?

Solution _____

17 Karina read a total of $20\frac{2}{4}$ pages in her science and social studies books combined. She read $12\frac{3}{4}$ pages in her science book. How many pages did she read in her social studies book?

Show your work.

Sometimes counting up or back can help you solve problems like this.

Pair/Share
How can you tell if your answer is reasonable?

Solution _____

---

18 Which of the following shows a correct way to subtract $15\frac{4}{5} - 9\frac{3}{5}$? Circle the letter of the correct answer.

A Subtract the whole numbers, then subtract the fractions. Subtract the differences.

B Add the whole numbers, then add the fractions. Subtract the sums.

C Subtract the whole numbers, then subtract the fractions. Add the differences.

D Write the mixed numbers as fractions greater than one. Then add the fractions.

Solve the problem on your own, and then check for your answer!

Marella chose **A** as the correct answer. Did she do each step correctly? Explain why or why not.

_____

_____

Pair/Share
Draw a model to check your answer.

_____

_____

Practice > **Adding and Subtracting Mixed Numbers**

Solve the problems.

1 On Saturday, Shawn worked in his yard for $3\frac{5}{6}$ hours. On Sunday, he worked another $4\frac{1}{6}$ hours in his yard. How long did he work in the yard in all?

A $\frac{2}{6}$ hour

B 7 hours

C $7\frac{5}{6}$ hours

D 8 hours

2 Ella ordered 16 pizzas for a party. After the party, there were $3\frac{5}{8}$ pizzas left. How many pizza were eaten?

A $12\frac{3}{8}$

B $13\frac{3}{8}$

C $13\frac{5}{8}$

D $19\frac{5}{8}$

3 Luis is writing recipes for soup that require cans of broth. Each can has $1\frac{3}{4}$ cups of broth. He needs each batch of soup to have an amount of broth within the range given below.

• Draw cans in each pot so that the amount of broth is within the given range.

• Leave the pot empty if the given range is not possible using an exact number of cans.

Small batch
3 to 4 cups of broth

Medium batch
6 to 7 cups of broth

Large batch
9 to 10 cups of broth

4 Four friends shared 3 orders of chicken wings.

- Alex ate $\frac{5}{8}$ of an order.
- Chase ate $\frac{7}{8}$ of an order.
- Ella ate $\frac{6}{8}$ of an order.

How much chicken is left for the fourth friend? _____

5 Marnel used $4\frac{2}{3}$ cups of cereal and $3\frac{1}{3}$ cups of marshmallows to make cereal bars. How many more cups of cereal did Marnel use than marshmallows?

Show your work.

Solution _____

6 Kieran ran the first part of a relay in $4\frac{4}{6}$ minutes. David ran the next part in $3\frac{5}{6}$ minutes. How long did they take to run both parts of the relay?

Show your work.

Solution _____

✔ **Self Check** Go back and see what you can check off on the Self Check on page 157.

Understand Fraction Multiplication

Think It Through

What's really going on when we multiply numbers?

Multiplication is finding the total number of objects in equal groups.

Think about how you would explain how to multiply 3 by 4 to a third grader. You could draw an area model with 3 rows and 4 columns, and then count the boxes.

When you multiply 4 × 3, you have four groups of three, or four copies of 3 boxes.

Think How is multiplying fractions like multiplying whole numbers?

When you multiply a fraction, like $\frac{1}{3}$, by a whole number, like 4, you are making 4 copies of $\frac{1}{3}$.

You can use a model to help you multiply $\frac{1}{3}$ by 4.

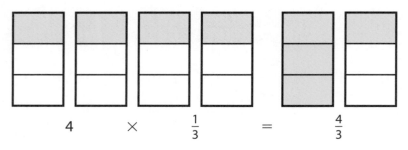

$$4 \qquad \times \qquad \frac{1}{3} \qquad = \qquad \frac{4}{3}$$

When you multiply $4 \times \frac{1}{3}$, you have 4 copies of $\frac{1}{3}$.

> ✏️ **Underline** the sentence that tells what you are doing when you multiply $4 \times \frac{1}{3}$.

Think Where does that product come from?

Look at the model of $4 \times \frac{1}{3}$ below.

 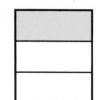

The parts are thirds and there are 4 shaded, so the model shows $\frac{4}{3}$!

The model shows four thirds. You can count four $\frac{1}{3}$ parts.

Notice that the denominator of the fraction $\frac{1}{3}$ and the denominator of the product $\frac{4}{3}$ are the same. The denominator tells the size of the equal parts in one whole. So the fraction and the product both have the same equal-size parts (thirds).

Suppose you have two groups of $\frac{4}{3}$s. To find the total number of $\frac{4}{3}$s in two copies of $\frac{4}{3}$s, you can multiply $\frac{4}{3}$ by 2.

$$2 \times \frac{4}{3} = 2 \times \left(4 \times \frac{1}{3}\right)$$
$$= (2 \times 4) \times \frac{1}{3}$$
$$= 8 \times \frac{1}{3}$$

This is the same as having eight copies of $\frac{1}{3}$.

Reflect

1 Explain what $5 \times \frac{1}{3}$ means.

_____

_____

_____

_____

Think About ▶ **Multiplying Fractions**

🔍 **Let's Explore the Idea** Repeated addition and using a model are two ways to think about multiplying fractions.

2 Fill in the blanks to find $5 \times \frac{3}{4}$ using repeated addition:

$$\frac{3}{4} + \frac{3}{4} + \underline{\hspace{1cm}} + \underline{\hspace{1cm}} + \frac{3}{4} = \underline{\hspace{1cm}}$$

Shade the model at the right to show $5 \times \frac{3}{4}$.

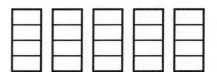

3 Fill in the blanks to find $2 \times \frac{5}{6}$ using repeated addition:

$$\frac{5}{\boxed{}} + \underline{\hspace{1cm}} = \underline{\hspace{1cm}}$$

Shade the model at the right to show $2 \times \frac{5}{6}$.

Use the models above to answer problems 4 and 5.

4 Fill in the blanks to show other ways to write problems with the same product as $5 \times \frac{3}{4}$.

$$\underline{\hspace{1cm}} \times \frac{1}{4} \qquad 3 \times \frac{\boxed{}}{4}$$

5 Fill in the blanks to show other ways to write problems with the same product as $2 \times \frac{5}{6}$.

$$10 \times \frac{\boxed{}}{6} \qquad \underline{\hspace{1cm}} \times \frac{2}{6}$$

Now try these two problems.

6 Draw a model to show $4 \times \frac{2}{3}$.

7 Draw a model to show $3 \times \frac{2}{4}$.

Let's Talk About It
Solve the problems below as a group.

8 Look at your model for problem 6. Draw another model that shows $8 \times \frac{1}{3}$.

How are the two models different?

_____

_____

_____

_____

What is the total number of thirds shaded in each model?

_____

9 Look at your model for problem 7. How many fourths are shaded in all?

_____

10 Think of a different model with a total of 6 fourths shaded. Fill in the blank to write a multiplication equation for this model:

$$\underline{\qquad} \times \frac{1}{4} = \frac{6}{4}$$

Try It Another Way Work with your group to use number lines to multiply fractions.

11 Fill in the blanks on the number line to show $4 \times \frac{3}{5}$.

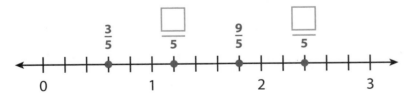

12 Label the number line below to show $6 \times \frac{2}{10}$.

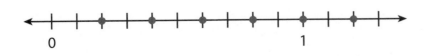

Connect ▶ **Ideas about Multiplying Fractions**

Talk through these problems as a class, then write your answers below.

13 Analyze How is $3 \times \frac{3}{6}$ the same as $9 \times \frac{1}{6}$?

_____

_____

14 Evaluate Violet solved the problem $4 \times \frac{7}{10}$ as shown.

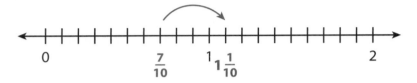

What did Violet do wrong?

_____

_____

15 Construct Fraction models and number lines are not the only models you can use to show fraction multiplication. Make a different kind of drawing to solve the problem below.

Anders filled a $\frac{1}{2}$-cup measure with flour 3 times for a recipe. How much flour did he use?

Answer Anders used _____ cups of flour.

Apply ▶ Ideas about Multiplying Fractions

16 **Put It Together** Use what you have learned to complete this task.

> Joaquin ran $\frac{4}{5}$ of a mile each day on Monday, Wednesday, and Friday. How many miles did he run in all?

Part A Describe two methods you could use to solve the problem $3 \times \frac{4}{5}$.

i _____

_____

_____

ii _____

_____

_____

Part B Write a different multiplication problem with the same product as $3 \times \frac{4}{5}$. Use $\frac{1}{5}$ instead of $\frac{4}{5}$. _____

Part C Allison is starting to run a little each day. She ran $\frac{1}{5}$ of a mile on all 7 days last week. Joaquin and Allison each wanted to run at least 2 miles during the week. Did they? Use a drawing or words to explain how you know.

_____

_____

_____

_____

Multiply Fractions

🅖 Use What You Know

In Lesson 18, you learned about multiplying fractions by whole numbers. In this lesson, you will multiply fractions by whole numbers to solve word problems.

One serving of crackers is $\frac{3}{10}$ of the whole box of crackers. Bella ate 3 servings last week. What fraction of the box of crackers did she eat?

3 parts = 1 serving

a. What fraction of the box is one serving? _____

b. How many servings did Bella eat? _____

c. Did Bella eat more or less than $\frac{3}{10}$ of the box of crackers? _____

d. What operation can you use to solve the problem? _____

e. If Bella ate 2 servings, you could multiply $\frac{3}{10}$ by 2 to find the fraction of the box of crackers she ate.

What is $2 \times \frac{3}{10}$? _____

f. Explain how you could find the fraction of the box of crackers Bella did eat.

_____

_____

_____

▷▷ Find Out More

To solve some word problems, you can multiply a fraction by a whole number. These problems include combining equal-size parts. In the cracker problem, the serving size $\left(\frac{3}{10}\text{ of the box}\right)$ is the equal-size part. You can add $\frac{3}{10}$ each time Bella eats a serving. Or, you can use multiplication.

Eating $\frac{3}{10}$ of the box **3 times** can be written as $\mathbf{3} \times \frac{3}{10}$, or $\frac{3 \times 3}{10}$.
Since $3 \times 3 = 9, \frac{3 \times 3}{10} = \frac{9}{10}$.

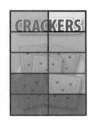
9 parts = 3 servings

The answer to a problem like the one above may be a fraction. You may be asked to tell between which two whole numbers the answer lies.

For example:

$\frac{9}{10}$ is less than 1 whole. $\frac{9}{10}$ is between 0 and 1.

$\frac{12}{10}$ is more than 1 whole, but less than 2 wholes. $\frac{12}{10}$ is between 1 and 2.

Situations for multiplying a fraction by a whole number are similar to ones you have seen for multiplying whole numbers. Some problems are about multiple groups of equal-size parts. Others are about comparing, such as "2 times as many."

▶ Reflect

1 Describe a real situation when you might want to multiply a fraction by a whole number.

_____

_____

_____

Learn About ▶ **Multiplying Fractions in Word Problems**

Read the problem below. Then explore different ways to solve the word problem.

> James is baking cookies. One batch of cookies needs $\frac{2}{4}$ of a teaspoon of vanilla. James wants 3 times the number of cookies in 1 batch. How much vanilla does James need?

▶ **Picture It** **You can use a drawing to help solve the word problem.**

Three times as many means 3 batches. The picture shows six $\frac{1}{4}$ teaspoons for 3 batches.

Batch 1   Batch 2   Batch 3

▶ **Model It** **You can also use fraction strips to solve the word problem.**

The fraction strip below is divided into fourths and shows $\frac{2}{4}$, the amount of vanilla in each batch.

$\frac{1}{4}$	$\frac{1}{4}$	$\frac{1}{4}$	$\frac{1}{4}$

The model below shows the amount of vanilla needed for **3 batches.**

Batch 1

$\frac{1}{4}$	$\frac{1}{4}$	$\frac{1}{4}$	$\frac{1}{4}$

Batch 2

$\frac{1}{4}$	$\frac{1}{4}$	$\frac{1}{4}$	$\frac{1}{4}$

Batch 3

$\frac{1}{4}$	$\frac{1}{4}$	$\frac{1}{4}$	$\frac{1}{4}$

Connect It Now you will solve the problem from the previous page using equations.

2 How much vanilla does James need for each batch? _____

3 How many batches does James want to make? _____

4 Write an equation to find how many teaspoons of vanilla James needs.

$$\underline{\hspace{2cm}} \times \underline{\hspace{2cm}} = \underline{\hspace{2cm}}$$

number of   teaspoon   teaspoons
batches   for 1 batch   needed

5 Explain how you can check your answer using repeated addition.

_____

_____

_____

_____

Try It Use what you just learned to solve these problems. Show your work on a separate sheet of paper.

6 Micah jogged $\frac{8}{10}$ of a mile. Sarah jogged 3 times this distance. How far did

Sarah jog? _____

7 On Monday, Sylvia spent $\frac{5}{12}$ of a day driving to her cousin's house. On Friday, she

spent the same amount of time driving home. What fraction of a day did Sylvia

spend driving to her cousin's house and back? _____

Study the example below. Then solve problems 8–10.

Example

Five friends shared a pizza. Each friend ate $\frac{2}{12}$ of the pizza. How much pizza did they eat altogether?

Look at how you could show your work using a model.

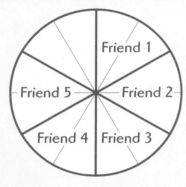

$$5 \times \frac{2}{12} = \frac{10}{12}$$

Solution The 5 friends ate $\frac{10}{12}$ of a pizza.

The student labeled the model to show each of the 5 friends!

 Pair/Share
How could you write the equation a different way?

---

8 A partially eaten bag of grapes weighs $\frac{5}{8}$ of a pound.

The bag of grapes weighed 4 times this amount before any were eaten. What was the original weight of the bag of grapes?

Show your work.

Was the original weight more or less than $\frac{5}{8}$ of a pound?

 Pair/Share
Check your answer using repeated addition.

Solution _____

9 Leo painted for $\frac{2}{3}$ of an hour each day on Monday, Tuesday, Thursday, and Friday. How long did Leo paint this week?

Show your work.

Did Leo paint for the same amount of time each day?

Pair/Share
Draw a model to show the problem situation.

Solution _____

---

10 Karime biked $\frac{3}{4}$ of a mile on Monday. On Tuesday he biked 5 times this distance. The number of miles Karime biked on Tuesday is between which two whole numbers? Circle the letter of the correct answer.

Make sure your answer is reasonable!

A 0 and 1

B 1 and 2

C 3 and 4

D 4 and 5

Lacey chose **A** as the correct answer. How did she get that answer?

_____

_____

_____

Pair/Share
How did you get the answer you chose?

_____

Practice Multiplying Fractions

Solve the problems.

1 A choir concert lasts for $\frac{5}{6}$ of an hour. The choir performed 3 concerts over the weekend. Find the number of hours the choir spent performing over the weekend. The answer is between which two whole numbers?

A 0 and 1

B 1 and 2

C 2 and 3

D 3 and 4

2 Tell whether each equation is *True* or *False*.

a. $3 \times \frac{4}{6} = 2$ ☐ True ☐ False

b. $2 \times \frac{4}{5} = \frac{8}{10}$ ☐ True ☐ False

c. $5 \times \frac{2}{9} = 5\frac{2}{9}$ ☐ True ☐ False

d. $2 \times \frac{3}{7} = 6 \times \frac{1}{7}$ ☐ True ☐ False

3 Melanie wrote an expression that has a value of $\frac{15}{4}$.

Choose *Yes* or *No* to tell whether each expression has a value of $\frac{15}{4}$.

a. $5 \times \frac{3}{4}$ ☐ Yes ☐ No

b. $1 \times \frac{5}{4}$ ☐ Yes ☐ No

c. $15 \times \frac{1}{4}$ ☐ Yes ☐ No

4 Morgan bought 6 tomatoes that each weigh $\frac{1}{4}$ of a pound. Russ bought 14 tomatoes that each weigh $\frac{1}{8}$ pound. Whose tomatoes weigh more?

Show your work.

Answer The tomatoes that _____ bought weigh more.

5 Mr. Nelson bought paint brushes for the art club. He gave each of the 6 club members $\frac{4}{12}$ of a box of paint brushes. What is the total number of boxes of paint brushes he gave to the club?

Show your work.

Answer Mr. Nelson gave the club _____ boxes of paint brushes.

✓ **Self Check** **Go back and see what you can check off on the Self Check on page 157.**

Use What You Know

In earlier lessons, you worked with equivalent fractions. This lesson will focus on equivalent fractions with denominators of 10 and 100. Take a look at this problem.

Doss is riding his bike home. He has seven tenths of a mile to go. Write an equivalent fraction to show how much Doss has left to ride in hundredths of a mile.

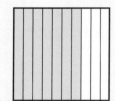

a. What fraction does the model show? Explain your reasoning.

_____

_____

b. What is the denominator of the fraction? _____

c. The distance is given in tenths. You need to find the distance in hundredths. Hundredths is how many times the number of equal parts as tenths? _____

d. What is the numerator of the fraction seven tenths? _____

e. Explain how you could use multiplication to find a fraction with a denominator of 100 that is equivalent to $\frac{7}{10}$.

_____

_____

_____

_____

▶▶ Find Out More

Every fraction with a denominator of 10 can also be written as a fraction with a denominator of 100.

The model on the previous page is divided into 10 equal parts, or **tenths**. If you split each of those 10 parts into 10 equal parts, the whole is divided into 100 equal parts, or **hundredths**.

When you divide the whole into 100 equal parts instead of 10, 70 parts are shaded. There are 10 times as many equal parts, so 10 times as many of them are shaded. You could also say the tenths model has $\frac{1}{10}$ as many equal parts as the hundredths model so it has $\frac{1}{10}$ as many parts shaded.

$$\frac{7}{10} = \frac{7 \times 10}{10 \times 10}, \text{ or } \frac{70}{100}$$

$$\frac{70}{100} = \frac{70 \div 10}{100 \div 10}, \text{ or } \frac{7}{10}$$

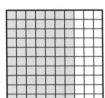

You can also use money to think about equivalent fractions with denominators of 10 and 100.

Think of 1 dollar, or 100 cents, as the whole.

- 1 dime = 10 cents, so 1 dime = $\frac{10}{100}$ of a dollar.

- 10 dimes = 1 dollar, so 1 dime = $\frac{1}{10}$ of a dollar.

So, $\frac{1}{10} = \frac{10}{100}$.

▶ Reflect

1 What fraction of the model at the right is shaded?
Write two different fractions to show the amount. Explain how to use multiplication to check that your fractions are equivalent.

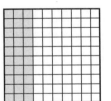

_____

_____

_____

Learn About ▸ Adding Tenths and Hundredths Fractions

Read the problem below. Then explore different ways to understand how to add fractions with denominators of 10 and 100.

> Carmen says that she has $\frac{4}{10}$ of a dollar. Troy says that he has $\frac{50}{100}$ of a dollar. Together, what fraction of a dollar do they have?

▸ **Picture It** **You can use a picture to help you add fractions with denominators of 10 and 100.**

You know that $\frac{4}{10}$ of a dollar is 4 dimes and $\frac{50}{100}$ of a dollar is 5 dimes.

Carmen's money

Troy's money

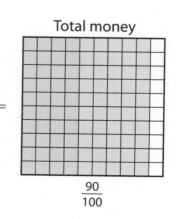

Together Carmen and Troy have 9 dimes.

9 dimes is $\frac{90}{100}$, or $\frac{9}{10}$, of a dollar.

▸ **Model It** **You can use a model to help you add fractions with denominators of 10 and 100.**

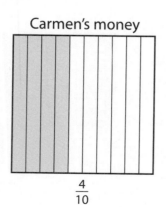

Carmen's money $\quad$ Troy's money $\quad$ Total money

$\frac{4}{10}$ $\qquad$ $\frac{50}{100}$ $\qquad$ $\frac{90}{100}$

Connect It Now you will solve the problem from the previous page using equivalent fractions.

2 What are the denominators of the fractions you are adding? Are they the same?

_____

_____

3 Complete the equation to use multiplication to find the hundredths equivalent to $\frac{4}{10}$.

$$\frac{4}{10} = \left(\frac{4 \times \square}{10 \times \square} \right) = \frac{40}{100}$$

4 $\frac{40}{100} + \frac{50}{100} =$ _____

5 Together, Carmen and Troy have what fraction of a dollar? _____

6 Explain how you can use equivalent fractions to add a fraction with a denominator of 100 to a fraction with a denominator of 10.

_____

_____

_____

_____

Try It Use what you just learned to solve these problems. Show your work on a separate sheet of paper.

7 Giselle spent $\frac{7}{10}$ of her money on a book and $\frac{10}{100}$ of her money on food. What fraction of her money did she spend altogether? _____

8 The winning car in a race beat the second car by $\frac{19}{100}$ of a second. The third car was $\frac{4}{10}$ of a second behind the second car. By how much did the first car beat the third car? _____

Practice **Adding Tenths and Hundredths Fractions**

Study the example below. Then solve problems 9–11.

Example

A farmer planted corn in $\frac{68}{100}$ of his field and beans in $\frac{3}{10}$ of the field. What fraction of his field did the farmer plant with corn and beans?

Look at how you could show your work using a model.

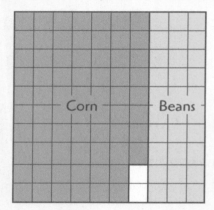

Corn   Beans

Solution The farmer planted $\frac{98}{100}$ of the field.

The student drew and shaded a model to show the sum of $\frac{68}{100}$ and $\frac{3}{10}$.

 Pair/Share

How can you solve the problem using equivalent fractions?

---

9 What is the sum of $\frac{7}{100}$ and $\frac{1}{10}$?

Show your work.

There is more than one way to solve this problem!

 Pair/Share

Can you explain the problem using dimes and pennies?

Solution _____

10 Jared, Consuela, and Reggie have an ant farm. Jared collected $\frac{25}{100}$ of the ants for the ant farm. Consuela collected $\frac{6}{10}$ of the ants. What fraction of the ants did Jared and Consuela collect altogether?

Show your work.

What do you notice about the denominators of these fractions?

Pair/Share
Draw a model to show the problem situation.

Solution _____

---

11 Heath has 100 trading cards. $\frac{7}{100}$ of his card collection is football cards and $\frac{7}{10}$ is baseball cards. Together, the football and baseball cards make up what fraction of Heath's card collection? Circle the letter of the correct answer.

A $\frac{7}{110}$

B $\frac{14}{100}$

C $\frac{77}{200}$

D $\frac{77}{100}$

Ezra chose **C** as the correct answer. How did he get that answer?

To solve this problem without a model, what should you do first?

_____

_____

_____

_____

Pair/Share
Chelsea chose D. How did she get that answer?

Practice ▶ **Adding Tenths and Hundredths Fractions**

Solve the problems.

1 Which equation is true?

A $\dfrac{3}{100} + \dfrac{8}{10} = \dfrac{11}{110}$

B $\dfrac{3}{100} + \dfrac{8}{10} = \dfrac{38}{100}$

C $\dfrac{3}{100} + \dfrac{8}{10} = \dfrac{83}{100}$

D $\dfrac{3}{100} + \dfrac{8}{10} = \dfrac{11}{10}$

2 Noelle rode her bike $\dfrac{5}{10}$ of a kilometer to the library, and then another $\dfrac{22}{100}$ of a kilometer to her friend's house. How far did Noelle ride her bike in all?

A $\dfrac{27}{110}$ of a kilometer

B $\dfrac{7}{10}$ of a kilometer

C $\dfrac{72}{100}$ of a kilometer

D $\dfrac{225}{100}$ kilometers

3 Fill in each box with either 10 or 100 to make the equation true.

$$\dfrac{4}{\square} + \dfrac{20}{\square} = \dfrac{60}{100}$$

▷▷ Find Out More

Tenths and hundredths can also be written as **decimals.**

Here is another way to think about the fraction $\frac{48}{100}$.

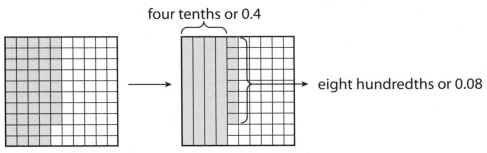

four tenths or 0.4

eight hundredths or 0.08

48 hundredths is 4 tenths and 8 hundredths.

You can use a place-value chart to understand the value of each digit. Decimals follow the same place-value pattern as whole numbers. A digit in any place has 10 times the value it would have in the place to its right and $\frac{1}{10}$ the value it would have in the place to its left.

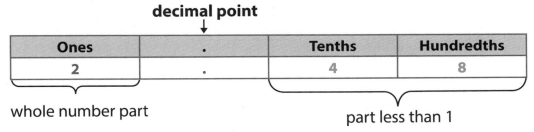

decimal point

Ones	.	Tenths	Hundredths
2	.	4	8

whole number part

part less than 1

To read the decimal 2.48:

    1. Say the whole number part, if there is one.   *two*

    2. Say *and* for the decimal point.   *and*

    3. Say the part less than 1 as a whole number.   *forty-eight*

    4. Say the place-value name of the last digit.   *hundredths*

You read 2.48 as *two and forty-eight hundredths.*

▶ Reflect

1 Explain how thinking about money can help you understand decimals.

_____

_____

Learn About ▶ **Fractions and Decimals**

Read the problem below. Then explore different ways to understand how to use fractions and decimals to name the same amount.

> A soccer camp has spots for 100 students. So far, 60 of those spots are filled. Write a fraction and a decimal in hundredths and tenths to show the amount of spots that are filled.

▶ **Picture It** You can use a model to understand how to write hundredths or tenths as a fraction.

Each model represents the fraction of the soccer camp spots that are filled.

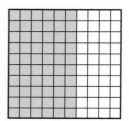   

The large square is 1 whole.

Each small square is $\frac{1}{100}$ of the whole.

Sixty small squares are shaded.

The large square is 1 whole.

Each section is $\frac{1}{10}$ of the whole.

Six sections are shaded.

▶ **Model It** You can use a place-value chart to understand how to write hundredths or tenths as a decimal.

The place-value chart shows the value of 0.60.

Ones	.	Tenths	Hundredths
0	.	6	0

Connect It Now you will use the models and what you know about fractions and decimals to solve the problem.

2 Look at *Picture It.* The model on the left shows 60 squares shaded.

Write a fraction for the model. _____

3 Divide the numerator and denominator by 10 and write the tenths fraction. How does the model on the right with six shaded sections show this fraction?

_____

_____

4 Look at the place-value chart. Write a decimal in tenths and the equivalent decimal in hundredths. How are the two decimals different?

_____

_____

_____

5 Write a number on each line below to describe how decimals relate to fractions with denominators of 10 and 100.

If the denominator of a fraction is 10, the equivalent decimal has _____ place after the decimal point.

If the denominator of a fraction is 100, the equivalent decimal has _____ places after the decimal point.

▶ Try It Use what you just learned to find related fractions and decimals. Show your work on a separate sheet of paper.

6 Write a decimal equivalent to $\frac{83}{100}$. _____

7 Write a decimal equivalent to $\frac{2}{10}$. _____

Draw a model that shows the fraction and the decimal.

Learn About ▷ **Writing Decimals as Equivalent Fractions**

Read the problem below. Then explore different ways to write a decimal as an equivalent fraction.

> Eli collects sports cards. He says 0.05 of his cards are baseball cards. What fraction of his cards are baseball cards?

▶ **Picture It** You can use a model to help write a decimal as an equivalent fraction.

The model shows 0.05.

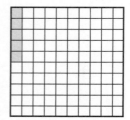

▶ **Model It** You can also use a place-value chart to help write a decimal as an equivalent fraction.

The place-value chart shows the value of 0.05.

Ones	.	Tenths	Hundredths
0	.	0	5

Connect It   Now you will use the model and the place-value chart to solve the problem.

8 How can the model help you write a fraction equivalent to 0.05?

_____

_____

_____

9 How can the place-value chart help you write a fraction equivalent to 0.05?

_____

_____

_____

10 Use words to describe the fraction of Eli's cards that are baseball cards.

_____

11 What fraction of Eli's cards are baseball cards? _____

12 Explain how you can write a decimal in hundredths as a fraction.

_____

_____

_____

Try It   Use what you just learned to write decimals as fractions. Show your work on a separate sheet of paper.

13 Write 0.9 in words and as a fraction. _____

14 Write 0.89 in words and as a fraction. _____

Practice **Relating Decimals and Fractions**

Study the example below. Then solve problems 15–17.

Example

Jayne read that it takes about two tenths of a second to blink an eye. She wrote that a blink takes about 0.02 of a second. Is Jayne correct?

Look at how you could show your work using a place-value chart.

Ones	.	Tenths
0	.	2

Two tenths as a decimal is 0.2, not 0.02.

Solution _Jayne is not correct. Two tenths written as a decimal is 0.2._

The student used a place-value chart. The tenths place is the first place to the right of the decimal point.

Pair/Share
How could you solve the problem using a model?

---

15 What is 0.7 written as a fraction?

Show your work.

How could drawing a model help you?

Pair/Share
How do you know if the decimal represents tenths or hundredths?

Solution _____

16 The number line below shows 1 whole divided into tenths. Write numbers in the boxes to label the missing fractions and decimals. Explain how you know what numbers to write.

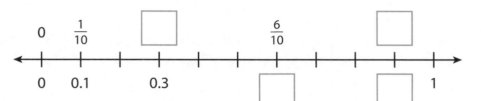

Could saying each number aloud help?

_____

_____

_____

_____

_____

Pair/Share
How could you show hundredths on this number line?

---

17 What decimal names the same amount as $\frac{50}{100}$? Circle the letter of the correct answer.

A 0.50

B 0.05

C 50.0

D 50.10

Abby chose **B** as the correct answer. How did she get that answer?

What does the denominator of the fraction tell you?

_____

_____

_____

_____

Pair/Share
What is a decimal in tenths that is equivalent to $\frac{50}{100}$?

Practice ▶ **Relating Decimals and Fractions**

Solve the problems.

1 What is 0.75 written as a fraction?

A $\frac{.75}{100}$

B $\frac{0}{75}$

C $\frac{75}{100}$

D $\frac{75}{10}$

2 Which fraction and decimal are equivalent? Circle all that apply.

A $\frac{4}{10}$ and 0.04

B $\frac{6}{100}$ and 0.60

C $\frac{3}{10}$ and 0.3

D $\frac{9}{100}$ and 0.09

E $\frac{7}{10}$ and 7.10

3 Model *A* is shaded to represent a value that is less than 1 whole.

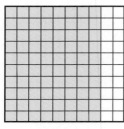

Model *A*

Choose *Yes* or *No* to indicate whether the value of the shaded part of Model *A* is equivalent to the value shown.

a. $\frac{8}{10}$ ☐ Yes ☐ No

b. $\frac{80}{100}$ ☐ Yes ☐ No

c. 0.08 ☐ Yes ☐ No

4 A test has 100 questions. Cora got 85 questions correct. What decimal shows the part of the test she answered correctly? What decimal shows the part of the test she answered incorrectly? Model the decimals below.

Show your work.

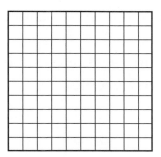

Solution _____

5 Kelly found some dimes and pennies in her dad's car. She found 5 coins in all. The coins totaled more than 20 cents, but less than 50 cents. What coins could Kelly have found? Write the amount as a fraction of a dollar and as an equivalent decimal. Model the fraction and decimal below.

Show your work.

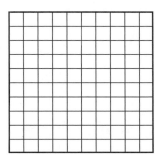

Answer Kelly could have found _____.

Fraction _____ *Decimal* _____

✓ **Self Check** Go back and see what you can check off on the Self Check on page 157.

Compare Decimals

Use What You Know

You know how to compare whole numbers and fractions. In this lesson, you will compare decimals. Take a look at this problem.

Kele and Kaci each bought equal-size bottles of water. They each drank some of their water. Kele now has 0.5 of his bottle left. Kaci has 0.4 of her bottle left. Who has more water left?

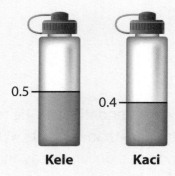

0.5 —

0.4 —

Kele   **Kaci**

a. Write 0.5 in words. _____

b. What fraction is equivalent to 0.5? _____

c. Write 0.4 in words. _____

d. What fraction is equivalent to 0.4? _____
Describe how to compare fractions that have the same denominator.

_____

_____

_____

e. Who has more water left? Explain how you know.

_____

▶▶ Find Out More

You can use the symbols >, <, or = to compare decimals.

0.5 > 0.4 means that 0.5 is greater than 0.4.
0.4 < 0.5 means that 0.4 is less than 0.5.

You can compare 0.5 and 0.4 in a place-value chart.

Ones	.	Tenths	Hundredths
0	.	5	0
0	.	4	0

Compare the places from left to right as you do
with whole numbers.
The ones are the same, so look at the tenths:
5 > 4, so **0.5 > 0.4**.

But what if Kaci's bottle of water was larger than
Kele's bottle? Then the comparison would not
make sense.

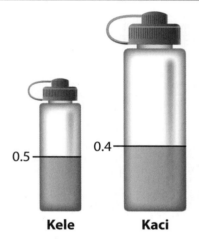

Comparing decimals is like comparing fractions.
When you compare fractions or decimals, you must
have the same-size whole.

▶ Reflect

1 Describe how to compare the two decimals 0.6 and 0.8.

_____

_____

_____

_____

Learn About ▶ **Comparing Hundredths Decimals**

Read the problem below. Then explore different ways to compare two decimals when both are in hundredths.

> Dora lives 0.35 mile from school. Katrina lives 0.53 mile from school. Who lives a greater distance from school?

▶ **Picture It** **You can use a model to help compare decimals in hundredths.**

Each large square is one whole. The shaded areas show 0.35 and 0.53.

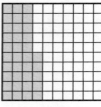   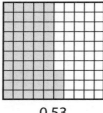

     0.35   0.53

0.35 is thirty-five hundredths.

0.53 is fifty-three hundredths.

▶ **Model It** **You can also use a place-value chart to help compare decimals in hundredths.**

The place-value chart shows 0.35 and 0.53.

Ones	.	Tenths	Hundredths
0	.	3	5
0	.	5	3

Compare ones: Both digits are the same.

Compare tenths: **5 > 3**.

Since the tenths digits are different, you don't need to compare hundredths digits.

Connect It Now you will solve the problem from the previous page by reasoning about the fractions that are equivalent to the decimals.

2 Look at the models on the previous page.

Write a fraction equivalent to 0.35: _____ ; to 0.53: _____

3 Which fraction is greater? Explain how you know. _____

_____

_____

_____

4 Write $>$, $<$, or $=$ in the circle to make a true statement: 0.35 $\bigcirc$ 0.53.

Who lives a greater distance from school? _____

Do the model and place-value chart support your answer? Explain.

_____

_____

_____

5 Explain how you can use fractions to compare two decimals when both are in hundredths. _____

_____

_____

Try It Use what you just learned to solve these problems. Show your work on a separate sheet of paper.

6 Compare 0.21 and 0.12 using $>$, $=$, or $<$. Explain how you got your answer.

_____

_____

_____

7 Which is less: 0.97 or 0.79? Use fractions to help solve the problem. _____

 **Learn About** ▶ **Comparing Tenths and Hundredths Decimals**

Read the problem below. Then explore different ways to compare decimals when one is in tenths and the other is in hundredths.

> Most bumblebees are about 0.75 of an inch long. A common hornet is about 0.8 of an inch long. Which insect is longer?

▶ **Picture It** **You can use a model to help compare decimals in tenths and hundredths.**

Each large square is one whole. The models show 0.75 and 0.8.

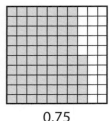   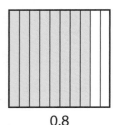

        0.75   0.8

▶ **Model It** **You can also use a place-value chart to compare decimals in tenths and hundredths.**

Notice that 0.8 has a 0 in the hundredths place in the chart. Remember that 8 tenths is equivalent to 80 hundredths.

Ones	.	Tenths	Hundredths
0	.	7	5
0	.	8	0

Compare ones: The digits are the same.

Compare tenths: **8 > 7.**

Since the tenths digits are different, you don't have to compare hundredths.

Connect It Now you will solve the problem from the previous page by reasoning about the fractions that are equivalent to the decimals.

8 Write fractions equivalent to 0.75 and 0.8. _____

9 How can you compare fractions with denominators of 100 and 10?

_____

_____

10 What fraction with a denominator of 100 is equivalent to $\frac{8}{10}$? _____

11 Compare the fractions. Then compare 0.75 and 0.8 using $>$, $<$, or $=$.

_____

Which insect is longer? _____

12 Explain how you can compare decimals when one is in tenths and the other is in hundredths. _____

_____

_____

Try It Use what you just learned to solve these problems. Show your work on a separate sheet of paper.

13 Compare 0.37 and 0.4 using $>$, $<$, or $=$. Explain how you got your answer.

_____

_____

_____

14 Which is greater: 0.9 or 0.92? _____

Show how you can use fractions to solve the problem.

_____

Practice ▶ **Comparing Decimals**

Study the example below. Then solve problems 15–17.

Example

Heath caught a bug that weighs 1.9 grams and Ty caught a bug that weighs 1.09 grams. Which bug weighs more?

Look at how you could show your work using equivalent fractions.

0.9 is nine tenths, or $\frac{9}{10}$.

0.09 is nine hundredths, or $\frac{9}{100}$.

$\frac{9}{10}$ is equivalent to $\frac{90}{100}$.

$\frac{90}{100} > \frac{9}{100}$, so 1.9 > 1.09.

Solution Heath's bug weighs more.

The student compared the decimal parts of the numbers because the whole number parts are the same.

Pair/Share
How do the values of the 9s compare in the two numbers?

---

15 Compare 0.3 and 0.8 using >, =, or <. Draw a model or number line to support your solution.

Show your work.

What models can you use to support your solution?

Pair/Share
Compare the models that you and your partner used.

Solution _____

©Curriculum Associates, LLC   Copying is not permitted.

16 Mika ran the 50-yard dash in 7.39 seconds. Felix ran it in 7.6 seconds. Who ran faster?

Show your work.

Does the greater number mean a faster or slower time?

Solution _____

Pair/Share
How did you and your partner decide what method to use to solve the problem?

17 Which statement and reasoning is true about the decimals 0.45 and 0.5? Circle the letter of the correct answer.

A $0.45 < 0.5$ because hundredths are greater than tenths.

B $0.45 < 0.5$ because $\frac{45}{100} < \frac{50}{100}$.

C $0.45 > 0.5$ because $45 > 5$.

D $0.45 > 0.5$ because hundredths are greater than tenths.

Make sure that the reasoning makes sense, too—not just the comparison.

Sarah chose **C** as the correct answer. How did she get that answer?

_____

_____

_____

_____

Pair/Share
Explain how you chose your answer.

Practice ▶ **Comparing Decimals**

Solve the problems.

1 Which change would make the following a true statement?

0.5 < 0.43

A Put a 3 in the hundredths place to change 0.5 to 0.53.

B Change the hundredths digit in 0.43 to 0.

C Put a 0 in the tenths place to change 0.5 to 0.05.

D Put a 0 in the hundredths place to change 0.5 to 0.50.

2 Which decimal is less than 0.75?

A 0.9

B 0.94

C 0.80

D 0.7

3 Which of the following decimals is greater than 0.07 but less than 0.3?
Circle the letter for all that apply.

A 0.02

B 0.34

C 0.27

D 0.73

E 0.1

4 Tell whether each statement is *True* or *False*.

a. $0.5 < 0.6$ because $\frac{5}{10}$ is less than $\frac{6}{10}$. ☐ True ☐ False

b. $0.25 > 0.3$ because 25 is greater than 3. ☐ True ☐ False

c. $0.89 > 0.8$ because $\frac{89}{100}$ is greater than $\frac{80}{100}$. ☐ True ☐ False

d. $0.06 = 0.6$ because 6 equals 6. ☐ True ☐ False

e. $0.4 < 0.14$ because 4 is less than 14. ☐ True ☐ False

5 Jana wrote two numbers that are between 0.4 and 0.45 on the board. What numbers could Jana have written?

Solution _____

6 Troy said that $0.9 > 0.90$ because tenths are greater than hundredths. Keith said that $0.9 < 0.90$ because 90 is greater than 9. How would you compare 0.9 and 0.90? Do you agree with either Troy or Keith? Write the symbol $<$, $>$, or $=$ on the line below to correctly compare the numbers.

Show your work.

Answer   0.9 _____ 0.90

 **Self Check**   Go back and see what you can check off on the Self Check on page 157.

Lesson 22 Compare Decimals

Unit 4
MATH IN ACTION

👥 **Introduction**

Use Fractions and Decimals

PS1 Make sense
of problems and
persevere in
solving them.

Study an Example Problem and Solution

**Read this problem involving fractions and decimals. Then look
at Luna's solution to this problem.**

Sand Jars

Luna made these notes after she made a sand art design in a 2-cup jar.

- · I used a glass jar that holds 2 cups.
- · I used less than 1 cup of yellow sand.
- · I filled less than 0.4 of the jar with pink sand.
- · I filled more than 0.2 of the jar with purple sand.

Luna wants to write specific instructions for making the
same kind of design that would work for a jar of any size.

- Find fractions or decimals to tell exactly what part of each jar to fill
  with pink, purple, and yellow sand.

- Write instructions using those numbers.

**Read the sample solution on the next page. Then look at the checklist
below. Find and mark parts of the solution that match the checklist.**

✏️ **Problem-Solving Checklist**

☐ Tell what is known.

☐ Tell what the problem
is asking.

☐ Show all your work.

☐ Show that the
solution works.

a. Circle something that is known.

b. Underline something that you need
to find.

c. Draw a box around what you do to
solve the problem.

d. Put a checkmark next to the part
that shows the solution works.

Luna's Solution

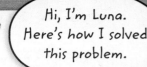

Hi, I'm Luna. Here's how I solved this problem.

▷ **I already know** the decimals for what fraction of the jar to fill with purple and pink. **I need to find** what fraction of the jar should be yellow.

▷ **The whole jar was 2 cups and yellow was less than 1 cup.**

1 cup is half of the jar.

Less than 1 cup means less than $\frac{1}{2}$ of the jar is yellow.

I had to choose either fractions or decimals. I chose fractions because I like them!

▷ **I can list all the information with fractions.**

pink: less than 0.4, so less than $\frac{4}{10}$ of the jar.

purple: more than 0.2, so more than $\frac{2}{10}$ of the jar.

yellow: less than $\frac{1}{2}$, so less than $\frac{5}{10}$ of the jar.

▷ **I can make a diagram with 10 equal parts.**

Then color it to find 3 fractions that are the right size and total $\frac{10}{10}$.

pink: $\frac{3}{10} < \frac{4}{10}$

purple: $\frac{3}{10} > \frac{2}{10}$

yellow: $\frac{4}{10} < \frac{5}{10}$

I drew a diagram to show all the parts and organize my thinking.

▷ **I can write an equation to show the sum is equivalent to 1.**

$$\frac{3}{10} + \frac{3}{10} + \frac{4}{10} = \frac{10}{10}$$

$\frac{10}{10} = 1$, so my fractions work.

▷ **So, here are instructions for any size jar.**

Fill any jar $\frac{3}{10}$ with pink sand, $\frac{3}{10}$ with purple sand and $\frac{4}{10}$ with yellow sand.

Try ▶ Another Approach

There are many ways to solve problems. Think about how you might solve the Sand Jars problem in a different way.

Sand Jars

Luna made these notes after she made a sand art design in a 2-cup jar.

> · I used a glass jar that holds 2 cups.
> · I used less than 1 cup of yellow sand.
> · I filled less than 0.4 of the jar with pink sand.
> · I filled more than 0.2 of the jar with purple sand.

Luna wants to write specific instructions for making the same kind of design that would work for a jar of any size.

• Find fractions or decimals to tell exactly what part of each jar to fill with pink, purple, and yellow sand.

• Write instructions using those numbers.

▶ Plan It Answer these questions to help you start thinking about a plan.

A. The example solution showed how to write all the amounts as fractions. How you could write all of the amounts as decimals? Explain and show.

_____

_____

_____

B. There is more than one possible solution for this task. Look back at the problem. How you can tell that a different solution is possible? Explain.

_____

_____

_____

Solve It Find a different solution for the Sand Jars problem.
Show all your work on a separate sheet of paper.

You may want to use the problem-solving tips to get started.

Problem-Solving Tips

- **Models**

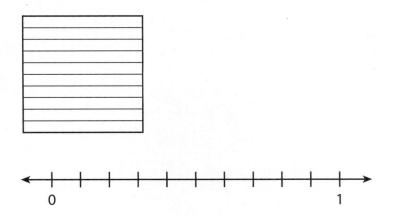

**Problem-Solving
Checklist**

Make sure that you . . .

☐ tell what you know.

☐ tell what you need
   to do.

☐ show all your work.

☐ show that the
   solution works.

- **Word Bank**

fraction	greater than	whole
decimal	less than	equivalent

- **Sentence Starters**

  • I can write fractions as _____

  • _____ is less than _____

Reflect
Use Process Standards As you work through the problem,
discuss these questions with a partner.

• **Use Structure** How can you use the relationship between fractions
  and decimals to solve the problem?

• **Use Repeated Reasoning** Can you think of problems that you have solved
  before that could help you solve this problem? Explain.

Discuss **Models and Strategies**

Read the problem. Write a solution on a separate sheet of paper.
Remember, there are lots of ways to solve a problem!

Coin Purses

Luna wants to make and sell small coin purses with gold braid around the perimeter. She will show a sample of each of the two styles at a craft fair. If people like them, she will make more.

Here are Luna's notes about the two styles.

Square style:

all sides are $2\frac{1}{2}$ inches

Rectangle style:

sides are $3\frac{1}{4}$ inches and $2\frac{1}{4}$ inches

Note: I will have to cut pieces of braid to fit, but I won't put together two small pieces for one side.

Length (inches)	Cost (dollars)
2	$2
4	$4
6	$6
8	$8
10	$10
12	$11
20	$17

Luna needs to buy enough gold braid to make one sample purse for each design. She wants to spend as little as possible.

How can Luna use this price chart to decide what lengths of gold braid to buy?

Plan It and Solve It Find a solution for Luna's Coin Purses problem.

Write a detailed plan and support your answer. Be sure to include:

- a diagram.
- the lengths of gold braid Luna should buy.
- how you used the cost to help make your decision.

You may want to use the problem-solving tips to get started.

Problem-Solving Tips

- ### Questions
  - What are some steps that I might take to solve the problem?
  - What step should I do first? Why?

- ### Word Bank

length	rectangle	whole
cost	square	perimeter

- ### Sentence Starters

  - The lengths of gold braid needed for each design is _____

  - The total length of gold braid is _____

  - The perimeter of the square is _____

  - I can add _____

Reflect

Use Process Standards As you work through the problem, discuss these questions with a partner.

- **Make Sense of Problems** How can you decide what to do first?

- **Make an Argument** What can you do to support your plan to show that it makes sense?

Read the problems. Write a solution on a separate sheet of paper. Remember, there are many different ways to solve a problem!

Hair Ribbons

Luna is teaching 3 friends how to make hair ribbons. She plans to use leftover ribbons from another project. She will share the ribbon between the 3 friends so they all get the same total length of ribbon. Luna's notes and the lengths of the pieces of ribbon she has are shown below.

- Cut the ribbons so each friend gets the same total length.
- Cut the pieces to be as long as possible.
- It doesn't matter how many pieces of ribbon each friend receives.
- It doesn't matter what color ribbon each friend receives.
- There are $4\frac{3}{4}$ feet of the blue ribbon, $6\frac{1}{4}$ feet of the purple ribbon, and 10 feet of the green ribbon.

How should Luna cut the ribbons?

▶ **Solve It** **Suggest a way that Luna could cut the ribbons so that each friend gets the same total length.**

Tell the number of pieces of ribbon each friend gets and the length of each piece. Explain how you got your answer, and how you made your decision.

▶ **Reflect**

Use Process Standards After you complete the task, choose one of these questions to discuss with a partner.

- **Persevere** Did you try approaching the task in different ways before deciding on a plan? Explain.

- **Real-Life Problems** Did you think about a real-life situation that is like this problem? Describe it.

Sports Picture Frame

Luna is designing a sports picture frame. Below are her instructions.

- Paint 6 craft sticks . Each stick is $\frac{3}{4}$ inch wide and $5\frac{3}{4}$ inches long.

- Glue the craft sticks side-by-side on a piece of cardboard.

- Glue a photograph $2\frac{1}{4}$ inches wide and $2\frac{1}{4}$ inches tall on the frame.

- Leave a space at least $2\frac{2}{4}$ inches wide to the right of the photo. Put your decorations here.

- There needs to be at least $\frac{2}{4}$ inch of space above and below the photo.

Will Luna's plan work?

▶ ## Solve It Help Luna design the picture frame.

- Copy the outline of the frame at the right and fill in all the measurements.

- Show and explain why your measurements work.

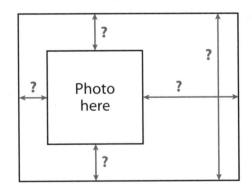

▶ ## Reflect

Use Process Standards After you complete the task, choose one of these questions to discuss with a partner.

- **Use a Model** How did the frame outline help you solve the problem?

- **Make an Argument** How did you show that your measurements work?

Solve the problems.

1 There are 6 plates on a table. Each plate has $\frac{1}{2}$ of an apple on it. Which equation does NOT show how many whole apples there are altogether?

A $6 \times \frac{1}{2} = 3$

B $6 \times \frac{1}{2} = \frac{6}{2}$

C $\frac{1}{2} \times 6 = \frac{3}{1}$

D $\frac{1}{2} \times 6 = \frac{3}{6}$

2 Which improper fraction is equivalent to $3\frac{5}{8}$?

A $\frac{29}{8}$

B $\frac{29}{5}$

C $\frac{24}{8}$

D $\frac{8}{5}$

3 Three sections of a fence need to be painted. Each section of the fence is made of 4 equal-sized boards. Alex paints $\frac{1}{6}$ of the fence. Bobby paints twice as much as Alex. Charles paints only 1 board. David paints the rest.

Who paints the largest part of the fence? _____

What fraction of the fence did he paint? _____

4 Emily made this table to show the number of pets owned by each of the 12 students in her dance class.

Student	A	B	C	D	E	F	G	H	I	J	K	L
Number of Pets	3	1	2	0	3	1	4	5	1	8	4	3

What fraction of the students own 3 or more pets? _____

5 Three points are labeled with fractions on the number line below. Label these three points with decimals.

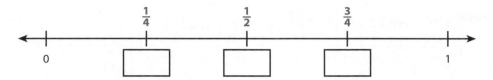

$\frac{1}{4}$ $\frac{1}{2}$ $\frac{3}{4}$

0   [ ]   [ ]   [ ]   1

6 Three people are kayaking. They started at the same point and rowed in the same direction for 20 minutes. Laura rowed $\frac{7}{8}$ mile. Daniel rowed $\frac{1}{2}$ mile. Annabelle rowed $\frac{1}{4}$ mile.

Draw a line from each person to show the distance he or she rowed.

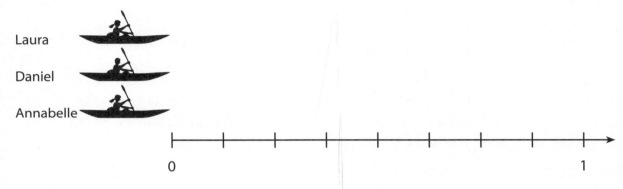

Laura

Daniel

Annabelle

0   1

Use <, >, or = to compare the combined distance Daniel and Annabelle rowed to the distance Laura rowed. _____

7 Jake and Sara each bought a carton of eggs. Some of the eggs were broken and some were not. How many broken eggs did Sara have?

Jake's carton has a total of 6 eggs and exactly 2 broken eggs.

Sara's carton has a total of 18 eggs and exactly _____ broken eggs.

Sara had the same fraction of broken eggs in her carton as Jake had in his carton. In the space below, draw pictures of the eggs in Jake's carton and the eggs in Sara's carton. Write the fraction of broken and unbroken eggs in each carton.

Performance Task

Answer the questions and show all your work on separate paper.

The fourth-grade classes in Hannah's school are making a quilt as a gift to the senior center in their community. The quilt is going to be made up of squares that students and teachers design and sew. The final quilt will be 8 squares by 12 squares.

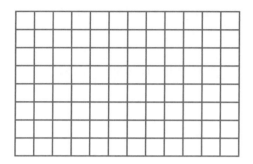

Checklist

Did you . . .

☐ use complete sentences in your explanation?

☐ draw a diagram?

☐ check that your plan makes sense?

24 of the squares will be made by teachers and will be white. The students will make the remaining squares. Each class has chosen a different color for their squares. Below is Hannah's plan for dividing the work.

- $\frac{1}{4}$ of the student squares will be made by the red class.

- $\frac{1}{3}$ of the student squares will be made by the blue class.

- $\frac{2}{3}$ of the student squares will be made by the green class.

- $\frac{1}{4}$ of the student squares will be made by the yellow class.

Hannah's teacher says Hannah's plan won't work. Explain what is wrong with Hannah's plan. Make a better plan and describe it using fractions as well as a diagram.

Reflect

Use Process Standards After you complete the task, choose one of the following questions to answer.

- **Reason Mathematically** What information did you need to find before deciding how to split up the student squares?

- **Argue and Critique** There are 5 groups making squares for this quilt: teachers and four classes. Could Hannah divide the work so that each group makes $\frac{1}{5}$ of the total number of squares? Explain your answer.

Unit 5
Measurement and Data Analysis

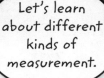

Let's learn about different kinds of measurement.

Real-World Connection A box seems like a pretty simple object. But what if you're building a sandbox? You need to know the lengths of all the sides. Before buying sand, you need to find out how much sand your box will hold. If you plan to carry the sand home from the store, you need to know how much each bag weighs and how many bags you can carry.

In This Unit You will use different measurements: length, weight, volume, area, and angle measure. You will practice ways of representing the same measurement. By the end of this unit, maybe you'll know enough about measurement to build a sandbox!

✓ Self Check

Before starting this unit, check off the skills you know below. As you complete each lesson, see how many more skills you can check off!

I can:	Before this unit	After this unit
convert units of length, weight, liquid volume, and time, for example: 5 feet = 60 inches.	☐	☐
solve word problems about time, money, distances, liquid volumes, and masses, for example: 4 L of juice + 300 mL of juice = 4,300 mL of juice.	☐	☐
use the area formula for rectangles, for example: $A = 9 \times 3$ for a rectangle with a length of 9 feet and a width of 3 feet.	☐	☐
use the perimeter formula for rectangles, for example: $P = (2 \times 12) + (2 \times 5)$ for a rectangle with a length of 12 feet and a width of 5 feet.	☐	☐
understand and use line plots and circle graphs.	☐	☐
collect and represent data.	☐	☐
measure angles using a protractor, for example: an angle on a stop sign is 135°.	☐	☐
solve addition and subtraction problems with angles, for example: 165° − 23° = 142°.	☐	☐

Lesson 23   👥 Introduction
Convert Measurements

🅖 Use What You Know

You have used basic units of measure like hours and minutes. Now you will learn how to express the same measurement using different units to solve problems. Take a look at this problem.

> Lydia heard the announcer on TV say, "We'll be back in 240 seconds." It takes Lydia 5 minutes to wash the dishes. Does Lydia have enough time to wash dishes during the commercial break?
>
>
>
> 1 minute = 60 seconds

a. Why can't you compare 5 minutes and 240 seconds without making some kind of change? _____

b. There are 60 seconds in each minute.

How many seconds are in 2 minutes? _____

In 3 minutes? _____

c. How many seconds does it take Lydia to do the dishes? Show how to add or multiply to find the answer.

_____

d. Is this more or less than the time the commercial takes?

_____

e. Does Lydia have enough time to wash the dishes during the commercial? _____

▶▶ Find Out More

On the previous page, you used the fact that there are 60 seconds in 1 minute to find that there are 300 seconds in 5 minutes.

When you compare seconds and minutes, seconds are the smaller unit and minutes are the larger unit. You can multiply to **convert** from a larger unit to a smaller unit within the same system of measurement. You just need to know how many smaller units make up one of the larger units.

The bar model below shows that there are 60 seconds in 1 minute.

5 minutes

1 minute	1 minute	1 minute	1 minute	1 minute
60 seconds	60 seconds	60 seconds	60 seconds	60 seconds

300 seconds

It also shows that 5 groups of 1 minute equals 5 groups of 60 seconds. So, the number of seconds in 5 minutes is 5×60 seconds, or 300 seconds. You can use a model like the one above to show the relationship between any pair of larger and smaller units in the same measurement system.

▶ Reflect

1 The bar model below shows there are 60 minutes in 1 hour.

1 hour	1 hour	1 hour	1 hour
60 minutes	60 minutes	60 minutes	60 minutes

Explain why you would multiply 60 by 4 to find how many minutes are in 4 hours.

_____

_____

_____

Learn About ▶ **Converting Units of Weight and Mass**

Read the problem below. Then explore different ways to convert from a larger unit to a smaller unit.

> Wanda is shopping for a pet carrier for her cat. One small carrier can hold 240 ounces. Her cat weighs 12 pounds. Can the carrier hold her cat?

▶ **Model It** **You can use a bar model to convert from a larger unit to a smaller unit.**

The bar model shows that there are 16 ounces in 1 pound.

12 pounds (lb)

1 lb	1 lb	1 lb	1 lb	1 lb	1 lb	1 lb	1 lb	1 lb	1 lb	1 lb	1 lb
16 oz	16 oz	16 oz	16 oz	16 oz	16 oz	16 oz	16 oz	16 oz	16 oz	16 oz	16 oz

192 ounces (oz)

Find the number of ounces in 12 pounds: $12 \times 16 = 192$.

▶ **Model It** **You can use a table to convert from a larger unit to a smaller unit.**

This table shows how many ounces are in different numbers of pounds.

Pounds (lb)	1	2	3	4	5	6	7	8	9	10	11	12
Ounces (oz)	16	32	48	64	80	96	112	128	144	160	176	192

The number of ounces in each column is equal to the number of pounds multiplied by 16.

Connect It Now you will solve the problem from the previous page by writing an expression.

2 The bar model shows that 1 pound equals how many ounces? _____

3 What do you multiply the number of pounds by to find the number of ounces?

_____

4 Write an expression that shows how to convert any number of pounds to ounces. Use P to stand for the number of pounds. _____

5 Use the expression to solve the problem from the previous page. Can the carrier hold the cat? Show your work. _____

_____

_____

6 Describe how to convert from a larger unit to a smaller unit.

_____

_____

_____

_____

Try It Use what you just learned to solve these problems. Show your work on a separate sheet of paper.

7 Steve buys 14 ounces of kiwis and 2 pounds of peaches. How many more ounces do the peaches weigh than the kiwis? _____

8 An empty suitcase has a mass of 2 kilograms. Draw a bar model to find its mass in grams. (1 kilogram = 1,000 grams) _____

Learn About ▶ Converting Units of Liquid Volume

Read the problem below. Then explore different ways to convert from a larger unit to a smaller unit of liquid volume.

> Julie made 4 liters of orange juice. How many milliliters of orange juice did Julie make?

▶ **Picture It** **You can use a picture to help convert from a larger unit to a smaller unit of liquid volume.**

Each beaker shows that 1 liter (L) is equal to 1,000 milliliters (mL).

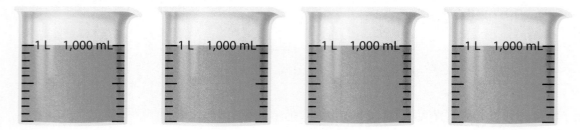

—1 L   1,000 mL—   —1 L   1,000 mL—   —1 L   1,000 mL—   —1 L   1,000 mL—

4 liters is equal to 4,000 milliliters.

▶ **Model It** **You can use a table to help convert from a larger unit to a smaller unit of liquid volume.**

The table below shows there are 1,000 milliliters in one liter. It also shows how many milliliters are in 2, 3, 4, and 5 liters.

Liters (L)	1	2	3	4	5
Milliliters (mL)	1,000	2,000	3,000	4,000	5,000

4 liters = 4,000 milliliters

Connect It Now you will solve the problem from the previous page using an equation.

9 Look at the picture of the beakers. How many milliliters are in 1 liter? _____

10 Look at the number pairs in each column of the table. Each number of milliliters is how many times the number of liters?

_____

Write an equation to describe the relationship between each pair of numbers in the table. _____

11 Use the equation to find the number of milliliters in 4 liters. _____

_____

How many milliliters of orange juice did Julie make? _____

12 Explain why the number of milliliters is always greater than the number of liters for each number pair in the table.

_____

_____

_____

_____

Try It Use what you just learned to solve these problems. Show your work on a separate sheet of paper.

13 Awan bought 3 liters of apple juice. He plans to drink all of it in 6 days, drinking the same amount each day. How many milliliters will Awan drink each day?

_____

14 Aliya made 8 quarts of punch for a party. Make a table or write an equation to find the number of cups of punch she has. (1 quart = 4 cups) _____

_____

Practice ▸ **Converting Measurements**

Study the example below. Then solve problems 15–17.

Example

A shed is 5 meters long. How many centimeters long is the shed?

Look at how you could show your work using a picture and an expression.

Think: 5 meters = ? centimeters

The drawing of a meter stick shows that 100 centimeters is equal to 1 meter.

0 cm   10   20   30   40   50   60   70   80   90   100
                                                    1 m

$100 \times m$
$100 \times 5 = 500$

Solution <u>500 centimeters</u>

The student substituted 5 for m: $100 \times 5 = 500$.

Pair/Share
How else could you solve this problem?

---

15 A bag of potatoes weighs 5 pounds. The bag is placed on a scale. The unit on the scale is ounces. What weight does the scale show?

Show your work.

There are 16 ounces in 1 pound.

Solution _____

Two pounds of potatoes are taken out of the bag. What weight does the scale show now?

Show your work.

Pair/Share
How could you use a table to solve this problem?

Solution _____

©Curriculum Associates, LLC   Copying is not permitted.

16 It took Miguel 7 minutes 38 seconds to run one mile. It took Jorja 9 minutes 13 seconds to run one mile. How many more seconds did it take Jorja to run one mile than Miguel?

Show your work.

There are 60 seconds in 1 minute.

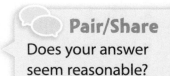

Pair/Share
Does your answer seem reasonable?

Solution _____

---

17 Aaron is 63 inches tall. In order to ride a roller coaster at an amusement park, a person must be 5 feet tall. Is Aaron tall enough to ride a roller coaster? How many inches shorter or taller is he than 5 feet? Circle the letter of the correct answer.

Remember there are 12 inches in 1 foot.

A Yes. He is 3 inches taller than 5 feet.

B Yes. He is 13 inches taller than 5 feet.

C No. He is 7 inches shorter than 5 feet.

D No. He is 17 inches shorter than 5 feet.

Tina chose **A** as the correct answer. How did she get that answer?

_____

_____

_____

Pair/Share
How can you check your answer?

_____

Practice ▶ **Converting Measurements**

Solve the problems.

1 Ming bought a watermelon with a mass of 6 kilograms. She cut off the rind. The remaining watermelon had a mass of 2,500 grams. What was the mass of the rind? (1 kilogram = 1,000 grams)

A 15,000 grams   **C** 3,500 grams

B 4,500 grams   **D** 500 grams

2 Choose *Yes* or *No* to indicate whether the measurement is equal to 2 yards, 1 foot.

a. 4 feet   ☐ Yes   ☐ No   (1 yard = 3 feet and

b. 84 inches   ☐ Yes   ☐ No   1 foot = 12 inches)

c. $2\frac{1}{3}$ yards   ☐ Yes   ☐ No

d. 1 yard, 2 feet, 24 inches   ☐ Yes   ☐ No

3 Suzie is measuring furniture for her bedroom, but she doesn't have a tape measure. Instead, she uses her book. She knows that her book is 8 inches long, as shown below.

|←8 inches→|

The table below shows the total number of book lengths that Suzie used to measure each object. Complete the table.

Object	Number of Book Lengths	Number of Inches
Bed	$10\frac{1}{2}$	
Dresser	6	
Bookcase	4	

4 Ramon has an 8-liter jug of water. He fills nine 750-milliliter pitchers with water. How much water is left? (1 liter = 1,000 milliliters)

A 250 mL

B 500 mL

C 1,000 mL

D 1,250 mL

5 Simone jogged 5 kilometers. How many meters did she jog?
(1 kilometer = 1,000 meters)

Show your work.

Answer Simone jogged _____ meters.

6 It took Sophia 1 hour to finish her homework. How many minutes did it take Sophia to finish her homework? How many seconds did it take her?
(1 hour = 60 minutes and 1 minute = 60 seconds)

Show your work.

Answer It took Sophia _____ minutes to complete her homework.

It took Sophia _____ seconds to complete her homework.

✓ **Self Check** **Go back and see what you can check off on the Self Check on page 265.**

4.M.3

🔄 Use What You Know

You have learned how to convert measurements to solve multi-step problems. Now you will solve multi-step problems involving time and money conversions. Take a look at this problem.

> Last week, Shing did chores for 3 hours and 15 minutes on Monday, 35 minutes on Wednesday, and 20 minutes on Saturday. What was the total number of minutes Shing did chores?

a. What do you need to do to solve the problem? _____

_____

b. Are all the times given in minutes only? Explain. _____

_____

c. How can you convert 3 hours to minutes? _____

_____

d. For the time that Shing did chores on Monday, convert hours to minutes and add the remaining minutes. How many minutes did Shing do chores on Monday? Show your work.

_____

_____

e. Show how to find the total number of minutes Shing did chores last week.

_____

_____

>> Find Out More

Math problems sometimes have multiple steps, like the problem with Shing's chores. If measurements are given in two different units, one of the steps is to convert units so the units are all the same.

Shing did chores for 3 hours and 15 minutes, 35 minutes, and 20 minutes. To find the total number of minutes, convert 3 hours to minutes before adding.

Hours	Minutes
1	60
2	120
3	180

Now you can add to find the total number of minutes Shing did chores.

(180 + 15) + 35 + 20 = 250 minutes

You solve real-life problems involving multiple steps and conversions in other ways. One way is to use a visual model like a number line. Below shows how you can use a number line to show Shing's times together to find the total.

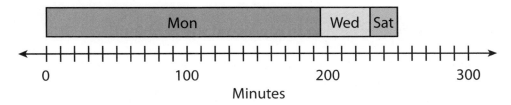

▶ Reflect

1 Explain why you need to know how to convert measurements in order to solve real-world measurement problems.

_____

_____

_____

_____

Learn About ▶ **Solving Problems About Time**

Read the problem below. Then explore different ways to solve time problems.

> Lucy has 2 hours to run errands. She has spent 15 minutes going to the post office and 45 minutes going to the grocery store. She has also spent 40 minutes going to get a haircut. How much time does Lucy have left to get her car washed?

▶ **Model It** **You can use a bar model to solve time problems.**

Since the errand times are in minutes, convert 2 hours to minutes.

2×60 minutes = 120 minutes

2 hours = 120 minutes			
15 minutes Post Office	45 minutes Grocery Store	40 minutes Haircut	? minutes Car Wash

▶ **Model It** **You can use a number line to represent the problem.**

You can count backward from the total amount of time Lucy has to run all her errands. First, convert 2 hours to minutes: 2×60 minutes = 120 minutes.

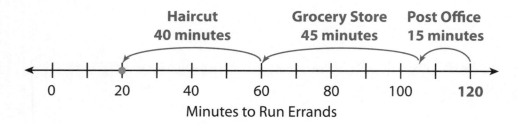

Connect It Now you will solve the problem on the previous page using time conversions and equations.

2 How much time, in minutes, does Lucy have to do all her errands?

_____

3 How can you find the total amount of time Lucy spent going to the post office, grocery store, and hair salon? _____

Write an equation to show this amount. _____

4 Write and solve an equation with an unknown to find the amount of time Lucy has left to get her car washed. _____

_____

5 How do you subtract 42 minutes from 1 hour 25 minutes? Explain what to do and why you do it. _____

_____

Try It Use what you just learned to solve these problems. Show your work on a separate piece of paper.

6 Chen spent 7 hours at school on Friday. He spent 30 minutes at lunch, 50 minutes at a school assembly, and the rest of the time in class. How much time did Chen spend in class? _____

7 Katrina took 3 minutes to get to her classroom after the bell rang. The table shows what she did along the way. How much time did she spend getting books from her locker? _____

Activity	Time
walk to locker	48 seconds
get books from locker	?
walk from locker to classroom	35 seconds

Learn About ▶ **Solving Problems About Money**

Read the problem below. Then explore different ways to solve money problems.

> Prim bought 3 muffins at the school bake sale. Each muffin cost $0.75. She also bought a cookie for $0.50. Prim gave Mr. Hall a $5.00 bill. How much change did she get?

▶ **Picture It** **You can use bills and coins to help solve money problems.**

Show the amount Prim spent using quarters. 1 quarter = $0.25

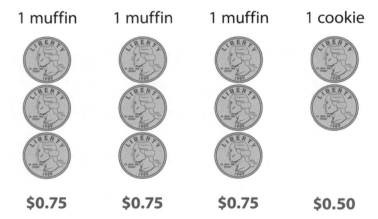

1 muffin	1 muffin	1 muffin	1 cookie
$0.75	$0.75	$0.75	$0.50

Show the amount Prim gave Mr. Hall in bills and quarters. There are 4 quarters in 1 dollar. Prim spent **11 quarters**.

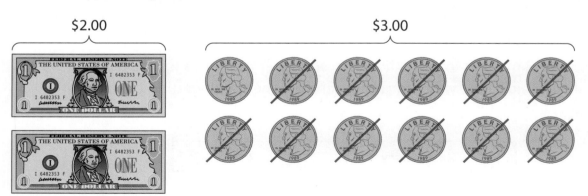

$2.00 $3.00

The amount that is not crossed out is the change that Prim got.

Connect It Now you will solve the problem on the previous page using money conversions and equations.

8 The money Prim used to pay is in dollars. The prices are in cents. Which is the larger unit? _____

9 Explain how you can convert $5.00 to cents.

_____

How many cents are in $5.00? _____

10 Each muffin cost $0.75, or 75 cents. The cookie cost $0.50, or 50 cents. Fill in the blanks to find how many cents Prim spent on 3 muffins and 1 cookie.

3 × _____ cents + _____ cents = _____ cents

11 Show how to find how many cents Prim got for change. _____

12 You have found Prim's change in cents. Explain how to find this amount in dollars and cents. _____

_____

_____

_____

Try It Use what you just learned to solve these problems. Show your work on a separate sheet of paper.

13 One pound of nuts costs $2.80. Aaron bought 2 pounds of nuts. He gave the clerk a $10.00 bill. How much change did he get? _____

14 Keisha bought 4 books and 2 bookmarks at the library book sale. Each book cost $2.50. Each bookmark cost $1.95. Keisha paid with a $20.00 bill. How much change did she get? _____

Practice ▶ **Solving Time and Money Problems**

Study the example below. Then solve problems 15–17.

Example

Marcel bought 4 DVDs. Each DVD cost $19.50, including tax. He has a coupon for $5.00 off the total cost. Marcel gave the clerk a $100.00 bill. How much change will he get?

Look at how you could show your work using words and numbers.

amount spent on DVDs: 4 × $19.50 = $78.00

amount spent after using coupon: $78.00 − $5.00 = $73.00

amount received in change: $100.00 − $73.00 = $27.00

Solution _Marcel will get $27.00._

What operation did the student use to represent the coupon for $5.00 off the total cost?

Pair/Share
How could you work backward to solve this problem?

---

15 It took Otis 6 hours to travel to the Grand Canyon. Along the way he took 18 minutes to get gasoline and 53 minutes to eat. How much time did Otis spend driving?

Show your work.

How many minutes are in one hour?

Pair/Share
How could you use a number line to solve this problem?

Solution _____

▷▷ Find Out More

Measurement problems can include many different units. If the units in the problem are different, you must convert at least one of the measurements so that all units are the same.

The problem on the previous page includes measurements in both inches and feet. To solve the problem, start by converting feet to inches.

To write $3\frac{1}{2}$ feet in inches, start by writing $3\frac{1}{2}$ feet as 3 feet $+ \frac{1}{2}$ foot.

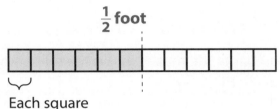

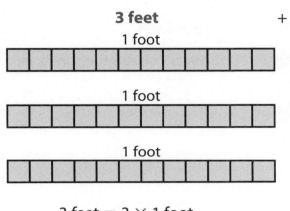

3 feet + $\frac{1}{2}$ **foot**

1 foot

1 foot

1 foot

Each square
is 1 inch.

$$3 \text{ feet} = 3 \times 1 \text{ foot}$$
$$= 3 \times 12 \text{ inches}$$
$$= \textbf{36 inches}$$

$$\frac{1}{2} \text{ foot} = \frac{1}{2} \times 1 \text{ foot}$$
$$= \frac{1}{2} \times 12 \text{ inches}$$
$$= \textbf{6 inches}$$

$3\frac{1}{2}$ feet $= \textbf{36 inches} + \textbf{6 inches} = 42$ inches

Now the only units in the problem are inches, so you can solve the problem.

▶ Reflect

1 Explain why it is important to look at the units for the measurements in a problem before you start to solve the problem.

_____

_____

_____

_____

Learn About ▷ Solving Length Problems

Read the problem below. Then explore different ways to solve length problems.

> Cindy buys a party sandwich that is 5 feet long. Her brother cuts off a piece of the sandwich that is $\frac{3}{4}$ foot long. Cindy wants to cut the remaining sandwich into 3-inch pieces to share with guests. How many pieces can she make?

▶ **Model It** **You can use a model to help solve length problems.**

The top bar of the model shows the full sandwich. The bottom bar shows the sandwich with $\frac{3}{4}$ **foot cut off** and the rest of the sandwich left to be shared.

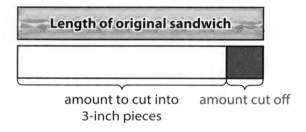

amount to cut into   amount cut off
3-inch pieces

▶ **Model It** **You can use a number line to solve length problems.**

The number line shows the length of the sandwich, 5 feet. Each foot is divided into four 3-inch sections.

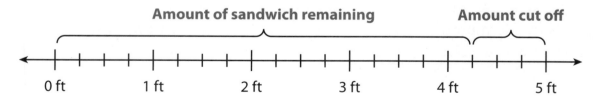

Amount of sandwich remaining   **Amount cut off**

0 ft   1 ft   2 ft   3 ft   4 ft   5 ft

Connect It Now you will use the number line to solve the problem from the previous page.

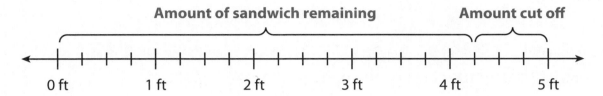

Amount of sandwich remaining   Amount cut off

0 ft   1 ft   2 ft   3 ft   4 ft   5 ft

2 Use the number line to find the length of the sandwich that is left. _____

3 How many inches are in 4 feet? _____

How many inches are in $\frac{1}{4}$ foot? _____

4 How many inches long is the sandwich that is left? _____

How many 3-inch pieces can be made from that? Write an equation to represent the problem. _____

Try It Use what you just learned to solve these problems. Show your work on a separate sheet of paper.

5 Cathy has 10 feet of ribbon that she wants to use to make bows. She needs $\frac{2}{3}$ foot of ribbon for each bow. She also needs to use 16 inches of the ribbon for another project. How many bows will she be able to make with the amount of ribbon that is left? (Remember, there are 12 inches in 1 foot.) _____

6 Tom is playing football. He carries the ball forward $7\frac{1}{3}$ yards and then goes backward 2 feet. How far forward did Tom carry the ball, in feet, after these two plays? (Remember, there are 3 feet in 1 yard.) _____

Learn About ▶ Solving Liquid Volume Problems

Read the problem below. Then explore different ways to solve liquid volume problems.

> Marco, Javier, and Jim are going to a party. Marco brings $1\frac{1}{2}$ liters of lemonade, Javier brings a 2-liter bottle of lemonade, and Jim brings 450 milliliters of lemonade. How many milliliters of lemonade will the boys bring to the party in all?

▶ **Picture It** **You can use a picture to help solve liquid volume problems.**

Think about the size of each measurement.

| $1\frac{1}{2}$ liters | 2 liters | 450 milliliters |

▶ **Model It** **You can use a model to help solve liquid volume problems.**

The bar model shows the measurements from the problem combined.

1 liter = 1,000 milliliters and $\frac{1}{2}$ liter = 500 milliliters

$1\frac{1}{2}$ liters	2 liters	450 milliliters

↓　　　　　↓　　　　　↓

1,500 milliliters	2,000 milliliters	450 milliliters

Connect It Now you will solve the problem from the previous page using models and equations.

7 Use the amounts given in the problem to write an equation that shows the total amount of lemonade, *T*, the boys bring to the party. _____

_____

8 What units are included in the equation? Which measurements will you convert so that all use the same unit? Explain. _____

_____

_____

9 Show how to find how many milliliters there are in $1\frac{1}{2}$ liters.

_____

_____

10 Show how to find how many milliliters there are in 2 liters.

_____

11 What is the total amount of lemonade the three boys brought to the party? Explain how you got your answer. _____

_____

_____

Try It Use what you just learned to solve these problems. **Show your work on a separate sheet of paper.**

12 Joanne is making punch. She uses $\frac{1}{2}$ gallon of orange juice, 3 quarts of lemonade, and $1\frac{1}{4}$ gallons of apple cider. How many quarts of punch will she have all together? (4 quarts = 1 gallon) _____

13 Matt has $4\frac{3}{4}$ cups of milk. He drinks 10 fluid ounces of it. How many fluid ounces of milk does Matt have left? (8 fluid ounces = 1 cup) _____

Learn About ▶ Solving Weight and Mass Problems

Read the problem below. Then explore different ways to solve mass and weight problems.

> Kyle has a jar filled with state quarters. He knows when the jar is empty it has a mass of 900 grams, but when it is filled with quarters it has a mass of 2 kilograms. If each quarter has a mass of about 5 grams, about how many quarters are in the jar?

▶ **Picture It** You can use a picture to help solve mass and weight problems.

| 5 grams | 900 grams | 2 kilograms |

▶ **Model It** You can use a model to help solve mass and weight problems.

2 kilograms

| Mass of Quarters
5n | Mass of Empty Jar
900 grams |

Use *n* to represent the number of quarters.

Mass of 1 quarter is 5 grams

Remember that 1 kilogram is equal to 1,000 grams.

Connect It Now you will solve the problem from the previous page using equations.

14 Remember that all the units need to be the same in order to add or subtract them.

The mass of the empty jar is _____ grams.

The total mass of the filled jar is _____ kilograms or _____ grams.

15 Write an equation to show that the mass of the quarters alone plus the mass of the empty jar equals the mass of the filled jar. _____

16 What is the mass of the quarters alone? _____

17 Write an equation to show that the number of quarters times 5 grams equals the total mass of the quarters. Then solve the equation to tell how many quarters are in the jar. _____

_____

18 Describe the three steps you used to solve this problem.

_____

_____

_____

_____

Try It Use what you just learned to solve these problems. Show your work on a separate sheet of paper.

19 The recipe for a large batch of cookies uses 1 kilogram of flour. Another recipe uses 700 grams of flour. How much flour is needed to make two batches of each recipe? _____

20 A can of nuts weighs 1 pound, 1 ounce. The empty can weighs 3 ounces. If you pour out half the nuts into a bowl, how many ounces of nuts are in the bowl?

(1 pound = 16 ounces) _____

Practice > **Solving Measurement Problems**

Study the example below. Then solve problems 21–23.

Example

Charlie is having a breakfast party. He buys 3 quarts of milk. All 11 people at the breakfast want an 8-fluid ounce glass of milk. Explain if Charlie bought enough milk.

Look at how you could show your work using a picture.

1 quart   =   32 fluid ounces

 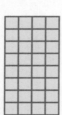

Charlie has 3 quarts, and 3 × 32 = 96.

Each glass holds 8 fluid ounces, and 11 × 8 = 88.

Solution Yes; he has 96 fluid ounces and needs 88 fluid ounces.

Charlie needs to know how many fluid ounces of milk are needed to fill the 11 glasses.

Pair/Share
How else could you solve the problem?

---

21 Mary has $7\frac{1}{4}$ yards of fabric. She cuts off $\frac{3}{4}$ foot of fabric to make the edge even. Mary wants to end up with 3 pieces of fabric that are the same size. How long will each piece be? (1 yard = 3 feet)

Show your work.

Will Mary add, subtract, multiply, or divide to get 3 equal pieces of fabric?

Pair/Share
How did you solve the problem? Why did you choose that method?

Solution _____

22 A wildlife sanctuary has two elephants. One has a weight of 11,028 pounds and the other has a weight of $5\frac{1}{2}$ tons. A platform can hold 22,000 pounds. Can the platform hold both elephants? Explain your reasoning. (1 ton = 2,000 pounds)

Show your work.

Will the combined weight be measured in pounds or tons?

Pair/Share

Did you and your partner solve the problem the same way?

Solution _____

_____

_____

---

23 Jessica is making punch. She mixes 132 ounces of juice and 15 cups of seltzer. How many 6-ounce glasses can she fill? Circle the letter of the correct answer.

There are 8 fluid ounces in 1 cup.

A 20 glasses

B 22 glasses

C 24 glasses with 3 ounces left over

D 42 glasses

Jason chose **C** as the correct answer. How did he get that answer?

_____

_____

_____

Pair/Share

Does Jason's answer make sense?

Practice ▷ **Solving Measurement Problems**

Solve the problems.

1 Joe has $3\frac{1}{4}$ gallons of punch. He adds $1\frac{1}{2}$ quarts of juice to the punch. He drinks $\frac{1}{4}$ quart of punch. Which expression can be used to find the number of quarts of punch Joe has left? (1 gallon = 4 quarts)

A $13 + 1\frac{1}{2} + \frac{1}{4}$

B $13 + 1\frac{1}{2} - \frac{1}{4}$

C $3\frac{1}{4} + 1\frac{1}{2} + \frac{1}{4}$

D $3\frac{1}{4} + 1\frac{1}{2} - \frac{1}{4}$

2 Jean made 5 gallons of lemonade for a picnic. If Jean plans to save $\frac{1}{2}$ gallon for her ride home, how many 8-fluid-ounce glasses of lemonade can she serve at the picnic? (1 gallon = 128 fluid ounces)

A 576

B 88

C 80

D 72

3 Clara had lengths of ribbon in different colors that she used to make bows for a craft fair. Each bow required 6 inches of ribbon. She used all of the ribbon. Complete the table below to show how much ribbon she had in yards and in inches and how many bows of each color she made. (1 yard = 3 feet and 1 foot = 12 inches)

Color of ribbon	Length of ribbon (yards)	Length of ribbon (inches)	Number of bows made
Red	3		
Yellow		54	
Blue			24

4 John is mixing paint for an art project. He combines 4 quarts of white paint with $3\frac{1}{2}$ gallons of blue paint. He uses 2 quarts. How much paint does he have left? Circle the letter for all that apply. (1 gallon = 4 quarts)

A 16 quarts

B $5\frac{1}{2}$ gallons

C $5\frac{1}{2}$ quarts

D $2\frac{1}{2}$ gallons

E 4 gallons

5 Nancy is making cookies for a bake sale. She needs a total of 4 pounds of chocolate chips. She has a 28-ounce bag of chocolate chips, but the store now only has 10-ounce bags. How many bags of chocolate chips does Nancy need to buy? (1 pound = 16 ounces)

Show your work.

Solution _____

6 Kelly has $7\frac{1}{4}$ yards of rope. She cuts 3 inches off each end of the rope. Kelly will divide the remaining rope into 5 equal pieces for a craft project. What will be the length of each piece of rope? (1 yard = 36 inches)

Show your work.

Solution _____

 **Self Check** Go back and see what you can check off on the Self Check on page 265.

🔄 Use What You Know

You have learned that you can find the perimeter of a rectangle by adding the lengths of the sides. Take a look at this problem.

Marissa has 64 feet of fencing. She is using the fencing to border a rectangular flower garden. Marissa wants the length of the garden to be 20 feet. If she uses all of the fencing, what will be the width of the rectangular garden?

? feet   20 feet

a. To solve the problem, do you use perimeter or area? Explain how you know.

_____

_____

b. How do you find the perimeter of a rectangle? _____

c. How much fencing is there in all? _____

d. What is the length of the garden? How many sides of this length does the garden have? What is the total length of these sides?_____

e. How much fencing is left to make the other two sides? Explain how to find this length. _____

_____

f. Explain how you can find the length of the other two sides of the rectangle.

_____

_____

▶▶ Find Out More

Rectangles have length and width.

To find the perimeter of a rectangle, you can add the sides in any order.

Perimeter = **length + length + width + width**

Since the opposite sides of a rectangle are the same length, you can rewrite the equation as:

Perimeter = **2 × length + 2 × width**

Use P to stand for perimeter, ℓ to stand for length, and w to stand for width:

$$P = 2 \times \ell + 2 \times w \qquad \text{or} \qquad P = 2\ell + 2w$$

The equation above is called the **perimeter formula**. Here is how to solve the problem from the previous page using the formula.

$$64 = (2 \times 20) + (2 \times w)$$
$$64 = 40 + (2 \times w)$$

Now subtract: $64 - 40 = 24$.

With 24 feet of fencing left, the width of the rectangle must be $24 \div 2$, or 12 feet.

Later in the lesson, you will solve problems about area.

▶ Reflect

1 The perimeter of a rectangular poster is 14 feet and the length is 4 feet. Describe how to use the perimeter formula to find the width. _____

_____

_____

_____

_____

Learn About ⟩ **Solving Perimeter Problems**

Read the problem below. Then explore different ways to solve perimeter problems.

> Keegan is building a rectangular play area in his backyard for his dog. The length of the rectangle is 30 feet and the width is 24 feet. What amount of fence does Keegan need to buy to make the play area?

▶ **Picture It** **You can use models to help solve perimeter problems.**

Draw a picture to represent the fence.

You can use color to highlight the sides that have the same length.

24 ft ☐ 30 ft

Add the lengths to find the amount of fence Keegan needs to buy.

30 feet + 24 feet + 30 feet + 24 feet

▶ **Model It** **You can also use words to help solve perimeter problems.**

In this rectangle, the length is 30 feet and the width is 24 feet.

There are two sides that have a length of 30 feet and two sides that have a length of 24 feet.

amount of fence = **length + length + width + width**
= **30 feet + 30 feet + 24 feet + 24 feet**

Connect It Now you will solve the problem from the previous page using a formula.

2 What formula can you use to find the amount of fence Keegan needs? Why?

_____

_____

3 Use the formula to find the amount of fence Keegan needs for the dog's play area.

_____

_____

4 Keegan uses the formula $P = 2(\ell + w)$ to find the amount of fence he needs. Does Keegan's formula work? Why or why not? _____

_____

5 Which formula do you think is easiest? Why? _____

_____

6 Explain when to use the formula for the perimeter of a rectangle.

_____

_____

_____

Try It Use what you just learned to solve these problems. Show your work on a separate sheet of paper.

7 Bianca is fencing in a garden. She wants the garden to be a rectangle 15 feet by 10 feet. How much fence does she need to buy to make her garden? _____

8 Michael glues pipe cleaners around the edges of a rectangular poster. He uses a total of 14 pipe cleaners with 5 pipe cleaners each on the longer sides of the poster. How many pipe cleaners does he use for each of the shorter sides of the poster?_____

Learn About ▷ Solving Area Problems

Read the problem below. Then explore different ways to solve area problems.

> Kevin is making a rectangular mural using colored tiles. He buys enough tiles to cover an area of 112 square feet. Kevin wants the width of the mural to be 8 feet. If he uses all of the tiles, what is the length of the mural?

▶ **Picture It** You can use a picture to help solve area problems.

Make a sketch of the mural.

```
            ? feet
        ┌──────────────────────┐
        │                      │
8 feet  │   112 square feet    │
        │                      │
        └──────────────────────┘
```

Since you multiply the length and width of a rectangle to find the area, think: $8 \times ? = 112$.

▶ **Model It** You can use words to help understand the problem.

area of the mural = **length** × **width**

The area of the mural is 112 square feet.

It can be covered by 8 rows of units that are each 1 square foot.

The number of square-foot units in each row is the length of the mural.

Connect It Now you will solve the problem on the previous page using a formula.

9 Write an equation to represent the area of the mural.

_____

10 Describe how you can find the length of the mural. _____

_____

_____

11 If Kevin uses all the tiles, what is the length of the mural? _____

12 Kevin notices another package of tiles that makes a mural with an area of 152 square feet. Write an equation that can help you find the length of this mural if it is also 8 feet wide. _____

13 Find the length of the mural Kevin can make with the package of tiles that covers an area of 152 square feet. _____

14 Suppose that you know the length and area of a rectangle. How would you find the width? _____

_____

_____

Try It Use what you just learned to solve these problems. Show your work on a separate sheet of paper.

15 Carla wants to create a garden in her backyard. She wants the width of the garden to be 9 meters and the area to be 162 square meters. What length should she make the garden? _____

16 Bill is building a deck. He wants the length of the deck to be 7 feet. If he wants the area of the deck to be 105 square feet, what will be the width of the deck? _____

Practice Solving Perimeter and Area Problems

Study the example below. Then solve problems 17–19.

Example

Jen drew a rectangle with a length of 12 inches and a width of 10 inches. Then she drew another rectangle by doubling the length and width of the first one. What is the perimeter of the second rectangle?

Look at how you could show your work using a formula for perimeter.

$P = 2(\ell + w)$

length and width of first rectangle: $\ell = 12$ inches and $w = 10$ inches

length and width of second rectangle: $\ell = 12 \times 2$, or 24 inches, and $w = 10 \times 2$, or 20 inches.

Perimeter of second rectangle $= 2(24 + 20)$
$$P = 2 \times 44$$
$$P = 88$$

Solution ___The perimeter of the second rectangle is 88 inches.___

The student uses a formula for perimeter of a rectangle and labels the work to keep it organized.

 Pair/Share
How else could you solve the problem?

---

17 A designer is adding a border around the edge of a rectangular swimming pool. He measures the pool and finds that the length of the pool is 52 meters and the width is 26 meters. How long is the tile border?

Show your work.

Are you looking for the perimeter or the area of the pool?

 Pair/Share
How did you solve the problem? Why did you choose that method?

Solution _____

18 Zachary is getting new carpet in his bedroom. The dimensions of his room are 9 feet by 13 feet. How much carpet does he need to cover the whole floor?

Show your work.

Are you finding the perimeter or the area of the room?

Pair/Share
How do the units in the answer tell whether you found area or perimeter?

Solution _____

---

19 Tricia wants to create a path using pebbles. She has 8 bags of pebbles and each bag covers an area of about 6 square feet. If she wants to make the path 2 feet wide, about how long can she make the path? Circle the letter of the correct answer.

A 3 feet

B 22 feet

C 24 feet

D 48 feet

Tricia chose **A** as the correct answer. How did she get that answer?

How much area can Tricia cover with all the bags of pebbles?

_____

_____

_____

_____

_____

_____

Pair/Share
Does Tricia's answer make sense?

Practice Solving Perimeter and Area Problems

Solve the problems.

1 A playground in the park is rectangular and has a length of 40 feet. The width of the playground is half the length. What is the area of the playground?

A 120 square feet

B 800 square feet

C 1,600 square feet

D 3,200 square feet

2 The diagram shows the garden Mike has next to his garage. He wants to put a fence around the three sides of the garden that do not border the garage. Which expression does NOT represent the amount of fence Mike needs to buy?

A $6 + 21 + 6$

B $2w + \ell$

C $2w + 2\ell$

D $2 \times 6 + 21$

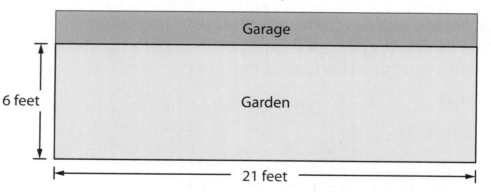

6 feet

Garage

Garden

21 feet

3 Maya is finding the perimeter of the rectangle at the right. Which expression(s) can be used to find the perimeter? Circle the letter for all that apply.

A $(2 \times 16) + (2 \times 12)$

B $2 \times 16 + 12$

C $2(16 + 12)$

D 16×12

E $16 + 12 + 16 + 12$

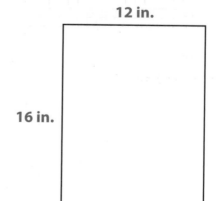

12 in.

16 in.

4 A rectangle is 22 feet long and has a perimeter of 56 feet. What is the width of this rectangle? _____

5 Ms. Leone decides to make a raised garden bed for her backyard. Her plan for the garden bed includes the following:

- It will be in the shape of a rectangle.

- The sides of the bed will use a total of 30 feet of cedar boards.

- Each side will be longer than 1 foot.

- The length and width will measure whole feet.

Part A Use the grid below to draw three different rectangles that can each represent Ms. Leone's garden bed. Be sure to use all 30 feet of the boards for each bed.

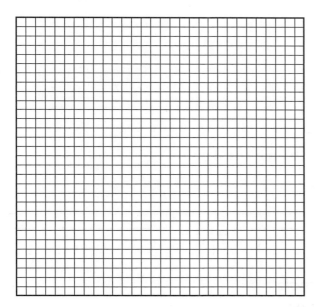

Key
□ = 1 square foot

Part B Write the length and width of each garden bed you drew. Then find the area of each garden bed.

Garden Bed 1:

Length: _____

Width: _____

Area: _____

Garden Bed 2:

Length: _____

Width: _____

Area: _____

Garden Bed 3:

Length: _____

Width: _____

Area: _____

✔ **Self Check** **Go back and see what you can check off on the Self Check on page 265.**

Use What You Know

You already know how to make line plots. Now you will make line plots with fractions and use them to solve problems. Take a look at this problem.

Emma's class has a jar of earthworms in their classroom. The class measures the length of each earthworm and records the data in a line plot. What is the difference between the lengths of the shortest and the longest earthworms?

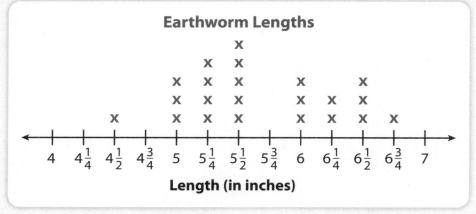

Earthworm Lengths

Length (in inches)

a. What do the numbers below the number line represent?

The numbers below tells the lengths of the Earthworms

b. How do you know which are the longest and shortest earthworms?

You would see the longest lenth out of the whole chat and the shortest length out the whole chat

c. What are the lengths of the longest and shortest earthworms?

longest earthworm _____ $6\frac{3}{4}$ _____ shortest earthworm _____ $4\frac{1}{2}$ _____

d. Explain how to find the difference between the lengths of the shortest and longest earthworms. *you can use greater than and less than.*

▷▷ Find Out More

To find the difference between the lengths of the longest and shortest earthworms on the previous page, you have to subtract $6\frac{3}{4} - 4\frac{1}{2}$. The fractions have different denominators. But, you can write equivalent fractions on the number line so that all the fractions have the same denominator.

The number line is labeled with halves and fourths. You can see that the distance between two whole numbers is divided into 4 equal sections. So, the number line can be labeled with fourths.

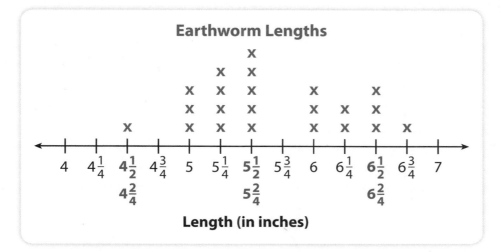

Earthworm Lengths

Length (in inches)

Now you can see that the difference between the lengths of the longest and shortest earthworms is $6\frac{3}{4} - 4\frac{2}{4}$, or $2\frac{1}{4}$ inches.

▶ Reflect

1 Which is the most common length of earthworm in Emma's class? What is the difference between this length of earthworm and the length of the shortest earthworm? Explain how you found your answer.

_____

_____

_____

_____

_____

Learn About ▶ **Representing Data on a Line Plot**

Read the problem below. Then explore different ways to help make a line plot.

The students in Mrs. Holbrook's class are growing plants. One day they measured the heights of the plants in inches. The heights are shown below. Make a line plot to represent the data.

$2\frac{5}{8}$	$2\frac{1}{8}$	$2\frac{3}{8}$	$2\frac{7}{8}$	2	$1\frac{1}{4}$	$1\frac{1}{2}$	$1\frac{7}{8}$	$2\frac{3}{4}$	$1\frac{3}{4}$
$1\frac{5}{8}$	$1\frac{3}{4}$	$1\frac{7}{8}$	$2\frac{1}{8}$	$2\frac{3}{8}$	$2\frac{3}{4}$	$1\frac{7}{8}$	$2\frac{1}{2}$	$1\frac{7}{8}$	$1\frac{5}{8}$

▶ **Model It** **You can count by fractions to help label a number line.**

The fractions in the data are in units of $\frac{1}{2}$, $\frac{1}{4}$, and $\frac{1}{8}$. Use the smallest unit, $\frac{1}{8}$, to label the number line. Divide the number line into 8 equal sections.

Count by eighths:

1 eighth, 2 eighths, 3 eighths, 4 eighths, 5 eighths, 6 eighths, 7 eighths, 8 eighths

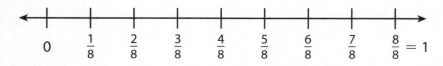

$$0 \qquad \frac{1}{8} \qquad \frac{2}{8} \qquad \frac{3}{8} \qquad \frac{4}{8} \qquad \frac{5}{8} \qquad \frac{6}{8} \qquad \frac{7}{8} \qquad \frac{8}{8}=1$$

▶ **Picture It** **You can use fraction bars to find equivalent fractions.**

$\frac{1}{2}$				$\frac{1}{2}$			
$\frac{1}{4}$		$\frac{1}{4}$		$\frac{1}{4}$		$\frac{1}{4}$	
$\frac{1}{8}$	$\frac{1}{8}$	$\frac{1}{8}$	$\frac{1}{8}$	$\frac{1}{8}$	$\frac{1}{8}$	$\frac{1}{8}$	$\frac{1}{8}$

The fraction bars show that the following fractions are equivalent:

$\frac{1}{2} = \frac{2}{4}$ and $\frac{1}{2} = \frac{4}{8}$

$\frac{1}{4} = \frac{2}{8}$

Connect It Now you will make a line plot to show the plant heights on the previous page.

2 Use *Picture It* to help you write these fractions as eighths.

$$\frac{1}{2} = \frac{\boxed{4}}{8} \qquad \frac{1}{4} = \frac{\boxed{2}}{8} \qquad \frac{3}{4} = \frac{\boxed{6}}{8}$$

3 Label the number line by eighths.

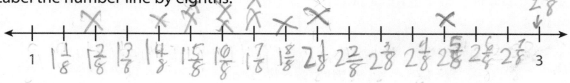

4 Use the number line in problem 3. Make a line plot of the plant heights below. Find equivalent fractions in eighths for data that include halves and fourths.

Plant highs

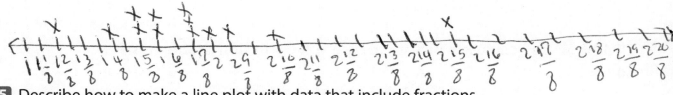

5 Describe how to make a line plot with data that include fractions.

_____

_____

Try It Use what you just learned to solve this problem. Show your work on a separate sheet of paper.

6 Al records the length of some fish in inches: $9\frac{1}{4}$, $10\frac{1}{2}$, $10\frac{5}{8}$, $9\frac{3}{4}$, $9\frac{7}{8}$, 10, $10\frac{1}{8}$, $9\frac{3}{4}$, $10\frac{3}{8}$.

Make a line plot of the data.

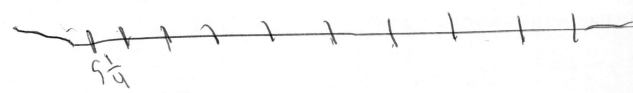

Learn About ▸ **Adding with Line Plots**

Read the problem below. Then explore different ways to solve addition problems with line plots.

Sophia is making a border for a quilt. She wants to use leftover strips of fabric that are all 2 inches wide. She measures the length of each strip and records the information in a line plot. If Sophia puts all the strips together, what will be the total length?

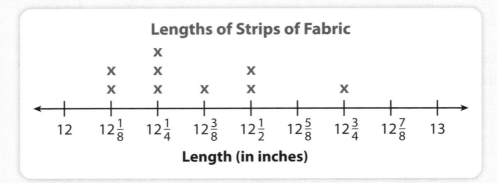

Lengths of Strips of Fabric

Length (in inches)

▸ **Picture It** You can use a picture to help solve addition problems with line plots.

The picture shows the strips of fabric placed next to one another to make one long strip.

$12\frac{1}{8}$	$12\frac{1}{8}$	$12\frac{1}{4}$	$12\frac{1}{4}$	$12\frac{1}{4}$	$12\frac{3}{8}$	$12\frac{1}{2}$	$12\frac{1}{2}$	$12\frac{3}{4}$

▸ **Model It** You can break up the whole numbers and fractions to help you add the lengths.

Add the whole numbers first: $12 + 12 + 12 + 12 + 12 + 12 + 12 + 12 + 12$

Then add the fractions: $\frac{1}{8} + \frac{1}{8} + \frac{1}{4} + \frac{1}{4} + \frac{1}{4} + \frac{3}{8} + \frac{1}{2} + \frac{1}{2} + \frac{3}{4}$

Connect It Now you will solve the problem on the previous page.

7 Write the fractions on the number line in eighths. Why should you do this?

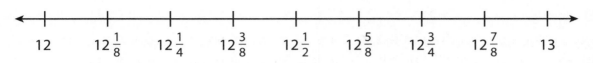

12	$12\frac{1}{8}$	$12\frac{1}{4}$	$12\frac{3}{8}$	$12\frac{1}{2}$	$12\frac{5}{8}$	$12\frac{3}{4}$	$12\frac{7}{8}$	13

_____

_____

8 Write an expression to find the total length if Sophia puts all the strips together. Write each fraction in eighths.

_____

9 What is the sum of the whole numbers? _____ What is the sum of

the fractions? _____ Write the sum of the fractions as a mixed number.

_____ What is the total length of all the strips? _____

10 How do you solve a problem about adding fractions or mixed numbers in a line plot?

_____

_____

_____

_____

Try It Use what you just learned to solve these problems. Use the line plot on the previous page. Show your work on a separate sheet of paper.

11 What is the length of all the $12\frac{1}{2}$-inch strips combined? _____

12 What is the length of all the $12\frac{1}{4}$-inch strips combined? _____

Learn About ▷ **Subtracting with Line Plots**

Read the problem below. Then explore different ways to solve subtraction problems with line plots.

There are many kinds of dragonflies that are different in length. A scientist measured the lengths of different kinds of dragonflies and made a line plot to show the measurements. What is the difference between the lengths of the longest dragonfly and the shortest dragonfly?

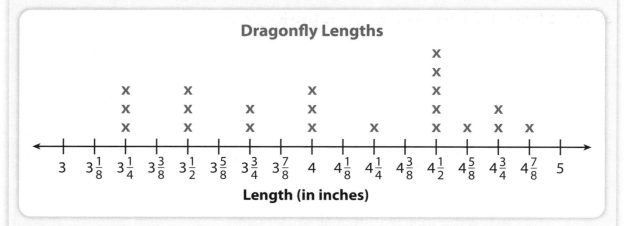

Dragonfly Lengths

Length (in inches)

▶ **Picture It** **You can use a picture to help solve subtraction problems with line plots.**

Length of longest dragonfly: $4\frac{7}{8}$ in.	
Length of shortest dragonfly: $3\frac{1}{4}$ in.	Difference in lengths: ? in.

▶ **Model It** **You can use a number line to solve subtraction problems with line plots.**

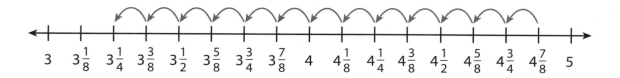

▶▶ Find Out More

Look at the bar graph on the previous page. You can also show the data in a **circle graph**. All the sections of a circle graph together equal one whole. You can quickly compare sections of a circle graph to each other or to the whole to interpret and compare data.

The circle graph at the right shows the data from the previous page. Each section shows the part of the class that picked that fruit.

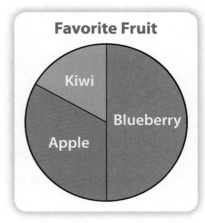

Favorite Fruit

You can describe the data in a circle graph using fractions.

- Look at the section labeled Blueberry in the circle graph. It takes up $\frac{1}{2}$ of the circle. This means that $\frac{1}{2}$ of the class chose blueberries as their favorite fruit.

- Look at the section labeled Apple. It takes up less than $\frac{1}{2}$ of the circle. So less than $\frac{1}{2}$ of the class chose apples as their favorite fruit.

You can also use the circle graph to make comparisions that do not include fractions or numbers.

- The green section is smaller than the red section. That means fewer students chose kiwis than apples.

- The blue section is larger than the red or green sections. So more students chose blueberries than any other fruit.

▶ Reflect

1 Do you think it is easier to tell that $\frac{1}{2}$ of the class chose blueberries as their favorite fruit from the bar graph or from the circle graph? Explain.

_____

_____

_____

Learn About ▶ **Reading Circle Graphs**

Read the problem below. Then explore ways to interpret circle graphs.

The 4th Grade teachers at Hill Elementary School asked their students where they would like to go on a field trip. The results are shown in the circle graph. Which field trip did about $\frac{1}{4}$ of the students choose?

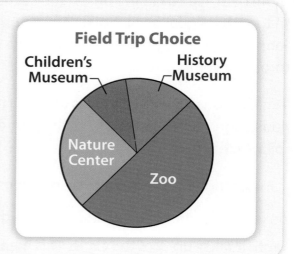

Field Trip Choice

▶ **Picture It** **You can use a picture to help you understand the problem.**

Look for a section that is close to $\frac{1}{4}$ of the circle.

Think about folding a circle into 4 equal sections. Compare the shape of $\frac{1}{4}$ of the circle to the sections of the circle graph.

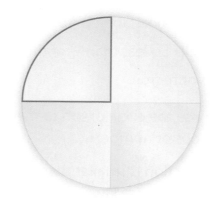

▶ **Picture It** **Use what you know about fractions to draw fourths.**

Divide the circle into fourths by drawing lines.

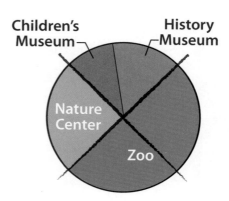

Use the circle graph for problems 4 and 5.

Colors of Cars Sold

4 Mr. Li made a circle graph to show the colors of cars he sold on Saturday.

Complete the following statements so they are true.

- Mr. Li sold more red cars than _____ cars.

- About _____ of cars sold were black.

- The color car that Mr. Li sold the most was _____ .

- Mr. Li sold about the same number of _____ and _____ cars.

5 About what fraction of the cars sold were either blue or gray? Explain.

Show your work.

Answer About _____ of the cars sold were blue or gray.

_____

_____

_____

_____

 **Self Check** Go back and see what you can check off on the Self Check on page 265.

Use What You Know

You already know different ways to represent data. Now you will learn more about collecting data. Take a look at this problem.

> Mrs. Collins observes the types of shoes worn by students in her class. One day, she counts 9 students wearing sneakers, 5 students wearing dress shoes, and 7 students wearing sandals. How can you use a bar graph to see what the most popular type of shoe is?

a. How many different types of shoes are worn by students in the class? Name each

type. _____

b. Represent the data using a bar graph.

c. Explain how to use this bar graph to determine the most popular type of shoe

worn by students in the class. _____

_____

_____

>> Find Out More

Mrs. Collins conducted an **observation** to answer the question, *What is the most popular type of shoe worn by students in the class?* She collected data by observing the shoes her students wore to school on a given day. The results of her observation are shown in the **frequency table**. This table shows how many times each type of shoe was observed.

Shoe	Number of Students
Sneaker	9
Dress Shoe	5
Sandal	7

The data could be used to answer many different questions, such as:

- How many students wear sneakers to school?

- What is the least popular type of shoe worn by students?

- How many more students wear sneakers than sandals?

An observation is one way to collect data. Other ways to collect data include conducting a **survey** or completing an **experiment**.

A survey gathers information by asking people questions. For example, you could survey your classmates by asking them about their favorite fruit.

An experiment is a procedure that can be repeated. Rolling a pair of dice multiple times to find how often doubles occur is an experiment.

The best method for collecting data depends on the question that is being asked.

▶ Reflect

1 How are observations, surveys, and experiments the same? How are they different?

_____

_____

_____

_____

_____

Learn About ▶ **Writing Questions to Collect Data**

Read the problem below. Then explore ways to write questions that can be answered using data.

Suppose you want to learn more about your classmates. One way to learn more about a group of people is to ask a question that can be answered by collecting data from the group. What questions could you ask your classmates that could be used to collect data?

▶ **Analyze It** **You can make a list of questions to ask your classmates. Then cross out the questions that will not collect data.**

What is your favorite school subject?

What time does school begin?

When is the next school field trip?

How many pets do you have?

What time do you go to bed?

▶ **Analyze It** **You can think of a topic you want to learn more about. Then write a question on that topic and list the possible data that could be collected.**

Think of a topic: last week's field trip

Write a question: On a scale of 1 to 5, how would you rate the field trip?

List possible data collected from classmates: 1, 2, 3, 4, or 5

Determine if the responses to the question, or data, vary from classmate to classmate. Also, make sure the question gives you the information you want.

Connect It Now you will solve the problem on the previous page by writing questions that can be answered using data.

2 What is a set of data? _____

_____

3 Look at the list of questions in the first *Analyze It*. To collect data, the question should have a variety of answers. Eliminate questions from the list that have a single answer. For which questions would you expect a variety of answers? Explain. _____

_____

_____

_____

4 Look at the second *Analyze It*. Use this method to write two questions that you could ask your classmates to collect data. _____

Topic: _____

Question: _____

Possible data: _____

Topic: _____

Question: _____

Possible data: _____

Try It Use what you just learned about writing questions to solve these problems.

5 *How many fourth-grade teachers are at my school?* Can you use this question to collect data? Explain. _____

_____

6 You want to collect data about playgrounds. Write a question you could use to collect data on this topic. _____

_____

Learn About ▸ **Collecting Data**

Read the problem below. Then explore how to determine the method that should be used to collect a set of data.

> Sadie wants to collect data to answer the question, *In what months were my classmates born?* Should Sadie use an observation, survey, or experiment to collect the data?

▶ **Analyze It** **You can analyze the given information to solve.**

Study the information given in the problem.

Determine the data that will be collected.

Sadie wants to collect information about the months her classmates were born. The data that is collected will be names of months: January, February, March, and so on.

Compare the possible methods for collecting data.

Observation: In this method, data is collected by watching people or events in a natural setting.

Survey: In this method, people are asked a question.

Experiment: In this method, you repeat a test or procedure.

Determine the best method for collecting the data.

Can Sadie observe her classmates to find out the months they were born?

Can Sadie ask her classmates a question to find out the months they were born?

Can Sadie repeat a procedure that will result in the months her classmates were born?

Connect It Now you will solve the problem on the previous page by evaluating each method.

7 Can Sadie observe her classmates to find out the months they were born?

_____

8 Can Sadie ask her classmates a question to find out the months they were born?

_____

9 Can Sadie repeat a procedure that will result in the months her classmates were born? _____

_____

10 Which method should Sadie use to collect the data? _____

11 How many different categories of data are possible? _____

_____

12 Explain how Sadie could collect data using this method. _____

_____

Try It Use what you just learned about the methods of collecting data to solve these problems.

13 Thomas kicks a soccer ball 10 times and records the distance of each kick. Is this an example of a survey, experiment, or observation? Explain. _____

_____

14 Leslie wants to find out how many televisions her classmates have at home. How can Leslie collect this data? _____

_____

15 Write a question about your classmates that you can answer using observation.

_____

_____

Learn About ▶ Representing and Interpreting Data

Read the problem below. Then explore different ways to represent a set of data.

> Marissa wants to answer the question: *How many commercial breaks are in a 30-minute television show?* She observed some television shows and recorded the number of commercial breaks for each show:
>
> 3, 3, 2, 1, 4, 3, 2, 3, 2, 3, 5, 1, 3, 2, 4
>
> How can Marissa represent the data? How can the data display be used to draw conclusions about the data?

▶ **Model It** **The data can be represented in a frequency table.**

List the data from least to greatest: 1, 1, 2, 2, 2, 2, 3, 3, 3, 3, 3, 3, 4, 4, 5

Number of Commercial Breaks	Number of Television Shows
1	2
2	4
3	6
4	2
5	1

▶ **Model It** **The data can be represented in a bar graph.**

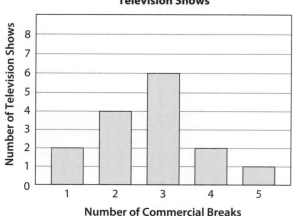

Commercial Breaks in 30-Minute Television Shows

Connect It Now you will solve the problem on the previous page by creating and analyzing a line plot of the data.

16 A line plot is another way to represent a set of data. How many Xs will you draw on a line plot of Marissa's data? _____

17 What numbers should you include on the number line? _____

18 Look at the bar graph in *Model It*. What is an appropriate title for the line plot? What is an appropriate label for the number line? _____

_____

19 Create a line plot of the data.

20 Use your line plot to analyze the data. What is the most common number of commercial breaks during a 30-minute television show? _____
How do you use the line plot to find this value? _____

_____

Try It Use what you just learned about representing a data set to solve these problems.

21 Use observation to collect and represent data from your classmates about their eye color. Write a question that can be answered by this data. Then observe your classmates and record the results of your observation. On a separate sheet of paper, create a bar graph to represent the data. _____

_____

Practice > **Collecting and Representing Data**

Study the example below. Then solve problems 22–24.

Example

Trevor wants to learn more about his school. Which of these questions could he ask to collect a set of data?

How old are the students at the school?

How many classrooms are in the school?

What lunch served by the cafeteria is the favorite among students?

Look at how you could determine the questions that could be used to collect a set of data.

The ages of students in Trevor's school vary from grade to grade, so this question can be used to collect a set of data. Students' favorite lunch served by the cafeteria will also vary, so this question can be used to collect data. The number of classrooms in the school is a single number, so this question cannot be used to collect a set of data.

Solution How old are the students at the school? What lunch served by the cafeteria is the favorite among students?

The student analyzed the possible responses for each question in the list, then eliminated he question with only one possible response.

Pair/Share
For each question, name the best method for collecting data: observation, survey, or experiment.

---

22 Suppose you want to learn more about the teachers at your school. Write a question you could ask to collect a set of data about the teachers. Name the best method for collecting the data.

Would you expect a variety of answers to the question you wrote?

Pair/Share
How did you determine if the data should be collected using an observation, survey, or experiment?

Solution _____

_____

_____

23 Gather data from your classmates using the survey. Create a frequency table that represents the data you collected.

What is your favorite season?
☐ Winter   ☐ Summer
☐ Spring   ☐ Fall

Is the sum of the numbers in the table equal to the number of classmates you surveyed?

Pair/Share
What is the most popular season among your classmates? What is the least popular season?

---

24 On the first day of school, students complete a questionnaire about their summer break. Some of the collected data is represented by the line plot. Which of the following statements is true? Circle the letter of the correct answer.

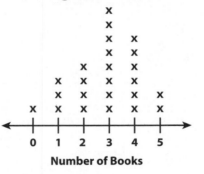

Books Read by Students During Summer Break

Number of Books

A The greatest number of books read by students during the summer was 8.

B The data was probably collected through observation.

C The most common number of books read by students during the summer was 3.

D An experiment was probably used to collect the data.

Gregory chose **D** as the correct answer. How did he get that answer?

_____

_____

Read each statement carefully and check it against the data and given information to see if it is true.

Pair/Share
Write two more questions students could have been asked on the questionnaire to collect data about their summer breaks.

Practice ▷ **Collecting and Representing Data**

Solve the problems.

1 Which question has an answer that is a set of data?

  A Which apple weighs the most?

  B How many letters are in the alphabet?

  C How tall is the slide on the playground?

  D How many pencils do students in my class keep in their desks?

2 What method was most likely used to collect the data in the table?

Number of Applications on Smartphone	Number of Smartphones
0–10	3
11–20	8
21–30	17
31–40	14

  A experiment

  B survey

  C observation

  D none of the above

3 Write a question that could be used to collect data on each of the following topics.

  text messages _____

  _____

  movies _____

  _____

  shoes _____

  _____

4 Collect and represent a set of data from your classmates about computers.

Part A Write a question that you can use to gather data from your classmates on this topic.

_____

_____

Part B Describe how you will collect data from your classmates.

_____

_____

Part C Create a line plot or bar graph to display your data. Write two or three sentences to summarize the data.

_____

_____

_____

✓ **Self Check** **Go back and see what you can check off on the Self Check on page 265.**

Think It Through

What is an angle?

Squares, rectangles, and circles are geometric shapes. An **angle** is another geometric shape.

Suppose you have two pencils lying straight across a table. You could put the erasers together to give the pencils a common endpoint. Then if you turned one pencil until it points straight up, you would form a **right angle**.

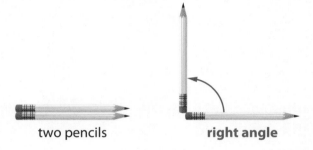

two pencils   right angle

This is the kind of angle you find at the corners of a square or rectangle. Trace the right angle with your finger. Name some right angles you see in your classroom.

Think You can describe other angles by comparing them to a right angle.

If you stop turning the pencil before it makes a right angle, you would form an **acute angle**. If you keep turning the pencil after it makes a right angle, but stop before it makes a straight line, you would form an **obtuse angle**.

acute angle   obtuse angle

Trace the acute and obtuse angles with your finger. Name some acute and obtuse angles you see in your classroom.

Think Angles and circles are related.

Suppose you turn the pencil clockwise and you keep turning the pencil until it is back at its starting position. If you trace the full turn, you trace a circle.

Two hands on a clock form an angle. The angle changes as the hands turn.

Think about the way a second hand travels around the face of a clock. It turns the same small amount each second. Imagine that you move the pencil like a second hand, except that you make each move so small that it takes 360 turns to go around the full circle. Each turn is an angle that measures one **degree**.

The size of the clock face and the length of the hands do not change the measure of the angle. The measure of the angle describes how wide the angle is open. The length of the sides of the angle does not change this.

Reflect

1 Describe and compare the circles and angles in the clocks below.

_____

_____

_____

_____

Think About **Measures of Angles**

🔍 **Let's Explore the Idea** The measure of any angle is equal to the number of one-degree angles one side has turned through.

2 There are _____ one-degree angles in a full circle.

3 An angle showing a full turn through a circle measures _____ degrees.

The drawing below shows an angle that turns through several one-degree angles. Use the drawing to answer problems 4 and 5.

— 1 degree

4 The angle shows a turn through 7 _____ -degree angles.

5 The angle measures _____ degrees.

Now try these two problems.

6 An angle shows a turn through 19 one-degree angles. What is the measure of the angle? _____

7 An angle measures 275 degrees. How many one-degree angles does the angle show a turn through? _____

Let's Talk About It

Solve the problems below as a group.

8 Why is it reasonable to use the same units to describe circles and measures of angles? _____

_____

_____

9 Mari lays a notebook flat on a table and opens it, as shown at the right.

How many one-degree angles did Mari turn the front cover through? _____

Think about the angle formed by the bottom edges of the front and back covers of the notebook. What does the angle look like? _____

_____

10 A second hand takes 60 equal turns to make a full circle around a clock face. How could you find the number of degrees the second hand turns through in one turn?

_____

_____

▶ Try It Another Way Work with your group to show the connection between fractions of a circle and angle measure. All three sections of the circle are the same size.

11 The angle shows a turn through $\dfrac{1}{\boxed{}}$ of the circle.

12 The angle shows a turn through $\dfrac{1}{\boxed{}}$ of 360 degrees.

13 The angle shows a turn through $\dfrac{1}{\boxed{}} \times$ _____ = _____ degrees.

14 The angle measures _____ degrees.

Connect ▸ **Ideas About Angle Measures**

Talk through these problems as a class, then write your answers below.

15 **Infer** Mr. Smith said, "Last week, Julia was against starting a Recreation Club at school. But, now she has done a 180." Use math terms to explain what Mr. Smith probably means.

_____

_____

_____

_____

_____

16 **Explain** Mark says that an angle showing a turn through $\frac{1}{4}$ of a circle that is 10 inches across is two times the measure of an angle showing a turn through $\frac{1}{4}$ of a circle that is 5 inches across. Is Mark correct? Explain your answer.

_____

_____

_____

_____

_____

17 **Compare** Which is greater: An angle showing a turn through $\frac{1}{6}$ of a circle or an angle showing a turn through $\frac{1}{5}$ of a circle? Explain your answer.

_____

_____

_____

_____

_____

Apply ▶ Ideas About Angle Measures

18 Put It Together Use what you have learned to complete this task.

Part A Use two 4-inch strips of cardboard, two 8-inch strips of cardboard, and two brass fasteners to make the "angle explorers" shown below.

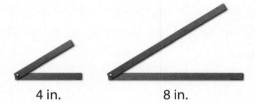

4 in.   8 in.

Angle explorers on this page are not life-sized.

Part B Use the 8-inch explorer to make an angle that turns through $\frac{1}{4}$ of a circle. Use the 4-inch explorer to make an angle that turns through $\frac{1}{2}$ of a circle. You can use the corner and edges of a piece of paper to help make the angles.

Describe the relationship between the measures of the two angles.

_____

_____

_____

_____

_____

_____

Part C Explain how you found your answer.

_____

_____

_____

_____

_____

_____

🔄 Use What You Know

In Lesson 28, you learned that an angle represents a turn through part of a circle, and that the measure of an angle is the number of degrees of that turn. Now take a look at this problem.

Both circles below are divided into 4 equal sections. Estimate the measure of the red angle in the circle on the right.

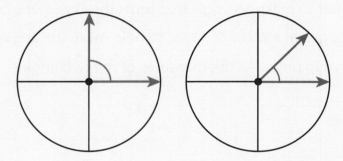

a. What fraction of a circle is one section? _____

b. How many degrees are in a circle? _____

c. How many degrees are in one section? _____

d. Look at the circle on the left. How many sections does the blue angle turn through? _____

e. What is the measure of the blue angle? _____

f. Explain how you could estimate the measure of the red angle.

_____

_____

_____

Angles that show a turn through 90 or 180 degrees are useful benchmarks for estimating the measures of unknown angles. But, sometimes you need a more precise measure.

If you want to know the number of inches in a line segment, you use a ruler. What tool could you use to measure the degrees in an angle? An angle shows part of a turn around a circle, so the measuring tool should be circular and be marked in degrees. A **protractor** is a tool used to measure angles. A 360-degree protractor is shown below.

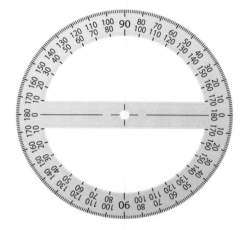

Most angles that you will measure are less than 180 degrees. So, most protractors you will use will be half-circles, like the one shown below.

You can use the symbol ° instead of the word *degrees*. So, 90° means "90 degrees."

▶ Reflect

1 How is a protractor like a ruler? How is it different? _____

_____

_____

_____

Learn About ▷ **Using a Protractor**

Read the problem below. Then explore how to use benchmarks and a protractor to measure an angle.

> Kara drew the angle below. What is the measure of the angle?
>
>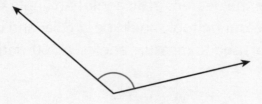

▶ **Picture It** **You can use benchmarks to estimate the measure.**

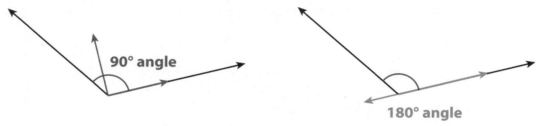

90° angle

180° angle

Kara's angle seems to be between 90° and 180°. It is obtuse.

▶ **Model It** **You can use a protractor to measure the angle.**

- First, line up either mark showing 0° with one ray of the angle.

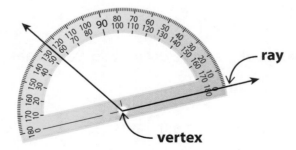

ray

vertex

- Next, line up the center point of the protractor with the vertex of the angle.

- Then, look at the other ray to read the number of degrees.

Connect It   Now you will use a protractor to solve the problem from the previous page.

2 Estimate the angle measure. _____

3 Why must you line up the protractor's center point with the vertex of the angle?

_____

_____

4 If you line up one ray with either mark showing 10° or 170° instead of either mark showing 0° or 180°, how would it change which mark the other ray points to?

_____

5 Line up either mark showing 0° or 180° with one ray. Which mark does the other ray point to? _____

6 Which number of degrees is the measure of the angle? Explain how you know.

_____

_____

Try It   Use a protractor to answer the questions below.

7 Phi draws a flag. What is the measure of the angle on the right end of the flag in the drawing? _____

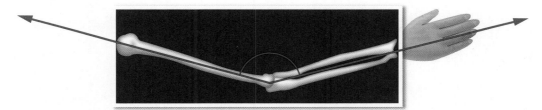

8 Dr. Ortiz checks an X-ray of a patient's elbow. What is the angle formed by the bones? _____

Learn About ▷ **Drawing Angles**

Read the problem below. Then explore how to draw an angle.

> Draw a 30° angle. Think about using two pencils to make an angle.

▶ **Picture It** **You know an angle is made up of two rays with a common endpoint, called the vertex.**

Think about using two pencils to make an angle.

▶ **Model It** **You can use a benchmark angle to get an idea of what your drawing should look like.**

Think about a right angle.
A right angle measures 90°.

90°

You know 30 × 3 = 90. Imagine rays that
split the 90° angle into 3 angles of equal measure.

A 30° angle will open about the same amount as
the angle shown at the right.

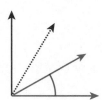

Connect It Now you will use a protractor to draw a 30° angle.

9 Draw a ray on a sheet of paper. Then place the protractor's center point on the endpoint of your ray. What part of the angle is that point? _____

10 Keeping the protractor's center point on the endpoint of your ray, draw a point on your ray at 0°.

11 There are two marks on the protractor labeled "30." Choose the one that is 30° from your 0° mark. Draw a point at this mark.

12 Use the straight edge of the protractor to draw a ray from the vertex through the point you drew at 30°.

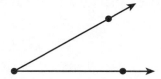

13 If you chose the other "30" mark and drew a point at that mark, what would be the measure of your angle? _____

14 Think about a right angle. Compare it to the angle you drew. How wide does your angle open compared to a right angle? _____

Try It Use what you just learned to solve these problems.

15 Draw a 75° angle.

16 Draw a 100° angle.

Practice ▸ **Measuring and Drawing Angles**

Study the example below. Then solve problems 17–19.

Example

What is the measure of the angle at the top of the roof in the drawing to the right?

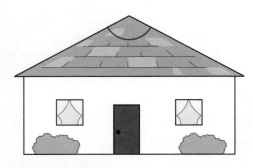

Look at how you could measure the angle.

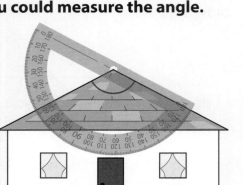

Solution _about 123°_

The center point lines up with the vertex of the angle, and the 0° mark lines up with one ray of the angle. The other ray points to the measure of the angle.

💬 **Pair/Share**
Does it matter which ray you choose to line up with the 0° mark?

---

17 What is the measure of the angle below?

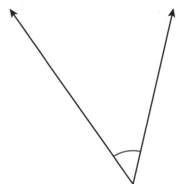

Solution _____

The angle looks like it opens less than a right angle. The measure will be less than 90°.

💬 **Pair/Share**
How did you and your partner decide where the vertex is?

18 Draw a 135° angle.

Show your work.

Pair/Share
If you had drawn a point at the other 0° mark, how would it change your angle?

19 Which set of points can be used to draw a 105° angle? Circle the letter of the correct answer.

Will a 105° angle be wider or narrower than a right angle?

A

C

B

D

Mia chose **C** as the correct answer. How did she get that answer?

_____

_____

Pair/Share
Does Mia's answer make sense?

_____

_____

Practice **Measuring and Drawing Angles**

Solve the problems.

1 Which point could be the vertex of an 80° angle that you could measure without moving the protractor?

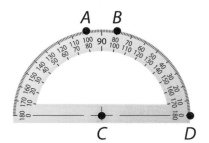

A point *A*

B point *B*

C point *C*

D point *D*

2 Which diagrams show a 25° angle? Circle the letter for all that apply.

A

D

B

E

C

F

3 What is the measure of this angle?

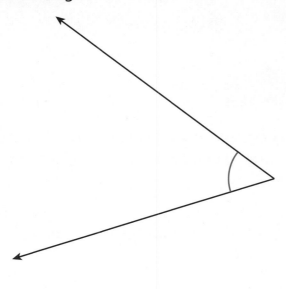

_____

4 Draw a 40° angle.

5 Ana placed a protractor over a ray so her protractor's center point is on the endpoint of the ray, and a second point on the ray is at 90°. What can she do next to make a 30° angle?

_____

_____

_____

_____

✓ **Self Check** Go back and see what you can check off on the Self Check on page 265.

Ⓖ Use What You Know

In Lesson 29, you learned how to use a protractor to measure and draw angles. Now you will learn about adding and subtracting angle measures. Take a look at this problem.

> Flora cuts a rectangular sheet of paper into two pieces on the dotted line.
>
>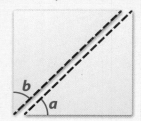
>
> What is the sum of angle *a* and angle *b*?

a. Angle *a* is _____ than 90°. Angle *b* is _____ than 90°.

b. Describe where the 90° angle starts and stops as it turns through the bottom left corner of the uncut sheet of paper. _____

_____

c. Describe where angle *a* starts and stops as it turns through the bottom left corner of the cut sheet of paper. _____

d. Describe where angle *b* starts and stops as it turns through the bottom left corner of the cut sheet of paper. _____

e. Compare where the turning starts and stops for the 90° angle with turning through angle *a* and going on through angle *b*.

_____

_____

_____

►► Find Out More

When Flora cut the sheet of paper, she split up a 90° angle into two smaller angles. You can **decompose**, or split up, any angle into smaller angles.

Remember that an angle's measure is the number of one-degree turns it shows. You can think of any angle as a group of one-degree angles with a common vertex.

Picture a 10° angle.

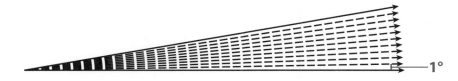

You can decompose a 10° angle in many different ways. Here are two possible ways.

$4° + 6° = 10°$

$3° + 7° = 10°$

► Reflect

1 Is it possible to decompose a 100° angle into two 60° angles? Explain.

_____

_____

_____

_____

Learn About ▷ **Combining Angles**

Read the problem below. Then explore different ways to understand combining smaller angles to form a larger angle.

Waylon and Andres play a game where the goal is to fill a tray with three same-size, triangular game pieces. There are no gaps and no overlaps. What is the measure of the bottom angle of the tray?

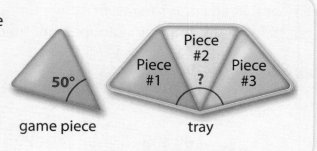

game piece   tray

▶ **Picture It** **You can use a sketch to help understand the problem.**

Imagine putting the three pieces together in the tray. The vertices of the 50° angles become the common endpoint of a larger angle. This is the angle at the bottom of the tray.

The three 50° angles **compose**, or combine to form, the larger angle.

▶ **Model It** **You can also use a protractor to help understand the problem.**

Look at a protractor. Start at 0°. Count three jumps of 50° each.

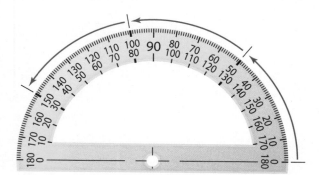

Connect It Now you will solve the problem from the previous page using an equation.

2 How many 50° angles compose the bottom angle of the tray? _____

3 Does addition or subtraction best express putting two or more angles together to make a greater angle? _____

4 You can write an equation to combine the 50° angles to compose the bottom angle of the tray.

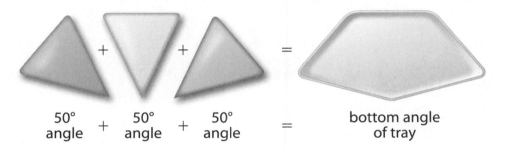

| 50° angle | + | 50° angle | + | 50° angle | = | bottom angle of tray |

The bottom angle of the tray measures _____ degrees.

5 Could you compose an angle that measures 150° from three angles with unequal angle measures? If so, give an example.

_____

_____

Try It Use what you just learned to solve these problems.

6 The angle between each spoke on a wheel of Sophia's bicycle measures 15°. Sophia puts reflectors on two spokes as shown to the right. What is the measure of the angle between the spokes with the reflectors?

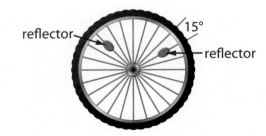

reflector

15°

reflector

_____

7 Gina sets two floor tiles as shown. What is the measure of the blue angle? _____

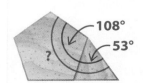

108°

53°

?

Learn About ▶ Finding Unknown Angle Measures

Read the problem below. Then explore different ways to understand using addition and subtraction to find unknown angle measures.

A door swings open 85° and then gets stuck. Randy pushes on the door, and it opens some more. Altogether, the door opens 100°. How many more degrees does the door open after Randy pushes it?

▶ **Picture It** **You can use a sketch to help you understand the problem.**

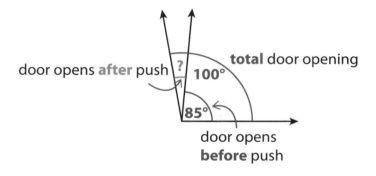

The **100°** angle is composed of two smaller angles.
One angle measures **85°**, and the other angle measure is **unknown**.

▶ **Model It** **You can use a protractor to help you understand the problem.**

Look at a protractor. Start at 0°. Count on 85°. How many more degrees do you need to count on to get to 100°?

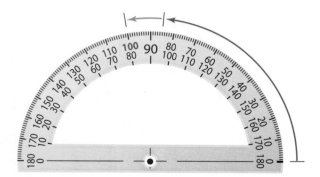

©Curriculum Associates, LLC   Copying is not permitted.

Connect It Now you will solve the problem from the previous page using an equation.

8 Write a sentence that describes how the unknown angle measure is related to the 85° and 100° angles. _____

_____

9 Does addition or subtraction best express this relationship? _____

10 Write an equation to describe how the unknown angle measure is related to the 85° and 100° angles.

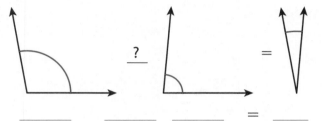

_____ _____ _____ = _____

11 How would the measure of the unknown angle change if the door opened a total of 120°? _____

_____

12 Imagine an angle that is composed of three smaller angles. If you know the measure of the composed angle and the measures of two of the smaller angles, explain how you could find the measure of the third small angle.

_____

_____

▶ Try It Use what you just learned to solve these problems.

13 A game includes an 8-second timer as shown at right. The timer's pointer turns through 135° as it counts down from 8 seconds to 5 seconds. How many more degrees does the pointer have to turn through to count down to 0? _____

14 A snake's mouth opens to form a 180° angle. The snake closes its mouth to form a 60° angle. By how many degrees did the angle formed by the snake's mouth change? _____

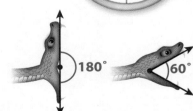

Practice **Adding and Subtracting with Angles**

Study the example below. Then solve problems 15–17.

Example

Halah turns a jar lid 60° and then 225° more. How many more degrees does Halah need to turn the lid to make one full turn?

Look at how you could show your work using a drawing and an equation.

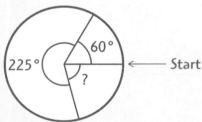

$$60 + 225 + ? = 360$$
$$285 + ? = 360$$
$$? = 75$$

Solution ___75°___

One full turn is equal to 360°. So the sum of 60, 225, and the measure of the unknown angle is equal to 360.

 Pair/Share
What operation did you use to solve the equation?

---

15 When the hands of a clock are on 12 and 4, they form a 120° angle. What angle is formed if the hands are moved to 4 and 6?

Show your work.

I know the hands make a 180° angle when they are on 12 and 6.

 Pair/Share
Once you know the angle from 4 to 6, how could you find the angle from 4 to 5?

Solution _____

16 Tyra's front door has a half-circle window. What is the measure of the angle of the center piece of glass?

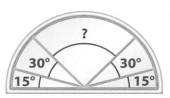

A circle has 360 degrees, so a half-circle has 180 degrees.

Show your work.

💬 **Pair/Share**
How could you check your answer?

Solution _____

---

17 A windshield wiper turns through 140°. The window cleaner sprays across 75°. If the wiper turns 40° before it gets to the sprayed area, how many degrees past the sprayed area does the wiper turn? Circle the letter of the correct answer.

The 140° angle is composed of 3 angles: 40°, 75° and ?°. The sum of the measures of these three angles must be 140.

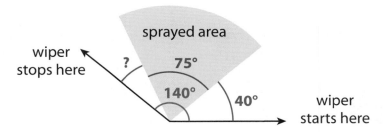

sprayed area

A 25°

B 35°

C 115°

D 255°

Ellen chose **D** as the correct answer. How did she get that answer?

_____

_____

_____

💬 **Pair/Share**
Does Ellen's answer make sense?

Practice ▶ Adding and Subtracting with Angles

Solve the problems.

1 Keith uses a can opener. Every time he twists the knob on the opener, the opener moves 36° around the can's lid. Which best describes how open the can is after 5 twists?

A one-tenth open

B one-fifth open

C half open

D completely open

2 A tire swing hangs straight down. Then a child gets on, swings forward 50°, and swings back 95°. How many degrees forward must the swing go to return to its starting position?

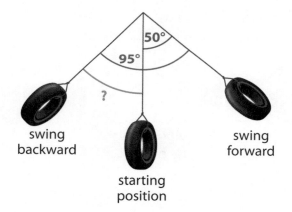

swing backward

swing forward

starting position

A 5°

B 45°

C 50°

D 95°

3 Choose either *Yes* or *No* to tell whether there is an angle of the given measure shown in the diagram.

a. 225° ☐ Yes ☐ No

b. 265° ☐ Yes ☐ No

c. 70° ☐ Yes ☐ No

d. 320° ☐ Yes ☐ No

e. 90° ☐ Yes ☐ No

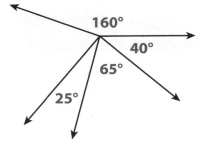

4 The measure of one angle is given in the figure below.

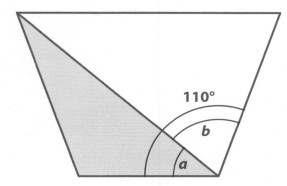

Use a protractor to measure angle *a*. Use this measure and the given angle measure to find the measure of angle *b*.

_____

5 Lilit opens a pair of scissors 65°. Then she closes the scissors 60° to make a cut. Then she reopens the scissors 100°. How many degrees open are the scissors now?

Show your work.

Answer The scissors are open _____ degrees.

✓ **Self Check**   Go back and see what you can check off on the Self Check on page 265.

Study an Example Problem and Solution

Read this problem about measurements. Then look at Alex's solution to this problem.

Birdcages

The zoo is planning to build a new area for birds. There will be three different-size rectangular cages as shown below.

Small cage: floor area of 12 square feet

Medium cage: floor area of 24 square feet

Large cage: floor area of 36 square feet

Alex needs to find a possible length and width for the floor of each size cage. What is a possible length, width, and perimeter for each cage's floor?

Read the sample solution on the next page. Then look at the checklist below. Find and mark parts of the solution that match the checklist.

✏️ **Problem-Solving Checklist**

☐ Tell what is known.

☐ Tell what the problem is asking.

☐ Show all your work.

☐ Show that the solution works.

a. Circle something that is known.

b. Underline something that you need to find.

c. Draw a box around what you do to solve the problem.

d. Put a checkmark next to the part that shows the solution works.

Alex's Solution

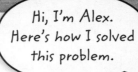

Hi, I'm Alex. Here's how I solved this problem.

▷ **I already know** the area of each cage floor in square feet. The area of a rectangle is the length times the width.

▷ **I need to find** two factors that can be multiplied to get the area of each rectangle. These factors can be the length and width of the rectangle.

▷ **I can use multiplication facts to find possible lengths and widths.**

$6 \times 2 = 12$

$8 \times 3 = 24$

$9 \times 4 = 36$

> I only wrote one fact for each area but there are others.

▷ **I can use the perimeter formula to find the perimeter of each rectangle.**

$$\text{Perimeter} = (2 \times \text{length}) + (2 \times \text{width})$$

small cage	medium cage	large cage
Length = 6 feet	Length = 8 feet	Length = 9 feet
Width = 2 feet	Width = 3 feet	Width = 4 feet
Perimeter = 16 feet	Perimeter = 22 feet	Perimeter = 26 feet

> I sketched the cages to help keep my answer organized.

▷ **I can also find the perimeters by adding the length and width, then multiplying by 2.**

For the small cage, the sum of the length and width is 8 feet.
So the perimeter is 2 × 8 feet = 16 feet.

For the medium cage, the sum of the length and width is 11 feet.
So the perimeter is 2 × 11 feet = 22 feet.

> Here's my final answer.

For the large cage, the sum of the length and width is 13 feet.
So the perimeter is 2 × 13 feet = 26 feet.

There are many ways to solve problems. Think about how you might
solve the Birdcages problem in a different way.

Birdcages

The zoo is planning to build a new area for birds. There will be three
different-size rectangular cages as shown below.

Small cage: floor area of 12 square feet

Medium cage: floor area of 24 square feet

Large cage: floor area of 36 square feet

Alex needs to find a possible length and width for the floor of each
size cage. What is a possible length, width, and perimeter for each
cage's floor?

▶ **Plan It** Answer these questions to help you start thinking about a plan.

A. What are all the factor pairs of 12? 24? 36?

_____

_____

_____

B. Think about each factor pair as the length and width of a rectangle. Which
factor pairs do you think would make the best rectangular shapes for the
birdcages? Explain.

_____

_____

_____

Solve It Find a different solution for the Birdcages problem.
Show all your work on a separate sheet of paper.

You may want to use the problem-solving tips to get started.

Problem-Solving Tips

- **Tools**

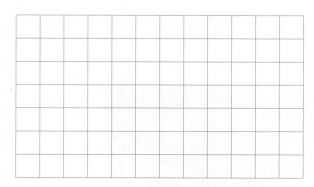

Problem-Solving Checklist

Make sure that you . . .
- ☐ tell what you know.
- ☐ tell what you need to do.
- ☐ show all your work.
- ☐ show that the solution works.

- **Word Bank**

factor	length	area
factor pair	width	perimeter
multiply	product	formula

- **Sentence Starters**

  - The factors of _____

  - To find the area _____

Reflect
Use Process Standards As you work through the problem, discuss these questions with a partner.

- **Persevere** How can you use your answers to the *Plan It* questions to decide on a solution path?

- **Use Tools** How can you use the grid paper to draw rectangles with the given areas?

Discuss ▸ **Models and Strategies**

Read the problem. Write a solution on a separate sheet of paper. Remember, there are lots of ways to solve a problem!

Bears

Alex is collecting data to show on the zoo's website. She has recorded information about three different kinds of bears.

Giant Panda

Average size at birth
Length: 18 centimeters
Mass: 113 grams

Average size of adult male
Shoulder height: 75 centimeters
Mass: 98 kilograms

Polar Bear

Average size at birth
Length: 30 centimeters
Mass: $\frac{1}{2}$ kilogram

Average size of adult male
Shoulder height: $1\frac{1}{2}$ meters
Mass: 449 kilograms

Black Bear

Average size at birth
Length: 28 centimeters
Mass: 320 grams

Average size of adult male
Shoulder height: 1 meter
Mass: 115 kilograms

How can Alex show the data so that visitors can easily compare the bears' sizes?

Plan It and Solve It Find a solution to Alex's Bears problem.

Alex wants to present the data about the three types of bears so that visitors can easily compare the sizes. She also wants to include two or three sentences that describe the sizes. Explain how Alex can do this. Then make a presentation that Alex can use.

You may want to use the problem-solving tips to get started.

Problem-Solving Tips

- **Question**
  - What units will you use to compare the four measurements given for each bear?

- **Models** You may want to use . . .
  - tables.
  - bar graphs.

- **References**
  1 meter = 100 centimeters
  1 kilogram = 1,000 grams

- **Sentence Starters**
  - _____ has a mass that is _____
  - _____ is _____ longer than _____

Problem-Solving Checklist

Make sure that you . . .
- ☐ tell what you know.
- ☐ tell what you need to do.
- ☐ show all your work.
- ☐ show that the solution works.

Reflect

Use Process Standards As you work through the problem, discuss these questions with a partner.

- **Be Precise** Why should you label all numbers with units as you work out the solution?

- **Use a Model** What do you need to do with the data? How can this help you decide what model to use?

Read the problems. Write a solution on a separate sheet of paper.
Remember, there are many different ways to solve a problem!

Feeding the Animals

Alex is helping the zookeepers plan meals for the hippos and pandas.
She wants to find how much food to buy to feed 1 of each animal
for 1 week. Here is the information that she has collected so far.

Amount of food the zoo animals eat:
· A hippo eats up to 40 kilograms of mixed vegetables each day.
· A panda eats between 20 and 35 kilograms of bamboo each day.

The table show the different packages of food the zoo can buy.

	Small Package	Medium Package	Large Package
Mixed Vegetables	50 kg	100 kg	250 kg
Bamboo	50 kg	100 kg	250 kg

How much of each type of food should be purchased to feed 1 panda
and 1 hippo for 1 week?

▶ **Solve It** **Suggest a way that Alex could feed the animals for a week.**

The food amounts for each animal are estimates.

• Estimate the amount of food each animal eats in 1 week.

• Decide which packages of food and how many to buy for each animal
  for 1 week. Explain the choices you made.

▶ **Reflect**

Use Process Standards After you complete the task, choose one
of these questions to discuss with a partner.

• **Be Precise** What would you have done differently if the daily food
  amounts for each animal were exact numbers and not estimates?

• **Use a Model** Did you choose to explain your thinking with equations,
  words, tables, or something else? Tell why you made that choice.

Snake Lengths

Alex records the lengths of the snakes in the Snake World exhibit.

Length of Snakes (in inches)				
$36\frac{1}{4}$	$37\frac{1}{2}$	$36\frac{1}{4}$	$37\frac{1}{4}$	38
$36\frac{1}{2}$	$36\frac{3}{4}$	$36\frac{1}{2}$	$38\frac{1}{2}$	37
37	$37\frac{3}{4}$	$36\frac{1}{4}$	$36\frac{3}{4}$	$37\frac{1}{2}$

Alex plans to post information about the snakes' lengths on the zoo's website. She wants to include a data display and a short summary about the lengths.

How can Alex compare the length of the snakes?

► **Solve It** Help Alex to compare the length of the snakes.

- Make a line plot to display the snake lengths.
- Write a summary of the data that Alex can put on the zoo website.
- Use subtraction to include at least one comparison statement in the summary.

► **Reflect**

Use Process Standards After you complete the task, choose one of these questions to discuss with a partner.

- **Use Tools** How did making the line plot help you write a summary of the data?

- **Use Structure** How did you decide what labels to use on the number line?

Solve the problems.

1 What is the total measure of the angles in the figure below?

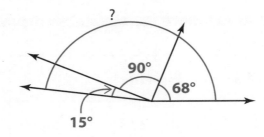

A 83°

C 163°

B 158°

D 173°

2 Which statement is true? Circle the letter for all that apply.

A When you convert a measurement from inches to feet, you multiply by 12.

B 3 kilometers − 70 meters = 230 meters

C 10 seconds = 600 minutes

D 1 week = 168 hours

12 inches = 1 foot
1,000 meters = 1 kilometer
60 seconds = 1 minute
7 days = 1 week
24 hours = 1 day

3 A sketch of Jane's rectangular garden bed is shown below. The perimeter of the garden bed is 34 feet.

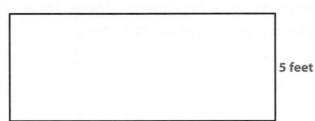

5 feet

Jane can plant 4 lettuce plants per square foot. How many lettuce plants can she plant in her garden bed?

_____

4 A camp counselor at Camp Horseshoe asked campers to name their favorite activity. The circle graph shows the data the counselor collected.

Favorite Camp Activities

Part A Answer the following questions.

- What fraction of the campers chose riding horses?

  _____

- What fraction of the campers chose crafts?

  _____

- What activity was chosen by about twice as many campers as swimming?

  _____

Part B Did the counselor use an observation, survey, or experiment to collect the data? Explain.

_____

_____

5 **Part A** A sprinkler is set up to turn through a full circle to water the grass. The sprinkler turns through $\frac{1}{4}$ of the circle. How many one-degree angles does it turn through?

Answer _____ one-degree angles

Part B The sprinkler turns through $\frac{3}{4}$ of the circle. What is the measure of the angle it turns through?

Answer _____ degrees

Performance Task

Answer the questions and show all your work on separate paper.

Ciara is using the recipe below to make 6 dozen cupcakes for a family party. She needs to buy flour, milk, and vanilla. Ciara will also need boxes to carry the cupcakes to the party. Each box holds one layer of cupcakes. Ciara has $25 to spend. Does she have enough money to buy everything she needs to make the cupcakes and bring them to the party? Explain how you know.

Recipe
Ciara's Vanilla Cupcakes

(makes 1 dozen cupcakes 3 inches across)

256 grams flour	200 grams sugar
1 teaspoon baking soda	4 eggs
5 tablespoons butter	5 milliliters vanilla
$\frac{1}{2}$ cup milk	

1 dozen = 12
1 foot = 12 inches
1 quart = 4 cups
1 liter = 1,000 milliliters
1 kilogram = 1,000 grams

Below are the products Ciara needs to buy and their prices.

FLOUR 1 kilogram — $2.50   MILK 1 quart — $2.00   VANILLA $\frac{1}{2}$ liter — $8.50   1 foot / $\frac{1}{2}$ foot / CUPCAKES — $1.00

Reflect

Use Process Standards After you complete the task, choose one of the following questions to answer.

- **Model** What equations did you use to help you solve this problem?

- **Be Precise** Why is it important to use labels for all of the amounts while you are solving this problem?

Unit 6
Geometry

Let's learn to identify different lines, angles, and shapes.

Real-World Connection The double yellow lines in the middle of the road, the fence posts that make up a garden gate, two of the lines that make up the letter H, and opposite sides of a rectangle: these are all examples of parallel lines. Lines that aren't parallel are easier to find around you: street intersections, the letter X, and two sides of a square next to each other that make an angle.

In This Unit You will describe lines and angles and look for different kinds of lines and angles in two-dimensional figures. You will also look for shapes that have a special property called symmetry.

✓ Self Check

Before starting this unit, check off the skills you know below. As you complete each lesson, see how many more skills you can check off!

I can:	Before this unit	After this unit
identify points, lines, line segments, rays, and perpendicular and parallel lines, for example: a plus sign has perpendicular lines.	☐	☐
draw and identify angles (right, acute, obtuse), for example: a square has 4 right angles.	☐	☐
classify two-dimensional figures based on sides and angles, for example: squares and rectangles have parallel sides.	☐	☐
draw and identify lines of symmetry in shapes, for example: a square has 4 lines of symmetry.	☐	☐

Lesson 31 👥 Introduction
Points, Lines, Rays, and Angles

↻ Use What You Know

In the past, you have learned about shapes like squares, rectangles, and triangles. Now you will learn more about the parts that make up these shapes. Take a look at this problem.

> Traci tries to teach her younger sister how to draw a rectangle. Traci tells her, "Draw a shape with four straight sides." Traci's sister draws the shape at the right.
>
> The shape includes 4 straight sides. Why is Traci's sister's drawing not a rectangle?

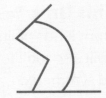

a. What is the total number of sides in a rectangle? _____

b. Are the sides of a rectangle straight, curved, or some of each? _____

c. How many corners does a rectangle have? _____

d. Are the corners of a rectangle like the corner of a sheet of paper, or are they narrower or wider? _____

e. Do some or all of the sides of a rectangle go on forever or do they all stop at a certain point? _____

f. Are all the sides of a rectangle the same length or can some be different lengths?

_____

_____

g. Explain how Traci could make her directions more clear. _____

_____

_____

_____

▶▶ Find Out More

Traci's directions are not clear and complete. In geometry, certain words are used to describe shapes in detail. Below are some of these words.

Point—A point is a single location in space. You can draw a dot to show a point. Name points with a capital letter: point *A*.

Line Segment—A line segment is a straight row of points that starts at one point and ends at another point. You can write "line segment *AB*" as $\overline{AB}$.

Line—A line is a straight row of points that goes on forever in both directions. You can write "line *AB*" as $\overleftrightarrow{AB}$. The arrows show that the line goes on forever in both directions.

Ray—A ray is a straight row of points that starts at one point and goes on forever in one direction. You can write "ray *AB*" as $\overrightarrow{AB}$. When you name a ray, you always start with the endpoint.

Angle—If rays, lines, or line segments meet at a common point, they form an angle. You can write "angle *A*" as $\angle A$. Notice that $\angle A$ is made up of $\overrightarrow{AB}$ and $\overrightarrow{AC}$ meeting at point *A*. You can also name this angle using three points: $\angle CAB$ or $\angle BAC$. The vertex is always the middle letter.

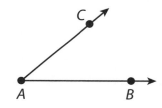

▶ Reflect

1 Use geometry words and symbols to describe the rectangle below.

_____

_____

_____

Learn About Points, Lines, Line Segments, and Rays

Read the problem below. Then explore different ways to understand points, lines, line segments, and rays.

Kent draws a shape with three sides. Use geometry words to describe each side of the shape.

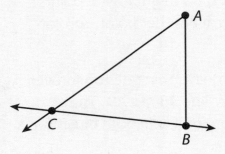

▶ **Picture It** **You can make some drawings to help describe the sides of the shape.**

Each side is straight. Draw the different kinds of straight rows of points that you know.

| line segment | ray | line |

▶ **Model It** **You can also use words to help describe the sides of the shape.**

Label the line segment, ray, and line that are drawn as the sides of Kent's shape. Look for endpoints and arrowheads.

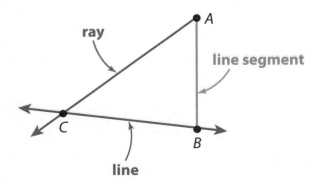

Connect It Now you will explore real-world examples of geometry words and solve a problem similar to the one on the previous page.

2 Name a real-world example of a line segment. _____

3 When two line segments, lines, or rays meet at a point, they form an angle. Name a real-world example of an angle. _____

4 Name a real-world example of a ray. _____

5 Explain how the drawing below represents one line, three line segments, four rays, and one angle.

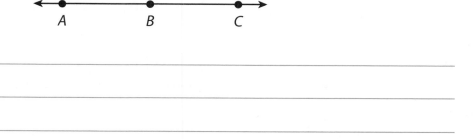

_____

_____

_____

_____

_____

Try It Use what you just learned to solve these problems.

6 How many lines are in this shape? _____ How many rays? _____

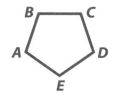

7 How many line segments are in this shape? _____

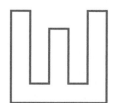

Read the problem below. Then explore different ways to understand angles.

The angle shown at the right is a **right angle**. A right angle looks like a square corner and measures 90°.

Look at the figure below. Name the rays that make up each of the angles listed.

1. A right angle
2. An angle that has a smaller opening than a right angle
3. An angle that has a wider opening than a right angle, but does not open as wide as a straight line

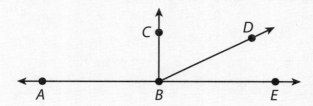

▶ Picture It You can make a drawing to help identify different types of angles.

Use shading to find the rays that make each angle.

A right angle is shaded. Look at the rays along the edges of the shaded area.

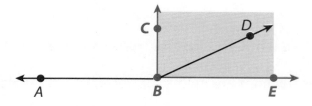

▶ Model It You can also use a model to help identify different types of angles.

Compare the opening of an angle to a right angle by holding the corner of a sheet of paper next to the angle. The angle below opens as wide as a right angle.

Connect It   Now you will extend your understanding of angles to identify them in the figure on the previous page.

8 *Model It* shows a right angle. Draw a right angle. Then use 3 points to name a right angle in the figure on the previous page. _____

9 An angle that has a smaller opening than a right angle is called an **acute angle**. Name an acute angle in the figure on the previous page. _____
Draw an acute angle.

10 An angle that has a wider opening than a right angle, but does not open as wide as a straight line, is called an **obtuse angle**. Name an obtuse angle in the figure on the previous page. _____ Draw an obtuse angle.

11 Explain how you could decide whether any angle is acute, right, or obtuse.

_____

_____

Try It   Use what you just learned to solve these problems.

12 How many acute angles are in the shape below? _____

13 How many obtuse angles are in the shape below? _____

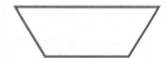

Learn About ▷ **Parallel and Perpendicular Lines**

Read the problem below. Then explore different ways to understand parallel and perpendicular lines and line segments.

Jordan looks at the street map below.

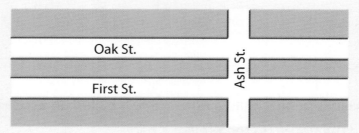

Describe the relationship between Oak Street and First Street. Then describe the relationship between Oak Street and Ash Street. How are they different?

▶ **Picture It** **You can use a sketch to help understand the problem.**

Sketch a picture of Oak Street and First Street. Shade the streets.

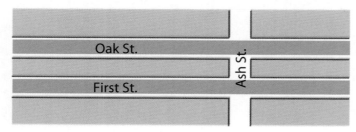

Notice that the streets do not cross.

▶ **Model It** **You can also use a model to help understand the problem.**

Look at Oak Street and Ash Street. Think of each street as a line. When the two lines cross, they form four angles.

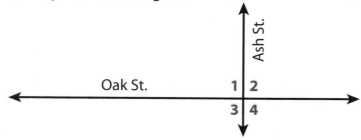

Connect It
Now you will use understanding of parallel and perpendicular lines to identify them in the map from the previous page.

14 Lines that are always the same distance apart and never cross are called **parallel lines.** Name a real-world example of parallel lines.

_____

15 Suppose each street keeps going in a straight line. If Jordan travels on Oak Street and makes no turns, can he ever get to First Street? Explain.

_____

16 Describe the angles that Oak Street and Ash Street make when they cross.

_____

17 Lines that cross and form a right angle are called **perpendicular lines.** Name a real-world example of perpendicular lines.

_____

18 Explain why 3 separate lines can all be parallel to each other, but 3 separate lines cannot all be perpendicular to each other. Use a drawing to show your answer.

_____

_____

_____

_____

_____

Try It
Use what you just learned to solve these problems.

19 How many pairs of parallel sides does the shape below appear to have? _____

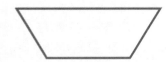

20 A rectangle is a parallelogram with _____ pairs of parallel sides.

Practice ▶ **Identifying Points, Lines, Rays, and Angles**

Study the example below. Then solve problems 21–23.

Example

In the shape below, list each pair of parallel sides and circle the letter marking each obtuse angle.

Even if the sides of the shape went on forever, the opposite sides would never cross each other.

Look at how you could show your work.

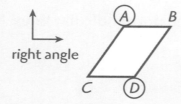

right angle

Solution $\overline{AB}$ and $\overline{CD}$ are parallel. $\overline{AC}$ and $\overline{BD}$ are parallel.

∠A and ∠D open wider than a right angle, so they are obtuse.

Pair/Share
What kind of angles are ∠B and ∠C? How do you know?

---

21 Put an X where each pair of perpendicular line segments meet in the shape below.

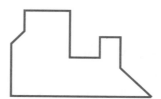

Perpendicular line segments meet to form right angles.

Pair/Share
Describe the angles that are NOT marked with an X.

22 A crosswalk is marked with a pair of parallel line segments. The distance straight across from point *A* to point *B* is 6 feet. What is the distance straight across from point *C* to point *D*?

Solution _____

---

23 Toshi cuts one fourth of a circle out of paper. How many angles does this shape have? Circle the letter of the correct answer.

A 0

B 1

C 2

D 3

Esme chose **D** as the correct answer. How did she get that answer?

_____

_____

_____

_____

Practice **Identifying Points, Lines, Rays, and Angles**

Solve the problems.

1 Think about a real-world example of where a wall meets the floor and where the same wall meets the ceiling. Which term describes the edge of the floor and the edge of the ceiling?

A parallel line segments

B perpendicular line segments

C right angle

D acute angle

2 Which drawing shows 3 lines?

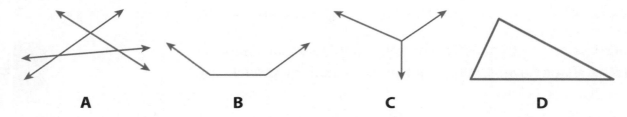

A　　　　**B**　　　　**C**　　　　**D**

3 Choose either *Yes* or *No* to tell whether there is an example of the given term in the diagram below.

a. parallel line segments ☐ Yes ☐ No

b. perpendicular line segments ☐ Yes ☐ No

c. right angle ☐ Yes ☐ No

d. acute angle ☐ Yes ☐ No

e. obtuse angle ☐ Yes ☐ No

4 Tell whether each sentence is *True* or *False*.

    a. A ray goes on forever in two directions.   ☐ True   ☐ False

    b. A line segment has exactly two endpoints.   ☐ True   ☐ False

    c. An obtuse angle has a wider opening
       than a right angle.   ☐ True   ☐ False

    d. Parallel lines meet to form an acute angle.   ☐ True   ☐ False

5 A triangle can have one pair of perpendicular sides. Can a triangle have one pair of parallel sides? Use drawings and words to explain your answer.

Show your work.

_____

_____

_____

6 Liz draws two shapes. Use words you have learned in this lesson to describe what the shapes have in common. How are they different?

_____

_____

_____

✔ **Self Check**   **Go back and see what you can check off on the Self Check on page 377.**

Use What You Know

In Lesson 31, you learned about parallel and perpendicular lines. Now you will use this understanding to classify two-dimensional shapes. Take a look at this problem.

Look at the shapes below. Put a check mark on all the shapes that appear to have at least one pair of parallel sides. Put a star on all the shapes that appear to have at least one pair of perpendicular sides.

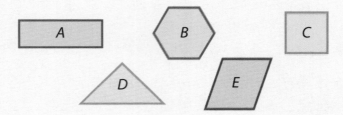

a. Which shapes have a pair of sides that are always the same distance apart?

_____

b. Lines, line segments, and rays that are always the same distance apart and never cross are called _____.

c. Which shapes have a pair of sides that form a right angle? _____

d. Lines, line segments, and rays that form a right angle when they meet are called

_____.

e. Explain how you could test your choices. _____

_____

_____

_____

©Curriculum Associates, LLC   Copying is not permitted.

▶▶ Find Out More

You know that there are many different kinds of shapes with straight sides, such as triangles and quadrilaterals. These shapes are types of **polygons**. There are many ways you can sort these shapes, such as by the number of sides the shape has. You can also sort them by the relationships between the sides.

Take another look at the shapes from the previous page. You can sort them by looking for pairs of parallel and perpendicular sides.

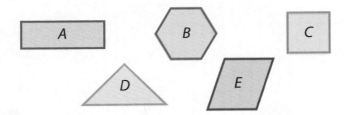

- Shapes with pairs of parallel sides *and* pairs of perpendicular sides: *A* and *C*

You can also sort the shapes by the kinds of angles they have. Here are some ways to sort the shapes by angles.

- Shapes with at least one right angle: *A, C,* and *D*

- Shapes with all right angles: *A* and *C*

- Shapes with at least one acute angle: *D* and *E*

- Shapes with at least one obtuse angle: *B* and *E*

- Shapes with all obtuse angles: *B*

▶ Reflect

1 Describe the sides and the angles of shape *C.* _____

_____

_____

_____

_____

Learn About ▸ **Sorting Shapes Based on Sides**

Read the problem below. Then explore different ways to understand sorting shapes into groups based on parallel and perpendicular sides.

Evan plays a board game. The board is divided into 3 sections.

parallel sides	perpendicular sides	parallel and perpendicular sides

These are Evan's cards. In which sections of the board do the cards belong?

hexagon	rhombus	parallelogram	trapezoid

▶ **Picture It** **You can use drawings to help sort shapes.**

Draw a pair of parallel lines and a pair of perpendicular lines.

 parallel lines   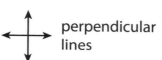 perpendicular lines

Draw lines along opposite sides of each shape. Compare these lines to the parallel lines you drew.

Draw lines along sides of each shape that form angles. Compare these lines to the perpendicular lines you drew.

▶ **Model It** **You can use a model to help sort shapes.**

Make a Venn diagram. Put each card's shape where it belongs in the diagram.

Evan's cards belong in the "parallel sides" section of the board.

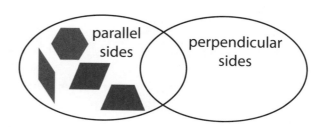

Connect It Now you will solve a problem similar to the one from the previous page. Evan gets different cards with a square and a quadrilateral. In which sections of the board do these shapes belong?

2 Look at the sides of the square. In which category does it belong?

_____

_____

square

3 Does the quadrilateral belong to any of the three categories? If not, name a category that can be used to describe this shape.

_____

_____

_____

_____

quadrilateral

4 Explain how to sort shapes based on parallel and perpendicular sides.

_____

_____

_____

Try It Answer the following questions using the shapes shown.

5 Describe the group these shapes belong in, based on the kinds of sides they have.

_____

6 Circle the shape that belongs in the group "no parallel sides."

Lesson 32 Classify Two-Dimensional Figures **393**

> **Learn About** **Sorting Shapes Based on Angles**

Read the problem below. Then explore different ways to understand sorting shapes into categories based on angles.

A classroom computer game shows the player a set of categories and a set of shapes. The player puts each shape in the correct category. Draw an arrow from each shape to the category it belongs to.

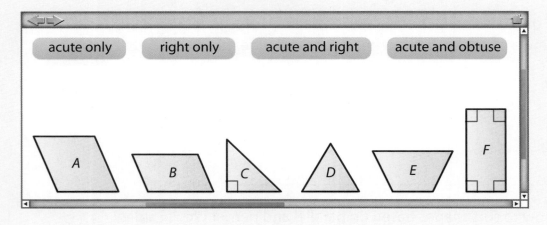

▶ **Picture It** **You can use a model to help sort shapes based on angles.**

Use the corner of a sheet of paper as a model of a right angle. Compare each angle to the paper corner.

For example, hold up the paper corner to the trapezoid.

This angle opens wider than a right angle. The angle is **obtuse**.

Then you can compare the corner to each of the other 3 angles in the trapezoid.

▶ **Model It** **You can label a picture to help sort shapes based on angles.**

Look at each shape. Mark each angle "a" for acute, "r" for right, or "o" for obtuse.

For example, mark the trapezoid like this:

The trapezoid has 2 acute angles and 2 obtuse angles. It belongs in the group "acute and obtuse."

Remember to look at all of the angles in a shape before you put it in a group.

Connect It Now you will sort shapes based on angles to solve the problem from the previous page.

7 Look at parallelograms *A* and *B*. Do they belong to the same group? Explain. Draw arrows to the correct group(s). _____

_____

8 Look at the two triangles. Describe the angles in each one. _____

_____

Draw arrows to match the triangles with their group(s).

9 Look at the trapezoid and rectangle. Which has right angles only? _____
Look at *Picture It*. To which group does the trapezoid belong?

_____ Draw arrows to the group(s).

10 Explain how to sort shapes based on whether they have acute, right, or obtuse angles. _____

_____

_____

Try It Use what you just learned to solve these problems.

11 Where does the rhombus at the right belong in the Venn diagram below? Mark the place with an X.

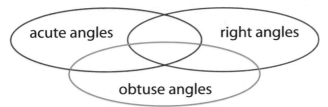

12 Circle the shape that has an acute angle, a right angle, and an obtuse angle.

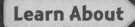

Learn About Sorting Triangles

Read the problem below. Then explore different ways to understand sorting triangles into groups based on kinds of angles and lengths of sides.

A website sells 7 kinds of triangular flags based on sides and angles.

Flag	Equal Sides	Angles
1	3	3 acute
2	2	2 acute, 1 right
3	2	2 acute, 1 obtuse
4	2	3 acute

Flag	Equal Sides	Angles
5	0	2 acute, 1 right
6	0	2 acute, 1 obtuse
7	0	3 acute

The triangle at the right is a model for which flag number? What is the name of this triangle?

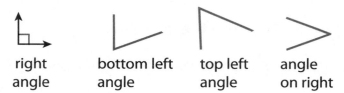

► **Picture It** You can use a picture to help describe the sides and angles of triangles.

Compare the angles of the triangle to a right angle. The triangle has 3 acute angles.

right angle   bottom left angle   top left angle   angle on right

The triangle has 2 sides of equal length (10 in.). Flag 4 has **2 sides of equal length** and **3 acute angles**. The triangle is a model for flag 4.

The tables below show triangle names based on the number of sides of equal length and kinds of angles.

Name	Description of Sides
equilateral	3 equal sides
isosceles	**2 equal sides**
scalene	0 equal sides

Name	Description of Angles
acute	**3 acute angles**
right	1 right angle
obtuse	1 obtuse angle

The triangle has 2 equal sides, so it's an isosceles triangle. Since it has 3 acute angles, it is an acute triangle. The triangle is an acute isosceles triangle.

Connect It Now you will explore naming triangles further.

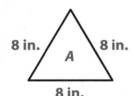
8 in. 8 in.
A
8 in.

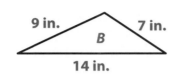
9 in. 7 in.
B
14 in.

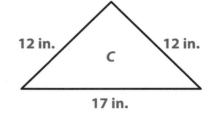
12 in. 12 in.
C
17 in.

13 Look at triangle *A*. How many sides are the same length? _____

What kinds of angles does it have? _____

What are two names for this triangle? _____

14 What are two names for triangle *B*? _____

Can this triangle also be called an acute triangle? Why or why not?

_____

_____

15 What are two names for triangle *C*? Explain.

_____

_____

16 Explain how to give a complete description of a triangle. _____

_____

_____

Try It Use what you just learned to solve these problems.

17 Give a complete description of
the triangle below.

_____

18 What do the triangles below have in

common? _____

How are they different? _____

_____

Practice Classifying Two-Dimensional Figures

Study the example below. Then solve problems 19–21.

Example

Do any of the shapes below have at least one pair of parallel sides and at least one right angle? If yes, list the shapes. If no, explain.

 A    B    C   D

Look at how you could show your work using a table.

Shape	Parallel Sides	Right Angle
A	X	X
B		X
C	X	
D	X	X

Solution _Yes; A and D_

The student listed each shape in a table and used an X to show that a shape had parallel lines or a right angle.

Pair/Share
How could you test for parallel lines?

---

19 Nate and Alicia play Draw My Shape. Nate says, "My shape has 2 pairs of parallel sides, 2 acute angles, and 2 obtuse angles." Alicia draws the rectangle below. Explain why Alicia's answer is incorrect.

I can test the angles to see if they are acute, right, or obtuse.

Solution _____

_____

Pair/Share
Can you have a 4-sided shape with 4 right angles and only 1 pair of parallel sides?

20 Compare and contrast the sides and angles of the shapes below.

square   rhombus

> All the square's angles look alike, but the rhombus looks like it has two different kinds of angles.

Solution _____

_____

_____

_____

> **Pair/Share**
> What does a rhombus have in common with a parallelogram?

---

21 Julio is missing one piece from the middle of the puzzle below. Circle the letter of the correct answer.

Which name best describes the missing piece?

A acute isosceles triangle

B acute scalene triangle

C right isosceles triangle

D right scalene triangle

Ricky chose **B** as the correct answer. How did he get that answer?

_____

_____

_____

_____

> How many right angles does a triangle have to have to be called a "right triangle"?

> **Pair/Share**
> Could a triangle ever have 2 right angles?

Practice Classifying Two-Dimensional Figures

Solve the problems.

1 Which is the best name for the group of shapes below?

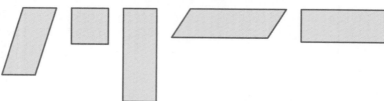

A shapes with acute angles

B shapes with right angles

C shapes with parallel sides

D shapes with perpendicular sides

2 Sort these four shapes. Use the characteristics labeled in the boxes below. Draw each shape in each of the boxes where it belongs. Some shapes may belong in more than one box.

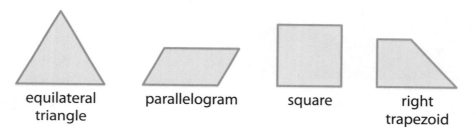

| equilateral triangle | parallelogram | square | right trapezoid |

Shapes with at Least One Acute Angle	Shapes with at Least One Pair of Perpendicular Sides	Shapes with at Least One Pair of Parallel Sides

3 Tell whether each sentence is *True* or *False*.

a. A right scalene triangle can have 3 different
   kinds of angles.   ☐ True   ☐ False

b. A right isosceles triangle has 2 right angles.   ☐ True   ☐ False

c. An equilateral triangle is also an acute triangle. ☐ True   ☐ False

d. A triangle cannot have two perpendicular sides.   ☐ True   ☐ False

4 Divide the shapes below into 2 groups. Give each group a title that tells what all the shapes in that group have in common. Then draw another shape that belongs to each group.

quadrilateral   square   hexagon

parallelogram   trapezoid   triangle

Show your work.

_____

_____

_____

✓ **Self Check**   **Go back and see what you can check off on the Self Check on page 377.**

🔄 Use What You Know

You have learned about shapes and lines. Now you will learn about a line with a particular purpose called a *line of symmetry*. Take a look at this problem.

Each of the figures below has a dashed line drawn across it. Imagine folding each shape along the dotted line. If the two parts would fit exactly on top of each other when the shape is folded, draw a star on that shape.

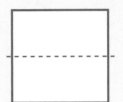   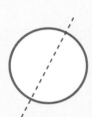 

a. Trace the square, including the dashed line. Cut out the square and fold it on the dashed line. Do the two parts fit exactly on top of each other? _____

b. Now trace and cut out the rectangle. Make sure you include the dashed line. When you fold on the dashed line, do the two parts fit exactly on top of each other? Why or why not?

_____

c. Which other shape(s) are divided into two parts that fit exactly on top of each other?

_____

d. Which other shape(s) are divided into two parts that do not fit exactly on top of each other? _____

e. Describe what parts that fit exactly on top of each other look like and what parts that don't fit look like. _____

_____

▷▷ Find Out More

In the problem on the previous page, you tested folding each figure along a line to see if the two parts fit exactly on top of each other. When you can fold a shape on a line and the parts line up with each other, the line is called a **line of symmetry**. Lines of symmetry were shown on the square, the isosceles triangle, and the circle.

Shapes can have more than one line of symmetry.

All of the lines of symmetry for a square are shown on the square at the right. Notice that all 4 lines of symmetry pass through the center point of the square.

This scalene triangle has no lines of symmetry. If you try drawing lines in the triangle so the parts fit exactly on top of each other, you'll see you can't.

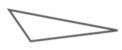

To the right are two different quadrilaterals. The rectangle has two lines of symmetry which go through the center point. The other quadrilateral has no lines of symmetry.

▶ Reflect

1 Describe a shape in your classroom that has at least one line of symmetry.

_____

_____

_____

_____

_____

Learn About ▶ **Finding a Line of Symmetry**

Read the problem below. Then explore different ways to find lines of symmetry.

Which of these shapes has at least one line of symmetry?

▶ **Model It** **You can trace and cut out the shapes. Then try folding the shapes in half.**

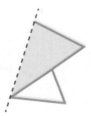  

The shaded parts show where one part is folded over the other part.

▶ **Picture It** **You can try drawing different lines in the shapes to find lines of symmetry.**

 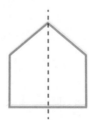 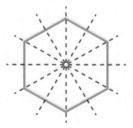

The lines drawn show all of the places you could fold each shape to make parts that fit exactly on top of each other.

Connect It Now you will describe the lines of symmetry you found to solve the problem from the previous page.

2 Does the parallelogram have any lines of symmetry? Why or why not?

_____

_____

3 How many lines of symmetry are shown on the pentagon? _____

4 Does the pentagon have any other lines of symmetry? How do you know?

_____

_____

5 The hexagon has 6 equal sides, 6 equal angles, and 6 lines of symmetry. Explain why you think this is true. _____

_____

_____

_____

6 Explain how you can figure out whether or not a line that divides a shape into two parts is a line of symmetry.

_____

_____

_____

Try It Use what you just learned to solve this problem.

7 Circle the figure below that has the greater number of lines of symmetry.

Learn About ▶ **Drawing a Line of Symmetry**

Read the problem below. Then explore different ways to draw lines of symmetry.

Draw all of the lines of symmetry for these shapes. How many lines of symmetry does each shape have?

▶ **Picture It** **You can use drawings to help draw lines of symmetry.**

The top and bottom of the oval match, so this shows a line of symmetry.

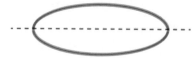

Another line can be drawn so that the left and right sides match.

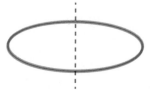

▶ **Picture It** **You can imagine folding the shape in different ways to draw lines of symmetry.**

Look at the plus sign. The lines show everywhere it could be folded to form parts that fit on top of each other.

 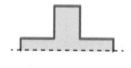 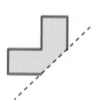

Connect It Now you will describe and draw lines of symmetry to solve the problem from the previous page.

8 On a separate piece of paper, trace the oval and show all lines of symmetry. What do you notice about the place where all lines of symmetry cross?

_____

_____

9 Now trace the plus sign and show all lines of symmetry. Where do the lines cross? How does this compare with the oval? _____

_____

10 How many lines of symmetry does the oval have? _____

11 How many lines of symmetry does the plus sign have? _____

12 Explain how you can decide when you have found all of the lines of symmetry in a figure. _____

_____

_____

_____

Try It Use what you just learned to solve this problem.

13 Draw all of the lines of symmetry on the hexagon below. All the sides of the figure have the same length.

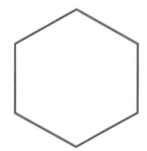

Lesson 33 Symmetry   **407**

Practice Finding and Drawing Lines of Symmetry

Study the example below. Then solve problems 14–16.

Example

Which of the figures below has fewer lines of symmetry?

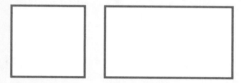

The student thought about folding the figures to decide where the lines of symmetry are!

Look at how you could explain your work.

The square has lines of symmetry connecting the corners and connecting both pairs of opposite sides.

The rectangle only has lines of symmetry connecting opposite sides, not opposite corners. So the rectangle has fewer lines of symmetry.

Solution _rectangle_

 Pair/Share
Why do you think that squares and rectangles have different numbers of lines of symmetry?

---

14 Name a kind of triangle that has a line of symmetry. Name another kind of triangle that doesn't have a line of symmetry.

Show your work.

What are the kinds of triangles that are named by their sides?

Solution _____

 Pair/Share
What's different about the triangle that has a line of symmetry and the one that doesn't have a line of symmetry?

15 Draw all of the lines of symmetry on the figure. How many lines of symmetry are there?

What point in a figure do all lines of symmetry pass through?

Pair/Share
Draw the figure on a piece of grid paper and cut it out to check the lines of symmetry.

Solution _____

---

16 Which figure shows the correct line(s) of symmetry? Circle the letter of the correct answer.

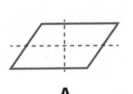

A

C

B

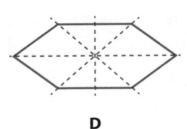

D

Imagine folding the figures in half along the lines.

Michael chose **D** as the correct answer. How did he get that answer?

_____

_____

_____

_____

Pair/Share
Discuss why the lines of symmetry that are incorrect don't work.

Practice **Finding and Drawing Lines of Symmetry**

Solve the problems.

1 Which shape always has 4 lines of symmetry?

    A an isosceles triangle

    B a rhombus

    C a square

    D a rectangle

2 Each shape below has side lengths labeled in units. Determine the number of lines of symmetry for each shape. Draw each shape in the correct box. Some boxes may have more than one shape. Some boxes may not have any shapes.

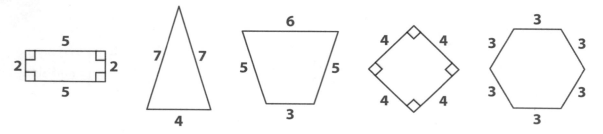

Number of Lines of Symmetry	0	Exactly 1	Exactly 2	Exactly 3	Exactly 4	More than 4
Shape						

3 Part of a figure is shaded on the grid below. Complete the figure by shading squares. Lines *r* and *s* are lines of symmetry for the completed figure.

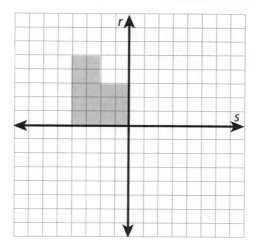

4 Draw all of the lines of symmetry on the figure below. Then draw a different quadrilateral that has more lines of symmetry than this figure. Show the lines of symmetry.

Explain your work.

_____

_____

_____

✓ **Self Check** Go back and see what you can check off on the Self Check on page 377.

Unit 6
MATH IN
ACTION

👥 **Introduction**

Classify Shapes and Angles

PS1 Make sense
of problems and
persevere in
solving them.

Study an Example Problem and Solution

Read this problem about shapes, symmetry, and angles. Then look at Bella's solution to this problem.

Wood Scraps

Bella cuts scraps of wood into different shapes and saves them to make mosaic art. Sometimes she looks for pieces with certain kinds of sides. Sometimes she looks for shapes with certain kinds of angles. Some of the pieces of wood that Bella needs to sort are shown below.

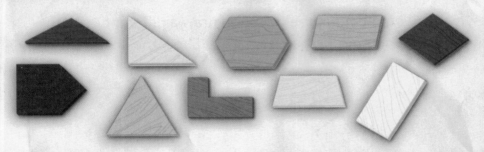

Show a way to sort all of the shapes. Have at least one category about the shapes' sides. Have at least two categories about the shapes' angles. Put each shape into every category it fits in.

Read the sample solution on the next page. Then look at the checklist below. Find and mark parts of the solution that match the checklist.

🖊 Problem-Solving Checklist

- ☐ Tell what is known.
- ☐ Tell what the problem is asking.
- ☐ Show all your work.
- ☐ Show that the solution works.

- **a. Circle** something that is known.
- **b. Underline** something that you need to find.
- **c. Draw a box around** what you do to solve the problem.
- **d. Put a checkmark** next to the part that shows the solution works.

Bella's Solution

▷ **I know I have to find one category for sides and two different categories for angles.**

▷ **I see some shapes with . . .**

sides the same length
parallel sides — These describe the sides.
perpendicular sides

right angles
acute angles — These describe the angles.
obtuse angles

I thought of the properties of the shapes. I used these to choose categories.

▷ **I'll use the properties to make angle categories and side categories.**

▷ **I'll organize the shapes in a table.**

A shape can be in more than one category.

At least 1 pair of parallel sides	
At least 1 right angle	
At least 1 acute angle	

The table shows my final answer.

I checked that each shape from the problem is in the table.
Each shape is included at least once.

Try ▶ Another Approach

There are many ways to solve problems. Think about how you might solve the Wood Scraps problem in a different way.

Wood Scraps

Bella cuts scraps of wood into different shapes and saves them to make mosaic art. Sometimes she looks for pieces with certain kinds of sides. Sometimes she looks for shapes with certain kinds of angles. Some of the pieces of wood that Bella needs to sort are shown below.

Show a way to sort all of the shapes. Have at least one category about the shapes' sides. Have at least two categories about the shapes' angles. Put each shape into every category it fits in.

▶ **Plan It** Answer these questions to help you start thinking about a plan.

A. What are some of the different categories you could use?

_____

_____

B. How can you be sure that the categories you choose will cover all of the shapes?

_____

_____

Solve It Find a different solution for the Wood Scraps problem.
Show all your work on a separate sheet of paper.

You may want to use the problem-solving tips to get started.

Problem-Solving Tips

- **Tools** You may want to use . . .

  - tables.

  - Venn diagrams.

- **Word Bank**

parallel	obtuse	right
perpendicular	acute	angle

- **Sentence Starters**

  - _____ has sides that are _____

  - The angles in _____

Reflect

Use Process Standards As you work through the problem, discuss these questions with a partner.

- **Persevere** How can you use the answers to the *Plan It* questions to decide on the categories to use?

- **Use Repeated Reasoning** Are there shapes that are more likely to fall into more than one category than others? Why do you think this is the case?

Discuss **Models and Strategies**

Read the problem. Write a solution on a separate sheet of paper.
Remember, there are lots of ways to solve a problem!

Symmetric Mosaic

Bella draws designs of different shapes for her mosaic art. This is a
drawing she started.

My Notes:

· The design has 1 line of symmetry.

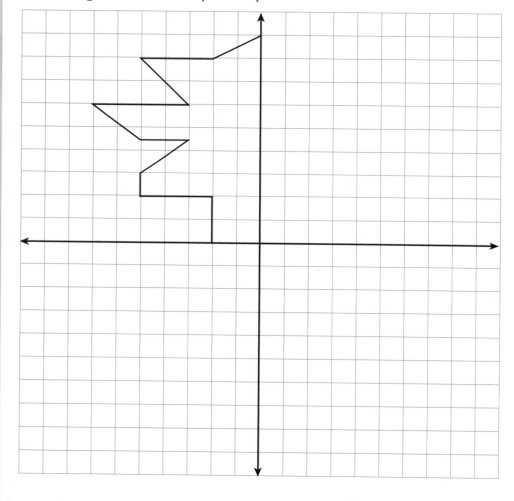

Draw the other half of the design and find ways to make the design with
mosaic shapes.

Plan It and Solve It Find a solution to Bella's Symmetric Mosaic problem.

Use the Symmetric Mosaic Activity Sheet to finish Bella's design.

- Pick a line to use as the line of symmetry. Then draw the other half of the shape.

- Break up the shape into triangles, quadrilaterals, pentagons, and/or hexagons. Use at least three different shapes.

- Write the name of each shape in your design. Tell how many of each shape you used.

You may want to use the problem-solving tips to get started.

Problem-Solving Tips

- **Questions**
  - How can you tell if a line is a line of symmetry?
  - What do the sides and angles of your shapes look like?

- **Word Bank**

right	acute	triangle
rectangle	square	trapezoid

  - The line of symmetry _____
  - I broke the shape into _____

Reflect

Use Process Standards As you work through the problem, discuss these questions with a partner.

- **Use Tools** What tools can you use to solve the problem? How could you use the tools?

- **Use Reasoning** How can you decide what shapes to use to create Bella's design?

Persevere ▶ **On Your Own**

Read the problems. Write a solution on a separate sheet of paper.
Remember, there are many different ways to solve a problem!

Mosaic Art

Bella is designing a wood mosaic piece. She wants the outline of the
mosaic to be a shape with the features listed below.

My Mosaic Plan

· at least 4 sides

· at least 2 lines of symmetry

· at least 1 pair of parallel sides

What shape could Bella choose for an outline?

▶ **Solve It** **Suggest a shape that Bella could use as an outline
for her mosaic.**

Draw a shape that has all of the features listed above.

• Label the shape to show that it has all of the features.

• Use as many geometry words as you can to describe your shape.

▶ **Reflect**

Use Process Standards After you complete the task, choose one
of these questions to discuss with a partner.

• **Make an Argument** How can you show or explain why your shape has all
of the features listed above?

• **Persevere** What different shapes did you try before deciding which one
to use in your solution?

Angle Cuts

When Bella cuts pieces of wood for a project, she always saves the scraps. The scraps make good pieces for making mosaics. The cut pieces have different angle measures. Bella sorts pieces by the angle measures. Here are the angle measures of the pieces she has saved.

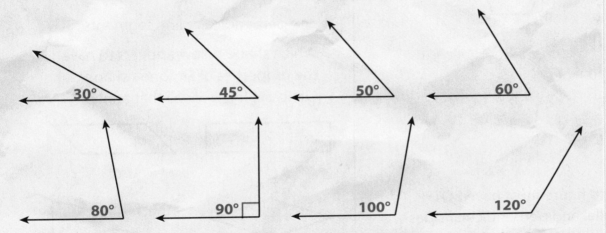

How can Bella put some of these angles together to make a straight line?

▶ **Solve It** Help Bella put some of the angles together to make a straight line.

Find a way Bella can put some pieces of wood together to make a 180° angle. Then measure and draw your angles to show that they make a straight line.

▶ **Reflect**

Use Process Standards After you complete the task, choose one of these questions to discuss with a partner.

• **Use Tools** How did you use tools to draw and measure angles?

• **Use a Model** What equations could you write to show the total measure of the angles you put together?

Solve the problems.

1 How many lines of symmetry does the shape have?

A 15

B 10

C 5

D 1

2 Which figure must have BOTH parallel and perpendicular sides?

A a parallelogram

B a rectangle

C a rhombus

D a right triangle

3 Simone drew a shape with the following properties.

- parallel line segments

- exactly 2 lines of symmetry

- no perpendicular line segments

Which shape below appears to have the properties of Simone's shape? Circle the letter for all that apply.

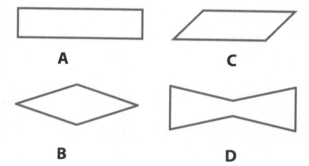

4 Draw a line of symmetry through the figure below.

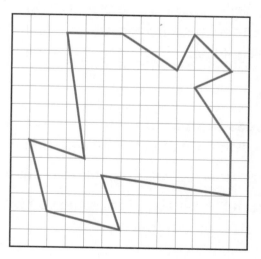

5 Margaret cut out six felt shapes in her craft class. She labeled each shape with a letter.

Part A Which shapes have one or more right angles?

Solution _____

Part B Describe shapes *A*, *B*, *C*, and *D* based on the kinds of sides they have.

_____

_____

6 **Part A** Draw all the lines of symmetry for each figure.

Part B Each figure has sides of equal length and angles of equal measure. For each figure, compare the number of sides, number of angles, and number of lines of symmetry. Write a sentence that describes the pattern.

_____

_____

Part C How many lines of symmetry can be drawn in a 7-sided polygon where all the sides are the same length and all the angles have the same measure? Sketch and check your solution.

Solution _____

Performance Task

Answer the questions and show all your work on separate paper.

Your Uncle Asher has a new bakery opening soon and has asked you to help him design a logo for the shop sign. He emailed you to say the shop will be called **Asher's Sweets** and described his idea for the shape of the logo:

> My logo is three shapes put together. One of the shapes is a 5-sided figure with exactly two parallel sides, exactly two right angles, and one line of symmetry. The other two shapes are exactly alike. Each one is an isosceles triangle. The bottom of each triangle—the side that is a different length from the other two—matches up to one of the parallel sides of the 5-sided figure.

Checklist

Did you . . .
- ☐ follow the instructions for the first logo?
- ☐ use a ruler?
- ☐ use vocabulary correctly?

Draw your uncle's logo idea on grid paper. Then use geometric shapes to create another logo for him to consider. Draw the logo and describe it in a note to your uncle using the terms *parallel, perpendicular, line of symmetry, acute, obtuse*, and any other geometry vocabulary from this unit.

Reflect

Use Process Standards After you complete the task, choose one of the following questions to answer.

- **Be Precise** Why is it important that you know the meaning of the geometry terms in your description?

- **Argue and Critique** Suppose you asked your uncle to draw a logo matching your description. Do you think his drawing will match what you had in mind? Explain your answer.

Glossary

AM morning, or the time from midnight until noon.

acute angle an angle with a measure less than 90°.

acute triangle a triangle that has three acute angles.

addend a number being added.

angle two rays that share an endpoint.

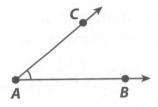

area the amount of space inside a closed, two-dimensional figure. Area is measured in square units such as square centimeters.

array a set of objects grouped in equal rows and equal columns.

☆☆☆☆☆
☆☆☆☆☆
☆☆☆☆☆

associative property of addition Changing the grouping of three or more addends does not change the sum.

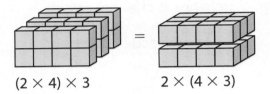

$(2 + 3) + 4 = 2 + (3 + 4)$

associative property of multiplication Changing the grouping of three or more factors does not change the product.

$(2 \times 4) \times 3 \qquad 2 \times (4 \times 3)$

attribute a characteristic of an object. Attributes of a shape include the number of sides and the length of the sides.

B

benchmark fraction a common fraction that you might compare other fractions to. For example, $\frac{1}{2}$ can be used as a benchmark.

capacity the amount of liquid a container can hold. Capacity is measured in the same units as liquid volume.

Glossary

centimeter (cm) a unit of length in the metric system. Your little finger is about 1 centimeter across. 100 centimeters is equivalent to 1 meter.

circle graph a graph that shows data divided into sections of a circle, showing how each data category is related to the whole and to other data categories.

closed figure a two-dimensional figure that begins and ends at the same point.

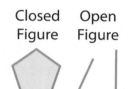

Closed Figure   Open Figure

column a top to bottom line of objects in an array.

common denominator a number that is a common multiple of the denominators of two or more fractions.

commutative property of addition Changing the order of the addends does not change the sum.

3 + 4   =   4 + 3

commutative property of multiplication Changing the order of the factors does not change the product.

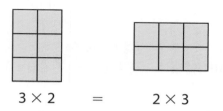

3 × 2   =   2 × 3

compare to decide if one number is greater than (>), less than (<), or equal to (=) another number.

compose to make by combining parts.

composite number a number greater than 0 that has more than one pair of factors.

convert to change from one measurement unit to another.

cup (c) a unit of liquid volume in the customary system. Four cups is equivalent to 1 quart.

customary system the measurement system commonly used in the United States. It measures length in inches, feet, yards, and miles; liquid volume in cups, pints, quarts, and gallons; and weight in ounces and pounds.

data information, often numerical information such as a list of measurements.

decimal a number containing a decimal point that separates the ones place from the tenths place.

decimal point the period or dot used in a decimal that separates the ones place from the tenths place.

decompose to break up into parts.

degree (°) a unit used to measure angles. There are 360° in one circle.

denominator the number below the line in a fraction. It tells how many equal parts are in the whole.

$$\frac{2}{5} \longleftarrow \text{denominator}$$

difference the result of subtraction.

digit a symbol used to write numbers. The digits are 0, 1, 2, 3, 4, 5, 6, 7, 8, and 9.

dimension length in one direction. A figure may have one, two, or three dimensions.

distributive property When one of the factors of a product is written as a sum, multiplying each addend by the other factor before adding does not change the product.

$$2 \times (3 + 6) = (2 \times 3) + (2 \times 6)$$

divide to separate into equal groups.

dividend the number that is divided in a division problem.

division an operation used to separate a number of items into equal-sized groups.

divisor the number you divide by in a division problem.

elapsed time the time that has passed between a start time and an end time.

equal (=) having the same value, same size, or same amount.

equation a mathematical statement that uses an equal sign (=) to show that two expressions have the same value.

equilateral triangle a triangle that has all three sides the same length.

8 in. 8 in.

8 in.

equivalent fractions two or more fractions that name the same part of a whole or the same point on a number line.

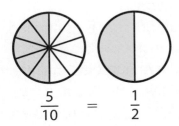

$$\frac{5}{10} = \frac{1}{2}$$

estimate (noun) a close guess made using math thinking.

Glossary

estimate (verb) to make a close guess based on math thinking.

even number a whole number that ends in the digit 0, 2, 4, 6, or 8. Even numbers have 2 as a factor.

expanded form a way of writing a number to show the place value of each digit.

$$254.3 = 200 + 50 + 4 + \frac{3}{10}$$

expression numbers or unknowns combined with operation symbols. For example, $5 + a$ or 3×6.

fact family a group of related math facts that all use the same numbers. The group of facts shows the relationship between addition and subtraction, or between multiplication and division.

$$5 \times 4 = 20$$
$$4 \times 5 = 20$$
$$20 \div 4 = 5$$
$$20 \div 5 = 4$$

factor a number that is multiplied.

factor pair two numbers that are multiplied together to give a particular product. For example, 1 and 12, 2 and 6, and 3 and 4 are all factor pairs of 12.

factors of a number whole numbers that multiply together to get the given number.

foot (ft) a unit of length in the customary system. One foot is equivalent to 12 inches.

formula a mathematical relationship that is expressed in the form of an equation. For example, the formula for the area of a rectangle is $A = \ell \times w$.

fourths the parts formed when a whole is divided into four equal parts.

fraction a number that names equal parts of a whole; a fraction names a point on the number line.

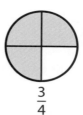

$$\frac{3}{4}$$

gallon (gal) a unit of liquid volume in the customary system. One gallon is equivalent to 4 quarts.

gram (g) a unit of mass in the metric system. A paper clip has a mass of about 1 gram. 1000 grams is equivalent to 1 kilogram.

greater than symbol (>) a symbol used to compare two numbers. It shows that the first number has a greater value than the second.

halves the parts formed when a whole is divided into two equal parts.

hexagon a polygon with exactly six sides and six angles.

hour (h) a unit of time. One hour is equivalent to 60 minutes.

hundredths the parts formed when a whole is divided into 100 equal parts.

improper fraction a fraction with a numerator greater than or equal to the denominator.

inch (in.) a unit of length in the customary system. A quarter is about 1 inch across. Twelve inches is equivalent to 1 foot.

isosceles triangle a triangle that has at least two sides with the same length.

8 in. 8 in.

6 in.

kilogram (kg) a unit of mass in the metric system. One kilogram is to equivalent to 1,000 grams.

kilometer (km) a unit of length in the metric system. One kilometer is equivalent to 1,000 meters.

length a measurement that tells the distance from one point to another, or how long something is.

less than symbol (<) a symbol used to compare two numbers when the first has less value than the second.

line (in geometry) a straight row of points that goes on forever in both directions.

line of symmetry a line that divides a shape into two mirror images.

line plot a data display that uses a number line to show measurement data.

Sea Lion Lengths

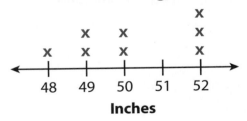

Inches

Glossary

line segment a straight row of points that starts at one point and ends at another point, or, a part of a line.

A   B

liquid volume the amount of space a liquid takes up.

liter (L) a unit of liquid volume in the metric system. One liter is equivalent to 1,000 milliliters.

mass the amount of matter in an object. Measuring the mass of an object is one way to measure how heavy it is. Units of mass include the gram and kilogram.

meter (m) a unit of length in the metric system. One meter is equivalent to 100 centimeters.

metric system the measurement system that measures length based on meters, liquid volume based on liters, and mass based on grams.

mile (mi) a unit of length in the customary system. One mile is equivalent to 5,280 feet.

milliliter (ml) a unit of liquid volume in the metric system. 1,000 milliliters is equivalent to 1 liter.

minute (min) a unit of time equivalent to 60 seconds.

mixed number a number with a whole part and a fractional part.

$$4\frac{1}{2}$$

multiple the product of a number and any other whole number. For example, 4, 8, 12, 16, and so on, are multiples of 4.

multiplication an operation used to find the total number of items in equal-sized groups.

multiplicative comparison a comparison that tells how many times as many. For example, $7 \times 3 = 21$ means 21 is 3 times as many as 7, and 21 is 7 times as many as 3.

multiply to find the total number of items in equal-sized groups.

numerator the number above the line in a fraction. It tells how many equal parts are described.

$$\frac{2}{5} \longleftarrow \text{numerator}$$

obtuse angle an angle that measures more than 90° but less than 180°.

obtuse triangle a triangle that has one obtuse angle.

odd number a whole number that ends in the digit 1, 3, 5, 7, or 9. Odd numbers do not have 2 as a factor.

operation a mathematical action such as addition, subtraction, multiplication and division.

ounce (oz) a unit of weight in the customary system. A slice of bread weighs about one ounce. Sixteen ounces is equivalent to 1 pound.

PM the time from noon until midnight.

parallel lines two or more lines that are always the same distance apart and will never cross.

parallelogram a quadrilateral with opposite sides parallel and equal in length.

partial products a strategy used to multiply multi-digit numbers. The products you get in each step are called "partial products".

```
      218
    ×   6
       48  (6 × 8 ones)
       60  (6 × 1 ten)
     1200  (6 × 2 hundreds)
     1308
```

partial quotients a strategy used to divide multi-digit numbers. The quotients you get in each step are called "partial quotients".

pattern a series of numbers or shapes that follow a rule to repeat or change.

pentagon a polygon with exactly five sides and five angles.

perimeter the distance around a two-dimensional shape. The perimeter is equal to the sum of the lengths of the sides.

period a group of three related place values, usually separated by commas. Examples are the ones period, the thousands period, and the millions period.

Thousands Period			Ones Period		
Hundred Thousands	Ten Thousands	Thousands	Hundreds	Tens	Ones
4	6	7	8	8	2

perpendicular lines two lines that meet to form a right angle, or a 90° angle.

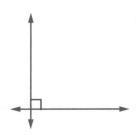

Glossary

pint (pt) a unit of liquid volume in the customary system. One pint is equivalent to 2 cups.

place value the value of a digit based on its position in a number. For example, the 2 in 324 is in the tens place and has a value of 2 tens, or twenty.

plane figure a two-dimensional figure, such as a circle, triangle, or rectangle.

point a single location in space. Two lines cross at a point, and two sides of a triangle meet at a point.

polygon a two-dimensional closed figure made with three or more straight line segments that do not cross over each other.

Polygons	Not Polygons
△ ⟨	○ ✕

pound (lb) a unit of weight in the customary system. One pound is equivalent to 16 ounces.

prime number a whole number greater than 1 whose only factors are 1 and itself. For example, 2, 3, 5, 7, and 11 are prime numbers.

product the result of multiplication.

protractor a tool used to measure angles.

quadrilateral a polygon with exactly four sides and four angles.

quart (qt) a unit of liquid volume in the customary system. One quart is equivalent to 4 cups.

quotient the result of division.

R

ray a straight row of points that starts at one point and goes on forever in one direction.

rectangle a parallelogram with four right angles. Pairs of opposite sides of a rectangle are the same length.

regroup to compose or decompose tens, hundreds, thousands, and so forth. For example, 10 ones can be regrouped as 1 ten, or 1 hundred can be regrouped as 10 tens.

remainder in division, the amount left over after equal groups have been made.

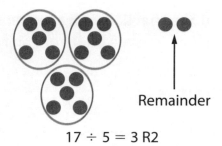

17 ÷ 5 = 3 R2

rhombus a parallelogram with all four sides the same length.

right angle an angle that forms a square corner and measures 90°.

right triangle a triangle with one right angle.

round to find a number that is close in value to the given number by finding the nearest ten, hundred, or other place value.

row a side-to-side line of objects in an array.

rule in a pattern, a procedure that describes the relationship between one number or shape and the next.

scale on a graph, the difference between the numbers labeling the graph.

scalene triangle a triangle that has no two sides with the same length.

second (s) a unit of time. Sixty seconds is equivalent to 1 minute.

side one of the line segments that form two-dimensional figures.

square a shape that has four sides of equal length and four right angles.

square unit a square with a side length of 1 unit that is used to measure area.

standard form the way a number is written using digits. For example, the standard form of *twelve* is 12.

sum the result of addition.

symbol any mark or drawing with a particular meaning, including numbers, letters, and operation signs. A symbol can be used to stand for an unknown number in an equation.

Glossary

tenths the parts formed when a whole is divided into ten equal parts.

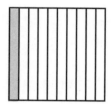

thirds the parts formed when a whole is divided into three equal parts.

three-dimensional solid, or having length, width and height. For example, cubes are three-dimensional.

trapezoid a type of quadrilateral. A trapezoid always has a pair of parallel sides.

triangle a polygon with exactly three sides and three angles.

two-dimensional flat, or having measurement in two directions, like length and width. For example, a rectangle is two-dimensional.

unit fraction a fraction with a numerator of 1. Other fractions are built from unit fractions. For example $\frac{1}{4}$ and $\frac{1}{10}$ are unit fractions.

unknown the piece or pieces of a problem that you are not given or do not know.

Venn diagram a drawing that shows how sets of numbers or objects compare.

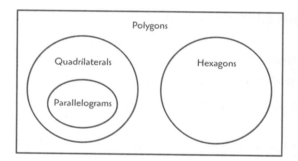

vertex the point where two rays, lines, or line segments meet to form an angle.

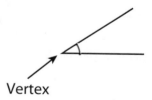

Vertex

W

weight the measurement that tells how heavy an object is. Units of weight include ounces and pounds.

word form (of a number) the way a number is written with words, or said aloud. For example, the word form of 105 is *one hundred five*.

Y

yard (yd) a unit of length in the U.S. customary system. One yard is equivalent to 3 feet.

Indiana Academic Standards Coverage by *Ready® Instruction*

The chart below correlates each Indiana Academic Standard to the *Ready® Instruction* lesson(s) that offer(s) comprehensive instruction on that standard. Use this chart to determine which lessons your students should complete based on their mastery of each standard.

Indiana Academic Standards for Grade 4 Mathematics Standards	*Ready®* Lesson(s)
Number Sense	
4.NS.1 Read and write whole numbers up to 1,000,000. Use words, models, standard form and expanded form to represent and show equivalent forms of whole numbers up to 1,000,000.	1
4.NS.2 Compare two whole numbers up to 1,000,000 using $>$, $=$, and $<$ symbols.	2
4.NS.3 Express whole numbers as fractions and recognize fractions that are equivalent to whole numbers. Name and write mixed numbers using objects or pictures. Name and write mixed numbers as improper fractions using objects or pictures.	13B
4.NS.4 Explain why a fraction, $\frac{a}{b}$, is equivalent to a fraction, $(n \times a)/(n \times b)$, by using visual fraction models, with attention to how the number and size of the parts differ even though the two fractions themselves are the same size. Use this principle to recognize and generate equivalent fractions. [In grade 4, limit denominators of fractions to 2, 3, 4, 5, 6, 8, 10, 25, 100.]	13A, 20
4.NS.5 Compare two fractions with different numerators and different denominators (e.g., by creating common denominators or numerators, or by comparing to a benchmark, such as 0, $\frac{1}{2}$, and 1). Recognize comparisons are valid only when the two fractions refer to the same whole. Record the results of comparisons with symbols $>$, $=$, and $<$, and justify the conclusions (e.g., by using a visual fraction model).	14
4.NS.6 Write tenths and hundredths in decimal and fraction notations. Use words, models, standard form and expanded form to represent decimal numbers to hundredths. Know the fraction and decimal equivalents for halves and fourths (e.g., $\frac{1}{2} = 0.5 = 0.50$, $\frac{7}{4} = 1\frac{3}{4} = 1.75$).	21
4.NS.7 Compare two decimals to hundredths by reasoning about their size based on the same whole. Record the results of comparisons with the symbols $>$, $=$, and $<$, and justify the conclusions (e.g., by using a visual model).	22
4.NS.8 Find all factor pairs for a whole number in the range 1–100. Recognize that a whole number is a multiple of each of its factors. Determine whether a given whole number in the range 1–100 is a multiple of a given one-digit number.	7
4.NS.9 Use place value understanding to round multi-digit whole numbers to any given place value.	4

The Process Standards for Mathematics are integrated throughout the instructional lessons.

Indiana Academic Standards (IAS) © 2016. Indiana Department of Education. All rights reserved.

Indiana Academic Standards for Grade 4 Mathematics Standards	*Ready®* Lesson(s)

Computation

4.C.1 Add and subtract multi-digit whole numbers fluently using a standard algorithmic approach.	3
4.C.2 Multiply a whole number of up to four digits by a one-digit whole number and multiply two two-digit numbers, using strategies based on place value and the properties of operations. Describe the strategy and explain the reasoning.	11
4.C.3 Find whole-number quotients and remainders with up to four-digit dividends and one-digit divisors, using strategies based on place value, the properties of operations, and/or the relationship between multiplication and division. Describe the strategy and explain the reasoning.	12
4.C.4 Multiply fluently within 100.	7
4.C.5 Add and subtract fractions with common denominators. Decompose a fraction into a sum of fractions with common denominators. Understand addition and subtraction of fractions as combining and separating parts referring to the same whole.	15
4.C.6 Add and subtract mixed numbers with common denominators (e.g. by replacing each mixed number with an equivalent fraction and/or by using properties of operations and the relationship between addition and subtraction).	17
4.C.7 Show how the order in which two numbers are multiplied (commutative property) and how numbers are grouped in multiplication (associative property) will not change the product. Use these properties to show that numbers can by multiplied in any order. Understand and use the distributive property.	5B

Algebraic Thinking

4.AT.1 Solve real-world problems involving addition and subtraction of multi-digit whole numbers (e.g., by using drawings and equations with a symbol for the unknown number to represent the problem).	3
4.AT.2 Recognize and apply the relationships between addition and multiplication, between subtraction and division, and the inverse relationship between multiplication and division to solve real-world and other mathematical problems.	9, 10
4.AT.3 Interpret a multiplication equation as a comparison (e.g., interpret $35 = 5 \times 7$ as a statement that 35 is 5 times as many as 7, and 7 times as many as 5). Represent verbal statements of multiplicative comparisons as multiplication equations.	5A
4.AT.4 Solve real-world problems with whole numbers involving multiplicative comparison (e.g., by using drawings and equations with a symbol for the unknown number to represent the problem), distinguishing multiplicative comparison from additive comparison. [In grade 4, division problems should not include a remainder.]	6
4.AT.5 Solve real-world problems involving addition and subtraction of fractions referring to the same whole and having common denominators (e.g., by using visual fraction models and equations to represent the problem).	16, 17
4.AT.6 Understand that an equation, such as $y = 3x + 5$, is a rule to describe a relationship between two variables and can be used to find a second number when a first number is given. Generate a number pattern that follows a given rule.	8

The Process Standards for Mathematics are integrated throughout the instructional lessons.

Geometry

4.G.1 Identify, describe, and draw parallelograms, rhombuses, and trapezoids using appropriate tools (e.g., ruler, straightedge and technology).	32
4.G.2 Recognize and draw lines of symmetry in two-dimensional figures. Identify figures that have lines of symmetry.	33
4.G.3 Recognize angles as geometric shapes that are formed wherever two rays share a common endpoint.	28
4.G.4 Identify, describe, and draw rays, angles (right, acute, obtuse), and perpendicular and parallel lines using appropriate tools (e.g., ruler, straightedge and technology). Identify these in two-dimensional figures.	31
4.G.5 Classify triangles and quadrilaterals based on the presence or absence of parallel or perpendicular lines, or the presence or absence of angles (right, acute, obtuse).	32

Measurement

4.M.1 Measure length to the nearest quarter-inch, eighth-inch, and millimeter.	25
4.M.2 Know relative sizes of measurement units within one system of units, including km, m, cm; kg, g; lb, oz; l, ml; hr, min, sec. Express measurements in a larger unit in terms of a smaller unit within a single system of measurement. Record measurement equivalents in a two-column table.	23
4.M.3 Use the four operations (addition, subtraction, multiplication and division) to solve real-world problems involving distances, intervals of time, volumes, masses of objects, and money. Include addition and subtraction problems involving simple fractions and problems that require expressing measurements given in a larger unit in terms of a smaller unit.	24, 25
4.M.4 Apply the area and perimeter formulas for rectangles to solve real-world problems and other mathematical problems. Recognize area as additive and find the area of complex shapes composed of rectangles by decomposing them into non-overlapping rectangles and adding the areas of the non-overlapping parts; apply this technique to solve real-world problems and other mathematical problems.	26
4.M.5 Understand that an angle is measured with reference to a circle, with its center at the common endpoint of the rays, by considering the fraction of the circular arc between the points where the two rays intersect the circle. Understand an angle that turns through $\frac{1}{360}$ of a circle is called a "one-degree angle," and can be used to measure other angles. Understand an angle that turns through n one-degree angles is said to have an angle measure of n degrees.	28
4.M.6 Measure angles in whole-number degrees using appropriate tools. Sketch angles of specified measure.	29

The Process Standards for Mathematics are integrated throughout the instructional lessons.

Indiana Academic Standards for Grade 4 Mathematics Standards	*Ready*® Lesson(s)
Data Analysis	
4.DA.1 Formulate questions that can be addressed with data. Use observations, surveys, and experiments to collect, represent, and interpret the data using tables (including frequency tables), line plots, and bar graphs.	27C, 30
4.DA.2 Make a line plot to display a data set of measurements in fractions of a unit ($\frac{1}{2}, \frac{1}{4}, \frac{1}{8}$). Solve problems involving addition and subtraction of fractions by using data displayed in line plots.	27A
4.DA.3 Interpret data displayed in a circle graph.	27B

The Process Standards for Mathematics are integrated throughout the instructional lessons.

Acknowledgments

Illustration Credits

page 244: Fian Arroyo

All other illustrations by Sam Valentino.

Photography Credits

page 114: Diana Taliun/Shutterstock

page 118: Videowokart/Shutterstock (flower A)

page 118: Koncz/Shutterstock (flower B)

page 118: Arsentyeva E/Shutterstock (flower C)

page 118: Barbol/Shutterstock (flower D)

page 118: oksana2010/Shutterstock (flower E)

page 118: tr3gin/Shutterstock (flower F)

page 118: Pavel Vakhrushev/Shutterstock (flower G)

page 118: Stephen B. Goodwin/Shutterstock (flower H)

page 120: Evgenyi/Shutterstock

page 150: Beata Becla/Shutterstock (bottles)

page 150: Nuttapong/Shutterstock (paper)

page 150: somchai rakin/Shutterstock (cans)

page 150: Africa Studio/Shutterstock (cardboard)

page 153: DeZet/Shutterstock (fuse)

page 153: Dmitrij Skorobogatov/Shutterstock (switch)

page 153: Rhonda Roth/Shutterstock (wire)

page 153: piotr_pabijan/Shutterstock (screw)

page 254: Eugenia Struk/Shutterstock

page 366: raybon/Shutterstock

page 370: irakite/Shutterstock (panda)

page 370: AndreAnita/Shutterstock (polar bear)

page 370: Dennis W. Donohue/Shutterstock (black bear)

page 372: Eric Isselee/Shutterstock (panda)

page 372: Anan Kaewkhammul/Shutterstock (hippo)

Background images used throughout lessons by Ortis/Shutterstock,
irin-k/Shutterstock, and Kritsada Namborisut/Shutterstock.